Discursive Constructions of the Suicidal Process

Also available from Bloomsbury

Applying Linguistics in Illness and Healthcare Contexts, edited by Zsófia Demjén
Corpus, Discourse and Mental Health, by Daniel Hunt and Gavin Brookes
Discourses of Men's Suicide Notes, by Dariusz Galasiński
Forensic Linguistics, by John Olsson
Investigating Adolescent Health Communication, by Kevin Harvey

Discursive Constructions of the Suicidal Process

Dariusz Galasiński and Justyna Ziółkowska

BLOOMSBURY ACADEMIC
LONDON • NEW YORK • OXFORD • NEW DELHI • SYDNEY

BLOOMSBURY ACADEMIC
Bloomsbury Publishing Plc
50 Bedford Square, London, WC1B 3DP, UK
1385 Broadway, New York, NY 10018, USA
29 Earlsfort Terrace, Dublin 2, Ireland

BLOOMSBURY, BLOOMSBURY ACADEMIC and the Diana logo are
trademarks of Bloomsbury Publishing Plc

First published in Great Britain 2020
This paperback edition published in 2022

Copyright © Dariusz Galasiński and Justyna Ziółkowska, 2020

Dariusz Galasiński and Justyna Ziółkowska have asserted their right under the
Copyright, Designs and Patents Act, 1988, to be identified as Authors of this work.

For legal purposes the Acknowledgements on p. ix constitute
an extension of this copyright page.

Cover design by Ben Anslow
Cover image: © Kathy Collins / Getty Images

All rights reserved. No part of this publication may be reproduced or transmitted
in any form or by any means, electronic or mechanical, including photocopying,
recording, or any information storage or retrieval system, without prior permission
in writing from the publishers.

Bloomsbury Publishing Plc does not have any control over, or responsibility for,
any third-party websites referred to or in this book. All internet addresses given
in this book were correct at the time of going to press. The author and publisher
regret any inconvenience caused if addresses have changed or sites have ceased
to exist, but can accept no responsibility for any such changes.

A catalogue record for this book is available from the British Library.

Library of Congress Cataloging-in-Publication Data
Names: Galasiński, Dariusz, author. | Ziółkowska, Justyna, author.
Title: Discursive constructions of the suicidal process / Dariusz Galasiński and Justyna Ziółkowska.
Description: London; New York, NY: Bloomsbury Academic, 2020. | Includes bibliographical references and index.
Identifiers: LCCN 2020015220 (print) | LCCN 2020015221 (ebook) | ISBN 9781350107694 (hardcover) | ISBN 9781350107700 (ebook) | ISBN 9781350107717 (epub)
Subjects: LCSH: Suicide victims–Correspondence. | Suicide victims' writings. | Discourse analysis.
Classification: LCC HV6545 .G356 2020 (print) | LCC HV6545 (ebook) | DDC 362.2801/4–dc23
LC record available at https://lccn.loc.gov/2020015220
LC ebook record available at https://lccn.loc.gov/2020015221

ISBN:	HB:	978-1-3501-0769-4
	PB:	978-1-3501-9768-8
	ePDF:	978-1-3501-0770-0
	eBook:	978-1-3501-0771-7

Typeset by Integra Software Services Pvt. Ltd.

To find out more about our authors and books visit www.bloomsbury.com
and sign up for our newsletters.

To us and ours

Contents

List of figures		viii
Acknowledgements		ix
1	Introduction	1
2	Conflict of discourses	25
3	Agency in the suicidal process	45
4	Suicide activities	71
5	Killing oneself	97
6	Future	119
7	The multimodality of suicide	143
8	Conclusions	169
Notes		184
References		186
Index		208

Figures

1	Timeline 1	154
2	Timeline 2	155
3	Timeline 3	157
4	Timeline 4	158
5	Timeline 5	160
6	Timeline 6	161
7	Timeline 7	163
8	Timeline 8	164

Acknowledgements

We would like to gratefully acknowledge the award of two grants by Poland's National Science Centre which were a significant part of the empirical basis of this book: SONATA 2012/05/D/HS6/02390 and OPUS 2013/09/B/HS6/02796.

1

Introduction

This book is about what a person does just before either taking their own life or attempting to. What happens a day, an hour, ten minutes before the suicidal act and death itself? We look at stories of the suicide process, accounts of what happens in the time leading to suicide. When does suicide start? When does it end? Who is involved? What does the act of suicide involve and mean?

We found to our continuing surprise that suicide and suicide attempts have so far been seen as events, moments outside time. They have never been studied as a process in which people do things which lead to their suicidal death and all those things which accompany them. Rather, in suicidology, the suicidal process is usually studied as the period between the first thoughts/wish of death and the suicidal act; others restrict the suicidal process to the last episode of thoughts/wish of suicide which preceded the particular suicide act. Suicidologists are interested in the chronology of events concomitant with subsequent elements of the process, as well as the relationship between the temporality of the process and psychological and socio-demographic variables.

We are interested in what happens in the time around the suicidal act. To date, no such insight has been offered. Suicide continues to be treated as a homogeneous event, outside time, without structure and 'contents'. It is seen as a dot on the timeline without reflection on what the person about to kill themselves does at the most critical and tragic moment of their life.

Despite repeated and more and more frequent calls from suicidology for a significant increase in qualitative bottom-up research (e.g. Hjelmeland & Knizek, 2010), qualitative research into suicide and/or suicide attempts remains rare, while research into the context-situated suicidal process does not exist. In this book, we aim to offer a narrative perspective on suicide and its process. With its discursive, qualitative perspective, we offer insight into the experience of the suicidal process from the point of view of those who have engaged in suicidal actions. We also want to continue arguing for text-based discourse analysis as an important tool in understanding and deconstructing suicide.

Furthermore, despite the fact that much of the evidence related to suicide and its process is textual, discourse analysis has barely engaged with the issue and such evidence. Therefore, our book is also an attempt to offer a new perspective for discourse analysis. We would like to show not only how useful discourse analytic insights into issues related to suicide can be but also that these insights can be of use in suicide prevention activities.

Aims of the book

The main aim of the book is to offer a discourse analytic insight into stories of the process of suicide, written both in the farewell letters of those who have killed themselves and in the narratives of those who have survived their suicide attempt. We are interested in unpicking what is constructed to happen in the time before the act, how the people involved are constructed and, finally, how the act of taking one's life is positioned in such narratives. In such a way, this book will focus on the basic model of the suicide process: the situation and activities immediately before a person takes their life.

And so, in this book we are interested in the narrated trajectory of the suicidal process. What are the constructions of its course, its beginning and its end? We are also interested in constructions of those involved in the suicide process. How does the person taking their life construct themselves at various stages of their journey? How do they position themselves in terms of control and agency? Finally, we are interested in how the act of suicide is constructed in the narratives of the process, and what the constructed role and function of communication about suicide is.

In sum, we shall be exploring discourses from people who were probably at the most dramatic juncture of their lives. We are interested in their accounts of that juncture as a time-extended process leading to an act aimed at killing them. We want to do this in a way which has not been done before: by analysing accounts of the suicide process focusing predominantly, though not exclusively, on the linguistic and discursive form through which the individuals construct themselves and the reality in which they position themselves.

But our book has another aim. To our knowledge, this is the first book in which an attempt is made to combine two sets of data: interviews with individuals with experience of a suicide attempt and suicide notes. Indeed, suicidology looking at suicide and suicidology interested in suicide notes seem to be almost entirely separate disciplines which barely come into contact with each other.

While research into suicide notes is quite large, it pales in comparison to the study of suicide itself (Scourfield et al., 2012 report 30,000 such articles since 1980). On the other hand, the voluminous *Oxford Textbook of Suicidology and Suicide Prevention* (Wasserman & Wasserman, 2009), containing 134 chapters and 872 pages, mentions suicide notes on one page. The later *International Handbook of Suicide Prevention* (O'Connor, Platt & Gordon, 2011), with only 36 chapters and 677 pages, contains no reference to suicide notes. The second edition of the handbook (O'Connor & Pirkis, 2016), with 823 pages, mentions suicide notes on only four pages and it is always just in passing. Suicide notes are not only not a priority in mainstream suicidology but also it seems they are hardly of interest.

By combining a corpus of interviews and a corpus of suicide notes, we want to show that the two corpora offer complementary insights and can and probably should be analysed next to each other. Since we suggest increased effort towards qualitative suicidology, the work on what seems to be separate areas of research should be combined in text-based suicidological research.

The book's projects

This book arises out of our frustration with the dominant discourses of suicidology. Time and again, we see suicide constructed as a single, largely uncomplicated event which can be explained by a set of risk factors. We want to challenge this assumed simplicity of suicide. Suicide does not just happen; it consists of a set of activities which are constitutive of it.

And so, in contrast to the dominant suicidological views, we want to show the drama of suicide. We want to show that suicide has a start, takes time and effort, has an end, and the end does not necessarily have to come with death or loss of consciousness. We want to show that the suicide process extends beyond the attempt or applying of lethal action to oneself. And so, the first project of the book is to bring attention to the complexity of suicide.

This book, as we intimated before, is about the most dramatic event of anyone's life. So, it is about people's suffering. The stories that we heard in interviews and read in suicide notes were heart-wrenching. They were stories of rejection and self-rejection, failure, concealment, topped with unconditional love and yearning for reciprocity which in most cases never came. We were in touch with raw human misery. We hope that this book will do them justice.

Also, as we delve into their suffering, we want to give it a voice. That is to say, we want to show their stories as they happened, not as we retell them. This is the second project of the book.

Now, even though our book is largely polemical, the third project is to offer a new perspective on suicide and suicide prevention. We see ourselves as critical friends of those endeavours and believe that qualitative perspectives in suicidology offer new and important contributions to efforts in preventing suicide. By understanding experiences of suicide, we begin to understand its social meanings and, through this, we begin to understand better how to design preventative interventions. And so, we are interested in setting up a dialogue between qualitative discourse analysis and the mainstream discourses of suicide, both in suicidology and in suicide prevention.

Suicide

'Each suicide drama occurs in the mind of a unique individual' (Shneidman, 1996: 5). Shneidman's famous words about suicide reflect well the perspective on suicide we want to take in this book. In contrast to the dominant suicidological view, we want to focus on the individual experiences of people who decide to take the step of killing themselves. We want to understand suicide and its process as a socially situated act which, in contrast to what Shneidman proposes, does not only happen in a person's mind but also happens in a particular social context through which suicide is made sense of by both the person who kills themselves and those who stay behind and must understand what happened.

Deaths by suicide are high. Every forty seconds someone in the world takes their life, making up not quite a million a year (WHO, 2019). Hudzik and Cannon (2014) report that more people die in suicidal acts than through wars or murder. According to Eurostat, in 2016 the suicide rate in the European Union was 10.33 suicides per 100,000 people. The lowest (3.89/100,000) was in Cyprus; the highest was in Lithuania (28.27/100,000). Moreover, researchers indicate that these figures are more than likely to be underestimated by at the very least 10 per cent, reaching, potentially, even 50 per cent (Silverman, 2006)! There are, of course, even more suicide attempts. Cautious estimates indicate that the number of suicide attempts is 10–15 times greater than the number of suicides; however, the American Foundation for Suicide Prevention (AFSP) estimates that 0.6 per cent of adults aged 18 or older have made at least one suicide attempt (AFSP, 2019).

Men commit suicide considerably more than women do and considerably so in high-income countries. This is the essence of the so-called gender paradox in suicide. Canetto and Sakinofsky (1998) observe that, while women have a higher incidence of suicide ideation and behaviour, more men kill themselves. The numbers are quite worrying. Men's suicide rates had been increasing in the twentieth century (Cantor, 2000; see also Lemieux, Saman & Lutfiyya, 2014; cf. Atkinson, 1978; see also Shiner et al., 2009). Globally, in 2016 the male–female suicide ratio was 1.75:1; in Europe, it reached 3.47:1 and is the highest in the world, whereas in some European countries it is significantly higher. For example, in our native Poland the male–female suicide ratio goes beyond 7:1; in Lithuania, it is just under 7 (WHO, 2018). More men than women take their lives in almost all countries in the world; according to the United Nations' World Health Organization (WHO) in 2016, there were only seven countries (from 183 listed) where women take their lives more frequently than men.

One could even say that being a man is the highest risk factor with regard to taking your life. Moreover, men's suicide rate is rising. Indeed, suicide amongst men has been described as a silent epidemic. These rates differ according to age. In the United Kingdom, suicide is the biggest killer of men under fifty and it is a very sobering fact that as many as 42 per cent of men considered taking their own life, as the UK's Office for National Statistics (ONS) reports (ONS, 2019a). To end with a particularly shocking US statistic, by age eighty-five the ratio of suicide between males and females was 53:1 (Szanto, Prigerson & Reynolds, 2001).

Over the centuries, attitudes towards suicide have changed significantly. In ancient Greece, suicide was accepted, especially if it was done for an important reason (e.g. bereavement, illness, honour; O'Connor & Sheehy, 2000). This tolerant attitude started to change with the rise of Christianity and the commandment not to kill, under which suicide fell. Suicide became an act against the 'natural law' (Hecht, 2013). In consequence, a person who killed themselves became a perpetrator of a crime (Marsh, 2013; Minois, 2001).

The beginning of the nineteenth century brought a new perspective on suicide. It was the first time that suicide was seen as either an illness or a symptom of an illness (Hacking, 1990; Marsh, 2010). Doctors received powers to secure, treat, control and assess suicide (Hacking, 1990). Nowadays, the common assumption is that suicide is a result of mental health problems (Battin, 1995; Marsh, 2010; Pridmore, 2011). A person who takes their life is represented as someone who suffers psychologically and kills themselves when in a bad psychological state. Common are publications in which authors state that you cannot commit suicide unless you are mentally ill (e.g. Harris

& Barraclough, 1997; Jamison, 2004; Mościcki, 1997). A medicalized view of suicide is adopted beyond psychiatry; it is, for example, adopted by WHO.

Indeed, the medical view of suicide has recently been strengthened. In the DSM-5, the American Psychiatric Association (APA) indicated that it would look into suicidal behaviour with a view to determine whether it should be treated as a mental disorder, called Suicidal Behavior Disorder (APA, 2013). This is underscored by claims that suicide ideation can now be reduced pharmacologically (Yovell et al., 2015).

As might be expected, further medicalization of suicide is controversial. Some argue that treating suicidal behaviour as a separate disorder will allow the development of uniform terminology and improve the quality of research (Oquendo & Baca-Garcia, 2014). Moreover, such a move, it is argued, would enhance suicide prevention. Indeed, as WHO estimates, as many as 165,000 people annually could have been protected from suicide if they had received adequate psychiatric help (Bertolote et al., 2003).

The counterargument is that medicine cannot always effectively deal with suicidal behaviour even if medical practitioners know there is a risk. People kill themselves despite psychiatric help, including medication (Khan et al., 2003; see also Fergusson et al., 2005; Gunnell, Saperia & Ashby, 2005; Maris, 2015), while arguments that suicide must result from a mental disorder are countered with research that there are suicides where no mental illness was ever determined (e.g. Chen & Dilsaver, 1996; Conwell et al., 1996; Phillips et al., 2002).

Furthermore, suicide prevention is largely based on the biomedical model of suicide. Despite much effort, suicide rates tend to stay the same, while predicting suicide is still in the realm of fanciful aspiration (Pokorny, 1983, 1993; see also Large et al., 2011). Indeed, it is the social understanding of suicide which seems to offer more promising perspectives on suicide and its prevention. The British ONS reports that there are more suicides in deprived communities than in their non-deprived counterparts (ONS, 2019b). Such research builds on earlier studies which suggest that unemployment (which is up to four times higher in deprived communities) and other economic factors such as indebtedness significantly increase the risk of suicide (Mäki & Martikainen, 2012; Reeves et al., 2014). The medicalization of suicide will hardly help here.

The final point we would like to make here is that, for years now, there have been calls for standardized terminology and classification (Dear, 2001; De Leo et al., 2006; Maris, Berman & Silverman, 2000b; O'Carroll et al., 1996; Rosenberg et al., 1988; Rudd & Joiner, 1998). There is no doubt that uniform criteria of classification are of crucial importance to both researchers and clinicians. For example, for clinicians such a classification could lead to better risk assessment and management, as well as to better interventions.

Silverman (2013) proposes that the first modern classification of suicide and suicidal behaviour was created by Aaron Beck and colleagues (Beck, Resnik & Lettieri, 1974). They assumed three concepts for describing the spectrum of suicidality: suicide ideas, suicide attempts and completed suicide. Each of these categories was also assessed on five dimensions: certainty of the assessor (0–100 per cent), lethality (zero, low, medium or high), intent to die (zero, low, medium or high), circumstances without which suicide could not have happened (zero, low, medium or high) and the method. The most difficult of those dimensions was the intent to die.

This classification was used by O'Carrol and colleagues (1996) for creating a new system. The authors decided to base descriptions of suicidal behaviour on three characteristics: suicide intent, evidence for self-inflicted injury and consequences of the act (injury, no injury or death). This, in turn, was modified by Silverman and colleagues (2007a, 2007b) who suggested the introduction of indeterminacy into the system (undetermined suicide attempt, undetermined suicide-related death and self-inflicted death with undetermined intent).

Finally, the Centers for Disease Control and Prevention (CDC) (Crosby, Ortega & Melanson, 2011; Posner et al., 2007, 2014) expands their classification onto self-harm distinguished between suicidal and non-suicidal self-directed violence, adding indeterminate self-inflicted death as a third category.

Significantly, despite many terminologies and classification systems, so far none has been adopted universally. It is clear, however, that an ideal system should be atheoretical, acultural and consist of mutually exclusive concepts which comprise the full spectrum of suicidal behaviours and ideation (De Leo et al., 2006; Silverman, 2006). And even though doubts are expressed as to the possibility of arriving at such a classification (De Leo et al., 2006), the goal remains an important one.

Suicide and suicide attempt

De Leo and colleagues (2006) point to four elements which occur in all definitions of suicide analysed by them. Suicide is defined (1) as death in consequence of one's behaviours; (2) through one's agency (an act directed at oneself); (3) by the involvement of an intention to die; and (4) as the awareness of the consequences of the action performed (see also Farberow, 1980; Maris, Berman & Silverman,

2000a). A suicide attempt, on the other hand, is defined on the basis of the definition of suicide. In other words, a suicide attempt is an act of suicide where death did not occur (Crosby, Ortega & Melanson, 2011; Posner et al., 2007). The crucial aspect of a suicide attempt is the existence of the suicide intention, that is to say, the intention to take one's own life, which, needless to say, raises difficult issues of how to determine such an intention after someone's death.

Despite the fact that the term 'suicide attempt' is said to be used so widely and without rigour that it might mean little (O'Carroll et al., 1996), both clinical and research interest in it remains high. It is the suicide attempt that is the most important predictor of suicide (Brown et al., 2000; Fushimi, Sugawara & Saito, 2006; Harris & Barraclough, 1997; Joiner, 2005; Sokero et al., 2005). Just this fact alone suggests the significance of research into suicide attempts, as it is such experiences that give significant insight into suicide and its process.

We realize that some researchers question the status of homogeneous suicide attempts. Meeham and colleagues (1992) demonstrated that only one in ten suicide attempts resulted in hospitalization, only another two required medical attention and the lethality of the remaining 70 per cent is unknown. Other research shows that over half of people who attempt suicide do not seek medical help (Crosby, Cheltenham & Sacks, 1999). It is reasonable to ask therefore whether suicide attempts resulting in such drastically different consequences are a group of similar events. Unfortunately, even though there are postulations that suicide attempts should also be assessed for their lethality (Williams, 2014), there is still no universal method of doing this. Interestingly, when asked to assess ten cases of possible suicide attempts, fourteen suicidologists and fifty-nine clinicians could not agree on much, even though half of the participants were provided with a definition of the suicide attempt. To a considerable extent, therefore, a suicide attempt is something that is socially constructed between the person who attempts to kill themselves (possibly, her or his family) and the clinician who acknowledges the attempt and admits the person for care.

In the next section, we introduce the main focus of this book: the suicide process.

The suicide process

According to Brüdern et al. (2016), the last ten years of suicidology have been dominated by the disease model of suicide. In this model, suicidal behaviour is considered to be a symptom of mental disorders (Marsh, 2010). It is also assumed that treatment of mental disorders reduces the risk of suicide. However, more and more research shows that the relationship between suicidal behaviour and mental disorders is more complex. As May, Klonsky and Klein (2012) have argued, although diagnoses of Axis I disorders (DSM) differentiated suicide ideators from non-suicidal controls and suicide attempters from controls, they failed to differentiate suicide attempters from suicide ideators (see also Kessler, Borges & Walters, 1999; May & Klonsky, 2016). To put it differently, although the diagnosis of major depression predicts suicidal thoughts, it does not predict suicidal plans or attempts (Nock et al., 2010). Only a fraction of depressed individuals with suicidal ideation act on their thoughts and progress to a suicide attempt (May, Klonsky & Klein, 2012). And so, this book offers an approach to the problem that looks at it from the perspective of those who engaged themselves in the process of taking their own life. While we cannot offer a clear answer as to what prompts suicidal ideators to put their plans into action, we can offer a platform upon which such further research can draw.

The suicidal process is usually studied as the period between the first thoughts/wish of death and the suicidal act (Portzky, Audenaert & Van Heeringen, 2005; Runeson, Beskow & Waern, 1996; Van Heeringen, Hawton & Williams, 2000). Some scholars take the first thoughts/wish of death in the individual's life history as the beginning of the process (Neeleman, de Graaf & Vollebergh, 2004; Runeson, Beskow & Waern, 1996); others restrict the suicidal process to the last episode of thoughts/wish of suicide which preceded the particular suicide act (Deisenhammer et al., 2009). So far, there have not been any studies that would reverse the top-down perspective, which is usually adopted in suicidological research, to a bottom-up perspective that puts the experience of the person with a suicide attempt history at the centre of investigation and explores their perspective as to when the suicidal process starts, proceeds and ends and, finally, what it means.

The foundations for the concept of the suicidal process were created by Pokorny (1974) who introduced the concept of suicidal behaviour as comprising suicidal thoughts, a suicide attempt and suicide. As Wasserman (2015) argues, further studies by Paykel and colleagues (1974) and Beskow (1979) led to the development of the concept and, although there are variations in definitions across studies, most suicidologists make a chronological link between suicidal ideation and suicide and define it as the 'suicidal process' (Runeson, Beskow & Waern, 1996; Schrijvers, Bollen & Sabbe, 2012; Van Heeringen, 2001). It is assumed that suicidal behaviour has a previous history and that the current process is a continuum of gradually increasing seriousness in suicidal behaviour, from weariness of life to death wishes, suicidal thoughts, attempts and a suicide (Wasserman, 2015).

The suicidal process, in both global (the path to suicide from the first thoughts/wish of death in a person's life history) and local terms (the last episode of thoughts/wish of suicide, which preceded the suicide act), is mostly studied in terms of its temporality. Suicidologists are interested in both the chronology of events concomitant with subsequent elements of the process and the relationship between the temporality of the process and the psychological and socio-demographic variables.

And so, with regard to the global understanding of the process, Neeleman and colleagues (2004) showed that serious psychological stressors may trigger the suicidal process but, later on in the suicidal process, these factors play a smaller role and psychopathological, socio-demographic and cultural factors have more significance. Additionally, the first suicidal behaviour in a person's life history is associated with socio-economic risk factors and negative life events to a greater extent than subsequent ones. It means that subsequent suicidal behaviour is more autonomous and is increasingly dependent on internal factors comparatively to initial suicidal behaviour (see Van Heeringen, Hawton & Williams, 2000).

The suicidal process, understood in global terms, is also shorter in men (median of twelve months) than in women (median of forty-two months) and its duration depended on the diagnosis of mental disorders; the median interval from first suicidal communication to the suicide was forty-seven months in schizophrenia, thirty months in borderline personality disorder, three months in major depression and less than one month in adjustment disorder (Runeson, Beskow & Waern, 1996). Another study showed that the depressive episode and borderline personality were diagnoses that affected progression of the suicide process, especially in women (Arsenault-Lapierre, Kim & Turecki, 2004; Bjerkeset, Romundstad & Gunnell, 2008). It has also been shown that 48 per cent of the patients hospitalized in psychiatric hospitals after a suicide attempt assessed that the suicidal process, which preceded the attempt, did not last more than ten minutes (Deisenhammer et al., 2009).

Despite continuing interest in the suicidal process, it is argued (Gordon, Stevenson & Cutcliffe, 2014) that, due to the emphasis on quantitative methodology and its focus on causation in contemporary suicidology, as well as the practical challenges associated with conducting qualitative research, understanding of the suicidal process is limited (see also Aldridge, 1998). The above-mentioned – mostly quantitative – studies provide knowledge about factors that affect the duration of the process and its successive stages, yet they do not allow us to fully understand how the suicidal process is subjectively perceived by people with a history of suicide attempts and their significant others. Qualitative analyses will afford us insight into the lived reality of the suicidal process and offer answers to questions which so far remain unanswered.

Furthermore, in this book we want to add the perspective of narrative constructions of the suicidal process that are significant to the individual who attempted to take their life, enriching our understanding through an external perspective on the process. Our approach to the suicidal process is in contrast to the research carried out hitherto, with regard to both the individuals who attempted suicide and their significant others. By focusing on lived perspectives, we heed the calls for a more methodologically diverse suicidology. For, in spite of the fact that suicidologists stress the importance of methodological diversity, which would lead to a greater understanding of suicide and suicidal behaviour (e.g. Leenaars, 2002a, 2002b; Rogers & Apel, 2010), bottom-up approaches in suicide research are still marginal (e.g. Hjelmeland, 2016).

Finally, discourse analytic studies are very rare in suicidology. This is despite the fact that an application of discourse analysis in suicide research seems to be eminently justifiable, as suicide attempts are extralinguistic phenomena which are mediated linguistically/discursively. It is almost exclusively through language, the narratives of those having tried to commit suicide or experienced suicidal thoughts, that researchers can have access to 'what happened', let alone to how the people concerned experienced these feelings or attempts. It is only through language that we can have access to how suicide and its ideation are positioned institutionally. And so, anchoring the study in discourse analysis, we draw upon its finely tuned methods of accounting not only for lexical choices but also for grammatical forms and larger syntactic and textual patterns. Thus, discourse analysis becomes a powerful tool in understanding how people construct their experience and relate it to the social and institutional-psychiatric reality in which they find themselves.

Reversing the perspective and focusing on the narrated experience of our informants allows us to obtain new insights into both the experience of the suicide process and the role of significant others within it. In the process, we shall be able to contextualize the existing knowledge about suicide. To date, no such research has been conducted.

Discourse analysis

This book is about how people communicate and the discursive resources they avail themselves of. We assume, following Bauman (1986), it is not the world which is the material of the narrative; rather, it is the narrative from which the world is abstracted. We are interested in people's experience of suicide, which includes the subject positions they constructed for themselves and in relationship to the act and those they left behind. We assume that their accounts give us insight into a host of meanings which allow us to understand suicide as a situated social situation experienced and given meaning by the person who performs it.

In what follows, we offer a brief account of a model of discourse analysis with which we have sympathy (for a much more comprehensive discussion, see Barker & Galasiński, 2001; for other such accounts, see Galasiński, 2004, 2008, 2013). In particular, the review we offer here is based upon our latest research (Galasiński, 2017; Ziółkowska, 2016).

We situate our analyses in a constructionist approach to discourse and within its critical strand (Krzyżanowski & Frochtner, 2016). Thus, we draw upon a tradition in discourse analysis which is an amalgamation of a number of approaches, including critical linguistics (Fowler, 1991; Fowler et al., 1979; Hodge & Kress, 1993); social semiotics (Hodge & Kress, 1988; Kress & van Leeuwen, 1996); sociocultural change and change in discourse (Fairclough, 1989, 1992, 1995, 2003); and socio-cognitive studies (e.g. Van Dijk, 1993, 1998). Linguistically, it is anchored within systemic-functional linguistics (e.g. Halliday, 1978, 1994; Halliday & Hasan, 1985) which complements the analyst's self-reflexivity (Wodak, 1999) and can help reduce the arbitrariness of interpretation by anchoring it in the linguistic form itself.

By saying that our discourse analysis is critical, we mean that our research tackles important problems of social life, traditionally issues around social inequalities. Indeed, we use the word 'discourse' in order to separate the more abstract semiotic system – language – to focus on the context-bound social practice of communication – discourse.

Discourse is a form of social practice (Fowler et al., 1979) and there is a dialectic relationship between discourse and social structure. On the one hand, discourse is shaped and limited by social structures such as social class, social norms or practices but, on the other hand, it is also constitutive of those structures (see below). And so, discourse is not only a set of practices of representing extralinguistic reality but also one of constructing it. It is as much the space for representation as it is for action. In such a way, every language use reproduces and, potentially, transforms the society which produced it.

We take a text-oriented approach (Fairclough, 1992). Thus, we focus upon the content and form of stretches of discourse, with an interest both in the semantics and syntax of an utterance and in the functions of what is said or written within the local context, as well as the social actions thus accomplished. Language users are not isolated individuals but are engaged in communicative activities as members of social groups, organizations, institutions and cultures. To a considerable extent, they speak and write in the ways it is appropriate (in many senses of this word) to speak or write.

Taking a text-oriented perspective means that we separate the analytic and interpretative stages of understanding the data we approach. This is to say that the initial and main approach to the data is focused upon the linguistic form of the texts, which is 'objectively' accessible. This focuses this stage of analysis on choices and patterns in vocabulary, grammar and text structures. Such an analysis can be supported by a hermeneutic-like interpretation of discourses in terms of the context in which they were submerged (see Titscher et al., 2000).

It is only after such analyses that the process of interpretation comes in. This consists of the process of 'making sense' of the data. This process is inevitably carried out from the point of view of the researcher who is involved in the process. In other words, while the analysis of the linguistic form can be accepted intersubjectively, the interpretation is underpinned by individual opinion and cannot be seen as better or superior to that done from another point of view.

Importantly, we are mindful that the very form of the notes – written language – was also a source of complication. As written texts, our data were more than likely to be different in text organization, vocabulary and genre from any spoken account (Linell, 2005). Yet, noting it, we do not explore this avenue. There cannot be spoken data to compare the suicide notes with. Moreover, we are not interested in tracing the characteristics of the genre of the suicide note. To some extent, this is what the 'traditional' research into suicide notes has done for years. In contrast, we are interested predominantly in the realities constructed in the notes, regardless of the medium in which it has been done.

And so, we are interested in the discourses (practices of representation) the interviewees and authors of the notes drew on when they spoke to us or wrote their notes. We want to discover the discourses of the suicide process in the three corpora we collected, the ways in which the process, including its main actor, is made social through the process of narrating it. In such a way, we set aside the issue of the representativeness of the data. We are not trying to make claims as to the extent the research is representative of how either people with the experience of a suicide attempt speak or authors of suicide notes write. Rather, we are interested in uncovering the discourses underpinning their narratives so as to shed light on the process of suicide or attempts. Making an assumption that people's discursive actions are rooted in social practices, we are uncovering the practices that construct the suicide process. Even though we cannot answer the question of how dominant these practices of representation are, the data we have must be seen as informing the social context in which they are rooted.

The following assumptions we make about discourse are relevant here.

(1) Discourse is socially constitutive. It enters into a 'dialectical' relationship with the contexts in which it occurs, so, as much as it depends on its context, it also creates social and political 'realities' (Fairclough & Wodak, 1997; van Leeuwen & Wodak, 1999). From the notorious case of homosexuality as a former mental disease (for the extraordinary story of how it was demedicalized, see Kutchins & Kirk, 1999), all the way to the newly, shall we say, written mental illnesses such as restless legs syndrome or so-called premenstrual tension (or PMT), one can quite easily see how the recent edition of the DSM invoked new diseases which psychiatrists will now treat.

As regards suicide, Marsh (2010) offers a fascinating account of the change in the discourses of suicide, from a personal choice, through criminalization, all the way to its medicalization – suicide is a symptom of mental illness. Moreover, the APA has announced in the current edition of the diagnostic manual that they are working on further medicalization of suicide. Suicide and suicidal behaviour are to become an illness in their own right.

Fairclough (1992) suggests that language has three main functions related to how it constitutes reality. First, discourse is constitutive of identities and subject positions of individuals as well as ways in which they are invoked in context. Second, discourse is constitutive of relationships between those individuals, how they are negotiated and reproduced. Third, it constructs systems of knowledge and beliefs.

(2) Discourse is a system of options from which language users make their choices. This is to say that, whatever can be said or written, it can be said or written differently. The construction of any representation of 'reality' is necessarily selective, entailing decisions as to which aspects of that reality to include and how to arrange them. Each selection carries its share of socially ingrained values so that representation is socially constructed (Hall, 1997; Hodge & Kress, 1993), and alternative representations are not only always possible but they carry divergent significance and consequences (Fowler, 1996). Nevertheless, texts

seek to impose a 'preferred reading' (Hall, 1981) or a 'structure of faith' (Menz, 1989) upon the addressee. As more and more social scientists claim to analyse 'discourse', as we have noted, linguistic discourse analysis tends to focus more upon its form.

(3) Discourse is ideological. The selective character of representation leads to the view that it is through discourse and other semiotic practices that ideologies are formulated, reproduced and reinforced. We understand the term ideology as social (general and abstract) representations shared by members of a group and used by them to accomplish everyday social practices: acting and communicating (Billig et al., 1988; Fowler, 1985; Van Dijk, 1998). These representations are organized into systems which are deployed by social classes and other groups 'in order to make sense of, figure out and render intelligible the way society works' (Hall, 1996b: 26), while, at the same time, they are capable of 'ironing out' the contradictions, dilemmas and antagonisms of practices in ways which accord with the interests and projects of power (Chouliaraki & Fairclough, 1999).

Ideology provides us with ways in which we can legitimize and accept social action (Van Dijk, 1988), regardless of its dominance and the social group which it underpins. The difference between ideologies and their social groups is the power to impose their ideological lens onto another groups (Foucault, 2002; see also Parker, 1989). It is power and its workings that make certain discourses limited to certain social groups (in our native Poland, for example, forms of psychological discourse such as questionnaires are only available to psychologists and only they can legitimately use them, regardless of their and others' competencies). It is through discourse that those ideologies are reproduced, reinforced and, in particular situations, replaced.

(4) Finally, we assume that text – the product of what one says or writes – is intertextual. Texts are full of other texts, accessing them for stylistic, ironic effect or for their ideological message. Intertextuality can be intentional, but it also can be unwitting, which suggests that certain texts have a dominant role in how certain contents or experiences are constructed.

We firmly situate the methodological perspective of this book in the qualitative research paradigm. That is to say, we take a bottom-up, 'inside' perspective. We want to look at reality through the eyes of those who were about to take their lives and, in the process, offer insight into the suicidal process which is still under-researched in suicidology as noted by Aldridge (1998), a critique which in our view is still valid. What is crucial about the approach we have taken is that the core of our endeavour is firmly based on the analysis of the lexico-grammatical structures of language. In such a way, regardless of our cultural background or life experiences, the initial linguistic analysis can be repeated and reproduced. This is because such analyses are not based on our beliefs or impressions but on the objectively accessible grammatical form and vocabulary.

As we reject the ontological assumption of discovering reality via an instrument and stress its social nature (see Denzin & Lincoln, 2000; see also Denzin, 1989), we want to take the 'inside' perspective, making our research more 'engaged'. This is particularly important in the case of research into vulnerable, disenfranchised perspectives. We take issue with Hammersley's (2008) critique of qualitative research, as he asks whose description is used in the ethnographic research. We take it as the question of the research perspective or – as Bloor (2001) would have it – one of the 'revolt of the subject'. To what extent can a person without disabilities understand a person with them (Oliver, 1996) or to what extent can we understand a person who is about to kill themselves? Put another way: viewing suicide through the eyes of someone writing a suicide note and preparing to die is very different from that of a researcher looking at suicide from a distance. Qualitative research brings us closer to the former perspective.

It is also noteworthy that, despite the fact that suicidologists stress the importance of methodological diversity, which would lead to a greater understanding of suicide and suicidal behaviour (e.g. Leenaars, 2002b; Rogers & Apel, 2010), bottom-up approaches in suicide research are marginal (e.g. Hjelmeland, 2016).

Qualitative suicidology

Our final methodological point is about the relationship between discourse analysis and suicidology. We locate our research in the qualitative suicidological strand which, even though still on the margins, is rapidly growing.

Although speaking of disciplines as homogeneous monoliths inevitably leads to oversimplification, it is possible to say suicidology is almost exclusively quantitative. Suicidological research can be grouped into three kinds of research: epidemiological, biological and interventionist (Hjelmeland & Knizek, 2010). These kinds of research account for 97 per cent of articles published in three leading journals in suicidology: *Archives of Suicide Research*, *Crisis* and *Suicide and Life-threatening Behavior* (Hjelmeland & Knizek, 2010; see also Goldblatt et al., 2012; White et al., 2016). The only two book-length suicidological studies which report qualitative research are our own recent books (Galasiński, 2017; Ziółkowska, 2016).

And so, the dominant perspective in suicidology is to see suicide as static and individual, probably resulting from mental illness and associated with identifiable risk factors, which became the main focal point of suicidological endeavours (White, 2017; White et al., 2016). Inevitably, suicide is seen outside its social context, let alone its meaning, as always to be prevented and controlled. This perspective was solidified in a recent declaration from the editor of a leading suicidological journal who stated that only the quantitative perspective could lead to progress in suicidological research (Joiner, 2011).

And yet, there is a growing unease within mainstream suicidology. Rogers and Lester (2010) point out that, after producing volumes of work, understanding of suicide is still elusive. Fitzpatrick (2011) suggests that insight into narratively constructed experience is crucial for extending suicidological knowledge onto meanings of suicide in its social context. Lester and Stack (2015; see also Hjelmeland, 2016) reinforce this message by saying that mere correlation of different variables does not bring suicidology closer to understanding suicide. They also call for more qualitative research.

In our view, the most interesting counterpoint to the mainstream suicidological view of suicide comes from the critical suicidological perspective. In contrast to mainstream suicidology, its critical counterpart suggests engagement with social anchoring of suicide, and in particular seeing it within social, historical, cultural and political contexts. Suicide no longer becomes an object for uncomplicated scientific inspection but an event which is socially entangled (Kirmayer, 2012; Marsh, 2010; White, 2017; White & Kral, 2014). White (2017) argues that critical suicidology introduces doubt into what the mainstream takes for granted. The self is no longer taken as the sole agent naturally doing away with its own existence (see also Jaworski, 2014). At the same time, it poses questions as to the inevitable positioning of suicide as unjustified and to be stopped (Button, 2016; for consideration of the notion of rational suicide, see also Mayo, 1986; Richards, 2017; Werth, 1999).

The two approaches should not be seen as separate from each other, though. Indeed, a recent critique of the most prevalent theory of suicide (Hjelmeland & Knizek, 2019) resulted as much in a defence of the interpersonal theory of suicide (Klonsky, 2019; Smith et al., 2019) but, more importantly, in an attempt to offer a platform for joining up the two approaches (Abrutyn & Mueller, 2019). Abrutyn and Mueller (2019) explicitly focus on the narrow understanding of science in mainstream suicidology and postulate inclusion of the softer qualitative perspective into the dominant research perspective.

In this book, we hope to reinforce the qualitative platform for a study of suicide and in such a way offer a new insight into experiences and the meaning of suicide (see Boldt, 1988; Colucci, 2013). If Lester (2000) was right that suicidology had reached its end and needed innovation (see also Rogers, 2003; Rogers & Apel, 2010; Rogers & Lester, 2010), we hope this volume will offer a new perspective in English.

And so, we see discourse analysis as capable of responding to calls for understanding the individuality of suicide in its social and cultural context (Münster & Broz, 2015). This is seconded by Marsh (2010, 2016) and Fullagar (2003) who make the point that the current psychiatric and suicidological discourses, by pathologizing suicide, distance researchers from suicide as an embodied social act (for a critique of scientism, see Fitzpatrick, 2015 and Hjelmeland & Knizek, 2011; for a social perspective, see also Roen, Scourfield & McDermott, 2008). Discourse analysis offers a much more holistic view and understanding of suicide through the perspective of those who constructed it in their suicide notes (see also Gavin & Rogers, 2006).

The data

There are three sets of data this book is based on. The first is a set of sixty-five semi-structured interviews conducted in sixteen medium-term wards in four hospitals in the south and south-west of Poland. They were conducted with patients who had been admitted to hospital after a suicide attempt. Thirty-six of the interviewees were male, twenty-nine were female. The interviews lasted between 7 and 115 minutes, and the mean duration was 28 minutes.[1]

The data collection was performed in accordance with the Declaration of Helsinki, with ethical approvals obtained from the ethics committee of the University of Social Sciences and Humanities in Poland. The participants received written information regarding the scope of the research, the identity and contact details of the researchers, the opportunity to withdraw from the studies at any point with no consequence, their confidentiality and anonymity, and all other information as required in accordance with Polish policies for research in a clinical context.

We have chosen not to represent our informants with fictional initials, let alone fictional first names as often is the practice in the literature. This is for two reasons. The stories we cite carry with them a number of sensitive details – we did not wish to create the possibility of false identities. Second, the default address form for adults in Polish is the polite form *pan/pani* (the equivalent of German *Sie* or Spanish *usted*) and referring to informants, adult people, only by first names (fictional or not) could be seen as patronizing and to a certain extent at least puts them in a position of lower or inferior status, something our informants, and probably most other people with mental illness, have to struggle with daily.

Moreover, throughout the book, we tend to refer to our informants as informants or participants rather than as patients. This is because the narratives they offered concerned non-clinical issues. When the context warrants it, we refer to them as patients (rather than, say, clients, service users or survivors) (see Costa et al., 2019). We realize that this is not an 'innocent' choice: there is a large literature on stigmatization of mental health users (for reviews, see Hayward & Bright, 1997; Rüsch, Angermeyer & Corrigan, 2005), their social and political isolation (Erdner et al., 2005; Kelly, 2006) and particularly the role of labelling in stigmatization (Corrigan, Kerr & Knudsen, 2005). Indeed, a number of studies were carried out into the very use of the expression 'mental patient', finding negative associations invoked by it (Johannsen, 1969; Rabkin, 1972). Also, we are mindful of Speed's (2006) analysis of self-labelling on the spectrum of patients-consumers-survivors, pointing out that it might reflect the position between passive acceptance and active resistance to the mental health system.

Still, we have made our choice precisely because our informants used the word 'patient' to refer to themselves. Also, we think that Speed's (2006) argument is somewhat tendentious in that he does not consider the possibility that accepting one's patienthood might be part of accepting one's illness (Davidson, 2003; Morse & Johnson, 1991) and part of a route towards recovery. It might also be part of 'coming out' and challenging the stigma (Corrigan & Matthews, 2003). We make these choices also as we reject the argument that uniform resistance towards psychiatric services is universally good or desirable. It can in fact be counterproductive.

All interviews were digitally recorded and later transcribed. The basis of our analyses is transcriptions. In qualitative research, the transcription of spoken data is considered significant, going beyond simple data processing (Atkinson & Heritage, 1984). We adopted a simplified version of the Jeffersonian system (e.g. Jefferson, 2004). The system allowed us to accurately render the contents and the form of what the informants say and to control the level of information needed for our analysis while making it transparent (Hepburn & Bolden, 2017).

The second set of data is the *Polski korpus listów pożegnalnych samobójców* (Polish Corpus of Suicide Notes, n.d.). It contains authentic suicide notes collected from regional prosecutors' offices in Poland in 2008. Only notes from people who killed themselves were put in the corpus (for a detailed account and description of the corpus, its sub-corpora and the process of data collection, see Zaśko-Zielińska, 2013).

The corpus contains 614 suicide notes, written between 1998 and 2008. Four hunded and fifty-six of those letters (74 per cent) were written by 290 men, while the remaining 256 notes were written by 92 women. The youngest author of a suicide note in the corpus was twelve years old (a girl), the oldest eighty-nine years old (a man). The corpus contains information about the time and the place of writing (finding), the age of the author, their gender and the medium (599 notes were handwritten), and sometimes includes their marital status.

We only had access to the processed version of the notes. In other words, we worked on digitized and fully anonymized texts of the notes, with no access to their material original or their facsimiles. The only aspect of the notes preserved in the corpus was the use of capital letters. We have preserved the capitalization in the Polish versions of the notes, which we have put in the appendices after every chapter. We have also preserved the spelling, punctuation and layout of the text as it was presented in the corpus.

Finally, we have the corpus of timeline visualizations of the suicidal process, collected between October 2018 and December 2018. We have twenty-six timelines collected from twenty study participants. Eleven participants were male, nine were female. They were patients hospitalized after a suicide attempt. The data were collected in psychiatric hospitals, during patients' first days in the hospital. Similarly to the first corpus of the data, the study was performed in accordance with the Declaration of Helsinki, with ethical approvals obtained from the ethics committee of the University of Social Sciences and Humanities in Poland. The participants received written information regarding the scope of the research, the identity and contact details of the researchers, the opportunity to withdraw from the studies at any point with no consequence, their confidentiality and anonymity, and all other information as required in accordance with Polish policies for research in clinical contexts.

It is important to stress that the originals of all the data we have are in Polish, raising the issue of the extent to which we write about Polish suicide notes or Polish interviews. However, we follow Barbagli (2015) who posits a 'Western' attitude towards suicide, one which would include Poland. Moreover, there is no evidence of significant national differences at least in the contents of suicide notes (indeed, suicide notes seem to have considerable similarities regardless of who wrote them and where), including those written in Poland. Alternatively, we do not know of any cross-cultural studies of interviews with people after suicide attempts. Perhaps our book will give rise to such research in the future. We would speculate, however, that perhaps because the notes are written at the most dramatic moment of a person's life, while stories we collected are about this very dramatic moment, the differences between certain identities fade away.

Finally, in the discussions we refer to our translations of the Polish originals. We attempted to render not only the content of the Polish originals but also their 'flavour' and 'gist'. Sometimes, this results in disjointed or 'bad' English, sometimes the language is barely intelligible. This is because the Polish originals were like that. Occasionally, we offer some information in square brackets (especially noting text which was removed for maintaining the anonymity of the authors). Moreover, we also decided not to use any contractions in the English translations. In contrast to English, Polish does not use contractions and their imposition on the translations would, in our view, be too interpretative. We do realize, however, that just as the presence of contractions carries meaning, so does their absence, and some of the English translations may seem unduly formal and stilted. Unfortunately, this could not be avoided. In most cases, we also introduce punctuation to the English translations. We also understand that this may offer an interpretation of the Polish originals, yet it also makes them more intelligible. Importantly, all our analyses were carried out on the Polish originals.

Vocabulary

As we come to the end of preparing the ground for the discussion in the book, we would like to make note of the vocabulary used in suicidology. There are two aspects of this. First, there is the terminology which is recommended for use by organizations such as the CDC, the second aspect is more to do with speaking of suicide.

The CDC, after much deliberating, recently announced a glossary of terms which should be used when referring to suicide and suicidal behaviour. Their effort is as much positive in recommending the use of certain terms (such as 'suicide' or 'suicide attempt') as it is negative in that they recommend not using a number of expressions. Thus, phrases such as 'completed suicide', 'failed attempt', 'successful suicide' are all deemed unacceptable (see Crosby, Ortega & Melanson, 2011; see also Posner et al., 2007). We think that such proposals are uncontentious.

The other initiative is more controversial in our view, and it concerns the use of the phrase 'commit suicide'. It is argued both in academic discourse (Nielsen, n.d.; Sommer-Rotenberg, 1998) and more widely in activist contexts (Caruso, n.d.; Olson, n.d.) that the use of the phrase places suicide very firmly in the legal, criminalized domain. Basically, commit suggests that suicide is a crime but, as it is not, 'commit' should be avoided. It is difficult not to agree with this, yet we still have two problems with removing the phrase from our vocabulary. First, we think that a number of people who are fully aware of the consequences can and want to use it. Having talked to people who have attempted to kill themselves, we know that they tried to 'commit suicide' while carrying the burden of doing something negative, socially sanctioned, perhaps not illegal, but still wrong. We are not certain at all that academics and activists should usurp the right to control the language people use outside such contexts.

The second issue, however, is more important. There are two main verbs which are suggested as replacements for 'commit': 'die' and 'complete'. We do not like either of them, as they change the object of which they speak. By using 'die' (as in 'died by suicide'), we remove the person's agency in taking their own life. 'Die by suicide' suggests that death just happens, and yet it does not. The person who kills themselves actually does something in order to 'die by suicide'. The suggested change of the verb significantly changes the way we are encouraged to see suicide. It no longer is an action of a person who takes their life, but an event that happens to them.

There are also problems with the other label which is proposed, admittedly, less frequently. We could say, for example: 'He completed suicide.' The word 'complete' takes care of the problem of agency – it does suggest an action a person takes and acknowledges the act of 'taking' life. The problem with it is that 'complete' has clear positive undertones. To complete something connotes something socially approved, such as exams, repairs, studying and the like. Thus, completing suicide does not make sense.

To a considerable extent, we think, the issue has no solution. In other words, as much as we agree with the arguments concerning the phrase 'commit suicide', we cannot see a 'natural' replacement. For these reasons, and for solving the problem for this book, we tend to speak of killing oneself and taking one's life. Of course, these phrases are not innocent either, as they obscure suicide, but, on balance, they are a reasonable solution. Yet occasionally we also use the phrase 'commit suicide', both as a reflection of how 'people speak' and because we find the other options more problematic than the use of the verb 'commit'.

One last terminological issue concerns the very word 'suicide'. In English, it refers to both the person who kills themselves and the act itself. Throughout the book, we use the word only in the latter meaning. This is predominantly for practical reasons – for avoiding ambiguity – as well as to be in line with the current practices in the literature on suicide. It mostly reserves the word for the act only.

Overview of the book

After this chapter, we begin the main discussion of the book. In Chapters 2 to 5, we discuss constructions of the period leading to the suicidal act. In Chapter 6, we discuss how the future is represented in the two corpora we have. In Chapter 7, we focus on multimodal representations of the suicide process, exploring how our informants negotiated their accounts on a visual timeline.

And so, in Chapter 2, we discuss suicidological definitions of suicide, exploring how the field constructs what is important and relevant in understanding suicide. We show that the key definitions of suicide construct it as an event which happens without human participation or with human participation only implied. We argue that their linguistic form has consequences not only for how suicide is constructed but also because it might set out dominant practices of suicidology. Backgrounding or removing the person and their actions from descriptions of suicide suggests that their experience is low in research priorities.

We also show that lived accounts of suicide, recorded in suicide notes, construct suicide in a different way. Lay representations of suicide are quite far from how it is rendered by suicidology. People writing those notes represent suicide as a time-extended process. We also argue for the notion of doing suicide, that is to say, engaging in a set of activities which eventually lead to the physical ending of the person's life.

In Chapter 3, we explore the narratively constructed agency of the person who takes their life. We begin our discussions by looking at how the definitions of suicide construct the person who commits it and argue that the person is either removed from the definitions altogether or their agency is backgrounded. For suicidology and suicide prevention, it seems, suicides only happen rather than are done by people anchored in social and political contexts.

We contrast those suicidological discourses with accounts of lived experience of suicide. We focus on accounts of decisions to commit suicide in interview data and in the corpus of suicide letters. While our informants spoke about the decision to kill themselves in very ambivalent ways, such ambivalence disappeared in suicide letters where their authors directly and explicitly ascribed agency to decide to themselves.

In Chapter 4, we continue the discussion of representations of the time before suicidal death and show such time is constructed as full of activity. Suicidal death is preceded by a series of actions and, in fact, also such actions are constructed as taking time, sometimes significant time. Particularly in Chapter 4 we would like to raise the question of when suicide starts. What constitutes the beginning of suicide?

Focusing on farewell letters, we discuss accounts of three stages of suicide: constructions of the beginning of the process, what happens during the time of 'committing suicide' and the end of the process. We also raise the issue of the communicative function of suicide notes.

Chapter 5 is about stories of the act of taking one's own life. First, we discuss stories in which the informants spoke about the instructions they gave themselves; these were stories about making sure that they do things effectively. Second, we explore stories in which the informants talked about the act itself. In contrast to the suicidological cognitive focus on suicidal death, we show stories in which the suicide attempt was constructed as a set of actions which had to be performed. Suicide was more of a physical and logistical problem than an emotional one.

In Chapter 6, we shift the focus onto constructions of the future in suicide notes and in our interview data. Our first finding was that suicide notes consistently constructed the future in very certain terms. We argue that in the way that suicide was rendered as more rational, as it was constructed as making sense, it also became more available for the authors of farewell letters. The chapter's second discussion is of the finality of suicide. We argue that, for our informants, suicide did not put an end to their physical or biological life. Rather, it put an end to the life they were living.

In Chapter 7, the last of the empirical chapters, we discuss verbal and visual representations of the suicide process on two timelines: a long-term one (extending at least beyond the day) and a short-term one (the day on which the suicide had taken place). We show that, on the long-term timescale, suicide and all other events were represented as event-objects, in a highly nominalized, non-narrative way. The suicide process became a punctuated series of objects. The short-term timescale, in contrast, was often ignored in order for the informants to be able to offer a narrative. Crucially, suicide became part of an ordinary day.

2

Conflict of discourses

In Chapter 1, we presented the dominant understanding of suicide and the suicide process. In this chapter and those that follow, we want to lay out the foundation of our argument in the book. We want to explore a conflict between the institutional/academic discourses of suicide and their lived counterpart. And so, on the one hand, we want to examine how suicide is constructed in the definitions of suicide and contrast this with how suicide is represented in suicide notes and interviews with those who attempted to kill themselves. In this chapter, we contrast the definitions with the representations of suicide in suicide notes.

Our argument in this chapter is two-fold. First, in the institutional and academic discourses, suicide is constructed either through its resulting 'condition' – death – or as an event which 'happens' outside any social or political reality. Second, suicide notes, as well as interviews, construct suicide as a series of events leading to the termination of life. In other words, the lived experience of suicide is of a process extended in time, with a beginning and an end. We finish with suggesting that suicide should not be seen only in terms of taking one's life but rather as a complex set of actions in which ending one's life is the last stage.

Definitions of suicide

Suicide is understood as the result of actions taken against the self by a person with the intention of ending their life. It assumes that in the person's knowledge and awareness they think the most likely consequence of their activities will be death. While definitions and descriptions of suicide and suicidal behaviour are linked to a number of factors (Silverman, 2006), De Leo and co-authors (2006) indicate that four elements are contained in all of the definitions of suicide they have analysed: (1) death as an outcome of the behaviour, (2) agency, (3) the intention to die and (4) awareness of the outcome of the act undertaken (see also Farberow, 1980; Maris, Berman & Silverman, 2000a). Therefore, in suicidal behaviours we have an actor independently taking the decision to end their own life, the individual is at the centre of the suicidal act, and it is their intent which leads to and defines suicide. As Andriessen (2006) writes, suicide is explicitly an individual decision and act (see also Jaworski, 2010). Even if we assume that the time preceding the suicide attempt is associated with an altered state of consciousness (e.g. close-mindedness and fixation on purpose; see, for instance, Baumeister, 1990; Shneidman, 1993, 1996), it is still accepted that the suicidal person is intentionally pursuing their own death and is the agent in the suicidal act.

However, the progressing medicalization of suicide and of suicidal behaviour (Marsh, 2010) has resulted in greater significance in terminology, classification, and a standardized approach. In consequence, the first calls by the National Institute of Mental Health for unifying systems of classification of suicidal behaviour were made in the 1970s (Pokorny, 1974). And yet, despite almost fifty years of debate, a common unified terminology and classification of suicidal behaviour remains rather elusive (Goodfellow, Kõlves & De Leo, 2018; Silverman & De Leo, 2016). This is so, despite the fact that, in order to understand, assess, predict and act preventively against suicide, it is necessary to come up with a consistent system of understanding suicide and its types, as well as classifying various related behaviours (Silverman, 2006; see also Leenaars et al., 1997; Rudd & Joiner, 1998; Shneidman, 1985).

And so, in the next section, we want to explore some definitions of suicide in order to see how it is rendered from the dominant suicidological perspective. Most of the definitions we analyse were taken from earlier articles offering reviews and systematic reviews of definitions of suicide in suicidology (De Leo et al., 2006; Goodfellow, Kõlves & De Leo, 2018; Maris et al., 2000b; Silverman, 2006). In addition, we also searched in suicidology's leading journals (*Suicide and Life-Threatening Behavior*, *Crisis*, *Death Studies* and *Archives of Suicide Research*) as well as looking for articles in the MeDLINE database (via PubMed). In such a way, we created a list of thirty definitions used in suicidological literature which we analysed along the lines described above.[1]

Suicide is death

The first kind of suicide representation is to construct it in terms of what happens to the person after they kill themselves. Consider the following definitions:

1. 'Death from injury, poisoning, or suffocation' (Goldsmith et al., 2002).
2. 'Death, arising from an act inflicted upon oneself with the intention to kill oneself' (Rosenberg et al., 1988).
3. 'Self-initiated, intentional death' (Ivanoff, 1989).
4. 'Suicide is, by definition, not a disease, but a death' (Silverman & Maris, 1995).

Focusing on the outcome, these definitions, and others like them, remove any focus on both the actions necessary to cause the death and the situation in which it happens. The act of suicide, the activity of the person who kills themselves, becomes relegated in considerations of what is relevant. In the extreme cases, as in examples 3 or 4, death happens as if it had not been preceded by anything.

By backgrounding all, for want of a better phrase, 'suicide activities', such definitions of the act of suicide construct it as an obvious and homogeneous state of not living. Suicide becomes a thing, not an activity. For instance, in example 1, what must be a tumultuous and emotional process, the 'injury, poisoning, or suffocation', is reduced to the easily inspected cause of death. Moreover, by defining suicide as death, to a considerable extent, the act is reduced to the state of not living. And, even though death and the causes of death are characterized in a number of ways, the only relevant aspect of suicide seems to be that the person is dead. Linguistically speaking, the four aspects of definitions of suicide mentioned by De Leo and colleagues (2006) are at best only implied and often very weakly.

Indeed, the use of nouns (e.g. 'death', 'injury', 'suffocation', 'act') in such definitions distances them from any lived experience of suicide, as it turns processes into things. Death resulting from injury or poisoning is unlikely to occur within seconds and, if one adds time for some preparations for the act of killing oneself, what must be a time-extended process is reduced to an atemporal event which seems to occur outside any time frame. The removal of any temporal component of what happens during the act of suicide backgrounds what seem to be crucial aspects of suicidal actions.

Suicide as an event

The 'uniformization' of suicide through the use of nouns is the second way in which suicide is represented and is explored in this section. Some definitions construct it as an event, that is to say as a unique occurrence, a point which is not extended in time and, indeed, is outside agency. What is most significant in these representations is that the event is inevitably placed in abstraction of any context. Consider the following examples:

5. 'Fatal self-inflicted self-destructive act' (IOM, 2001).
6. 'An act with a fatal outcome' (De Leo et al., 2004; WHO, 1986).
7. 'Suicide is a conscious act of self-induced annihilation' (Shneidman, 1985).
8. 'The act of killing oneself' (WHO, 1998).

In contrast to the definitions we discussed in the section 'Suicide is death', here suicide is no longer constructed through its result. Rather, the definitions focus on what happens before death occurs. Significantly, however, just as in the definitions in the previous section, these also offer a reduced representation of what happened. To reiterate, what is very likely to be a series of activities done over time is reduced to a singular event.

Moreover, linguistically, suicide becomes an object which remains unexplored, and the definitions do not offer a perspective through which such explorations might happen. The suicide-object is rendered by the noun 'act', a nominalization,[2] which allows the actor to be completely removed from the text. In other words, the definitions make no reference to the actor who not only must be behind the actions performed but also must intend the action to happen and must intend a particular result of the action to happen. The actions are reduced to an event which, it seems, simply occurs, as if out of thin air.

Now, three of the above-mentioned definitions contain expressions that imply human participation. The act is 'fatal' or has a 'fatal outcome', it is 'conscious' and 'self-inflicted', and yet there is no construction of who might be conscious or for whom the act might be fatal. Put differently, human participation in the act seems only an implied characteristic. Suicide, which must involve a person doing something in order to kill themselves is reduced in the definition texts to an abstract event which happens without human agency. Indeed, we would suggest that in such a way the definitions provide suicidology and other relevant disciplines with an object of central interest, with the actor at best being one of its characteristics.

And so, in examples 1 to 8, suicide is constructed in two ways. On the one hand, it is represented as death – namely, an outcome – on the other hand, as an abstract, singular act with no obvious actor. The common characteristic of such constructions is not only removal of any agency in suicide but, more significantly, removal of any human participation. In such a way, the definitions make it impossible to include any context in which suicide can be seen and, possibly, researched.

There is no obvious explanation of such constructions. We suggest, however, that constructing suicide as death or as an act enables representing it as an unproblematic object ready for scientific inspection. The definitions do away with problematic aspects of suicide such as, for example, intentionality, which is consistently postulated as a necessary condition for the assessment of whether someone's death resulted from suicide (e.g. Andriessen, 2006; Beck, Schuyler & Herman, 1974; O'Carroll et al., 1996). Focusing on suicide as an event makes it much less contested, as researchers need only establish the occurrence of self-inflicted death. This, in turn, makes studies of suicide more readily available.

Indeed, assessing the intent of the person who kills themselves is extremely difficult. This is particularly evident in the so-called Golden Gate studies which focus on people who survived jumping off the Golden Gate Bridge in San Francisco, a very well-known suicide spot. One of the studies reports that people, admittedly with a strong intent to kill themselves as judged by their actions, were not so sure during the flight down to the surface of the water (Rosen, 1975). If the act of suicide is seen as a process which is underpinned by intent, the notion that it is only death which constitutes suicide becomes at the very least problematic. This, in turn, poses significant methodological issues which disappear when suicide is constructed merely as a death or an occurrence. Removing the person from suicide makes studying it considerably easier.

Definitions offer a view of suicide which makes it unproblematic. They do away with issues such as intentionality or consciousness of the person committing it, which can potentially put a question mark over whether the death was or was not suicide. As suicide is reduced to death or an act resulting in death, determining whether it happened can be seen as made easier and dependent on a largely arbitrary decision. This is because suicidological research does not stop to consider the intentions behind the act, let alone their possible fluctuations, despite the fact that suicidology is well aware of people changing their minds during the suicidal act (Rosen, 1975).

In contrast to suicidological accounts, narrative accounts of suicide construct it differently. Suicide is represented as extended in time, an action which is far from the point outside of time.

The suicide process

In this section, we begin to discuss constructions of suicide as an action that takes time. Indeed, suicide is constructed as an act which takes place in a particular context in both space and time. In what follows, we discuss two groups of extracts, all coming from the corpus of suicide letters. The first group consists of extracts in which letter authors explicitly situate their suicide in time; the other contains fragments in which the writers position their actions happening in the present time.

Consider first the following extracts:

Extract 1

> I was writing this letter some time ago, but finally I have decided to take this step. Up till the day of [date] nothing has changed, she is still cheating on me and she is nasty towards me. My death happened at [time]. Approximately.

Extract 2

> I am aware of what I am doing. I am going to mum, because mum is waiting for me and I cannot put it off and procrastinate any longer. I want to spend with my beloved wife. Mum[3] tells me to come to her and we shall be together, she will be taking care of me as she had for us all. She never wanted anything bad for anyone, she took care of everything we leave for you.

Extract 3

> Forgive me, my beloved girls, for my disgraceful act, but I cannot differently, I cannot put it off any more, because in the end I would not have the strength to do what I want to do.

Extract 4

> It is hard to write anything at this moment. I am scared of what is going to happen in a moment. Very scared. But I cannot live knowing that I could so much hurt a person who loves me so such. I am nothing, a complete nothing. I do not want to hurt anyone, especially her.

All four extracts position suicide as part of a longer period of time which included writing, worrying, postponing or putting off the termination of life. Although the timescale the authors of the letters refer to is unclear, all four letters are fairly explicit in suggesting that the final suicidal act is the end of a journey. Interestingly, while the author of extract 1 positions the process in terms of days, in extracts 2 and 3 the length of time is unclear, equally likely to be days or minutes, while in extract 4 it is likely to be limited to the situation in which the letter author's life was terminated.

It is worth mentioning that all four extracts show the time before taking one's life as leading to the author's death. The writing of the note leading to the decision to commit suicide (extract 1) or the reference to what was going to happen (extract 4) suggests that the process has a vector, that is to say, it goes in one direction.

In a number of letters, such constructions were even stronger, with the process of suicide being shown to be inevitable; the authors of the letters found themselves on a sort of conveyor belt leading to their death. Witness:

Extract 5

> It is necessary to end, take care and do not worry.
> Bye, bye, bye, bye. Yours, [first name]
> [There is time for everyone].
> I am in the attic, but I will not be able to talk to any more.

Extract 6

> You are a really valuable person. I will remember every moment spent with you till the end of my life. Not much time.

Extract 7

> Not much time left for me. Farewell.

These notes offer a narrative view of the passing time, the last minutes before death. Suicide is not a moment, a dot on the timeline, but rather things happen, time passes before one takes one's life. What is fascinating about the stories of passing time, however, is that they construct the coming of suicide as independent from the men who wrote the notes. 'It's necessary to end,'[4] 'not much time' or 'not much time left for me' all show that the time before suicide is getting shorter and shorter. Death is coming closer and closer. The stories show the authors as moving on a sort of conveyor belt which ends in taking their lives. It is worth noting, incidentally, that such a positioning of suicide in time raises again the question of accessibility of suicide.

A reservation is needed here. In the previous paragraph, we suggest that the suicide notes in question position death (or suicide) as coming closer and closer. However, it is equally possible to suggest that it is the note authors that are moving towards death and the notes construct them as helpless. To return to the metaphor of a conveyor belt, they travel on it, almost without control. The references to time seem to underscore this, as they are vague and unclear.

Accessibility of suicide is constructed through it coming along in time as if outside the writing man's decision. It just draws closer, of its own accord. It is almost as if the men did not commit suicide; it just happened to them. However, we are not making an argument here for depersonalizing suicide or for removing references to the agency of the person about to commit suicide. Rather, we see such stories as offering insight into the social dimensions of suicide, its social anchoring as it is narrated.

Furthermore, the notes position the reader as a witness to the moments just before death as experienced by those about to take their lives. We have a 'privileged' view of the moments before the authors kill themselves. But this also suggests that we watch the process, not only the end of a person's life. The notes are stories of suicide as it was happening, and not as it happened. We can see the moments before suicide through the eyes of the writing author and the time passing.

Now, the above extracts construct the suicide process as directional, that is to say that things are moving towards the person's taking of their life. This was not always the case. In a number of suicide letters, directionality was absent. Consider:

Extract 8

> For courage I have smoked and not I feel good. You do not even know how many tears I have shed when writing this letter. I know you [plural] will be suffering. I know you [plural] will be crying. I am crying too.

Extract 9

> I had loved you till the last minute.

Extract 10

> 4.25. The end.

Extract 11

> Time is 2.30.

Extract 12

> Fate has so wanted.

All five extracts construct suicide as time-extended. The reference in extract 8 to shedding many tears constructs the time before the author took her life as emotional as well as long. Incidentally, the extract is consistent with many references to writing which construct it as taking a significant amount of time and energy, sometimes making references to death coming immediately after the end of writing.

Extract 9 also shows suicide as coming after a period of time. However, while it is unclear whether the letter author refers to his entire life or only to the time immediately before killing himself, we suggest the latter interpretation. This is because we think of the letter as drawing on notions of romantic love which is made more dramatic at the moments of death, much like in the myths of knightly love present till the knight is dead (Ossowska, 1986). The suicide note's reference to love makes it greater and more passionate, as if it were to be understood to last until the person's death.

We also see extracts 10 and 11 as implying suicide as running its course rather than happening. Extract 10 is perhaps more suggestive of the passing of time during the suicide action because of the word 'end', presumably marking the end of life or the process (the reference is ambiguous). Yet the act of recording the time – presumably, the time of the person's death – in itself, we would like to argue, implies a process. After all, the record serves a sort of punctuation of time, after which at least one action – the taking of life – must happen. In such a way, suicide is part of at least a two-stage process, the recording of time and taking one's own life. This, incidentally, is how we see the last of the above quotes, the reference to fate. Writing it constructs the process of killing oneself.

Incidentally, the reports in extracts 10 and 11 position the authors as witnesses-rapporteurs (on speaker positions, see Ziółkowska, 2009) who make a report of the end of the process. The suicide notes become almost an affidavit which is left behind. The process has ended and the suicide note stipulates it to this effect.

So far, we have discussed suicide letters which suggest that suicide is not solely the ending of one's life. Suicide is a process which lasts in time and the physical extinguishing of life is only a stage of the process. However, all the letters we have quoted so far more or less explicitly construct death as an ending of the process represented in the letters. We now turn to extracts that show different stories. This is a process which is captured by the narrative as if a photograph, or perhaps a video, had been taken at the time. The authors record what they do. Consider first the following letter, which we quote in its entirety:

Extract 13

> It's 17.26. From one moment to another I can see that my life makes no sense. I talked to [first name] a moment ago and she has depressed me even more. She said nothing, but I mean the tone of her voice. It was so unhappy, as if she had wanted to say I am so unhappy with you.

Extract 13 is poignant in showing the person about to kill himself as the time passes and he moves closer and closer to taking his life. We see someone not yet engaged in taking his life, only implying movement towards it. But what is particularly interesting is that the suicide note contains reference to a conversation with someone close to the letter author, a conversation which the letter implies made things even worse. Suicide is constructed not only to involve writing or just waiting to kill oneself; it involves interaction with others. The process, which presumably had already started (we will come back to considering this issue in the 'Conclusions' section of the chapter.), is not a solitary one.

Admittedly, this note is an exception in the corpus we have. There is no other letter which tells a story of conversations with others. We want to argue, however, that the absence of such references is not evidence for the absence of such interactions. In other words, to use a well-worn cliché, absence of evidence does not constitute evidence of absence. Thus, the process of committing suicide involves activities well beyond preparations or emotional work (which we discuss in Chapter 5).

The following extracts construct the suicide process in a similar way. The authors of the notes position themselves as taking part in an ongoing action of suicide. Consider:

Extract 14

I keep writing some more, because I want to persuade you that life and health are beautiful until one has them.

Extract 15

My hands are shaking a little, because I am scared of what I want to do. When you read this letter it means it is all over.

Extract 16

Sorry for my spelling and handwriting, but I am somewhat nervous as I write it.

Extract 17

I am aware of what I am doing. I am going to mum, because mum is waiting for me and I cannot put it off and procrastinate any longer.

Extract 14 not only shows writing as an activity which takes time but also shows that the activity is restarted a number of times. The person represents himself as someone who cannot finish writing, still wanting to write some more, as if aware of the fact that they would be his last words. The references to the ongoing action of writing in extracts 15 and 16 are similar; the note authors show themselves as not only writing but also, as in extract 15, anticipating what is about to happen.

Extract 17 takes the construction of suicide further. The author of the note positions himself as currently involved in suicide. Not only is he referring to suicide through the admittedly ambiguous 'what I am doing' but he also underscores it by reference to 'going to mum', his wife who had died (which is made clear earlier in the long note, not quoted here). Importantly, then, suicide is represented as something which is being done. The authors of the letters construct themselves as involved in a number of activities which will end with their death.

The final group of extracts we discuss are quite similar to extract 17. The authors position themselves as engaged in suicide. Consider:

Extract 18

I am going to the other world.

Extract 19

I am going. It should work out.

Extract 20

I am hanging myself. Do not look for me.

Extract 21

[first name] I am going to hang myself. Do not look for me.

Extract 22

I am taking my life. Please take your mobile phone.

We see these five extracts as a sound platform to argue for the notion of 'doing suicide'. In other words, we suggest that the authors position suicide as something one engages in; suicide can be performed in time, and not only completed. While extracts 18 and 19 are somewhat ambivalent as to what exactly they refer to, extracts 20 and 21 are much more explicit as to constructing their authors as engaged in the action of killing themselves. They are engaged in performing suicide. In other words, the reference to hanging oneself in extract 21, rendered in the present tense (which in Polish can be translated as both simple present and present continuous tenses), suggests that the act of hanging oneself involves more than simply the act of physical hanging. Hanging oneself seems to also involve writing about it and, presumably, some other activities.

Similarly, extract 22,[5] which is almost at its most explicit in constructing the author as 'doing suicide', once again demonstrates an activity which involves other things than solely extinguishing life. The most explicit note in this respect is the following extract:

Extract 23

I, [first name], am killing myself.

Before we comment on this, a note on translation is needed. As mentioned, in contrast to English, Polish does not differentiate between the present simple tense ('I kill') and the present continuous ('I am killing') and translations into English are based on the context of what is said or written. Here, the context is so minimal that any translation is much more of an interpretation rather than translation. It is important to note, however, that the note could well have been translated as 'I [...] kill myself'.

Regardless of the translation, the note is somewhat odd. The author was clearly not 'killing himself', because he was writing. But the note is reminiscent of performative sentences (Austin, 1962), which perform the act by virtue of saying the sentences. In other words, some utterances do not so much tell us about something as much as they do something. And so, if you say, given the right circumstances, 'I (hereby) take you to be my wife/husband', 'I sentence you to death' or 'I name this starship Enterprise', you actually also do this. In other words, you get married, you sentence the person to die or you name a starship, respectively. Interestingly, it is not only these highly ceremonial contexts in which this happens. We also use such sentences in very much everyday situations (Searle, 1969). 'I promise you', 'I forgive you' and 'I apologise' are a promise, an act of forgiving and an apology, respectively.

The question that can be asked at this moment is the extent to which a sentence such as 'I kill myself' in a suicide note is part of the act of killing oneself. Of course, we are not suggesting at all that the act of saying 'I kill myself' will actually kill the person; rather, we propose that the statement is part of doing the suicide. In other words, a note is a constitutive part of suicide. This has a number of consequences and suggests a rethinking of the dominant views on suicide as the termination of life. Instead, we suggest that suicide is a complex set of actions in which causing oneself to die is only one part.

In this section, we have discussed suicide notes which position suicide as a set of actions which end in someone's death. The authors of suicide notes constructed these actions in two ways. On the one hand, they showed actions preceding death as leading to it; the person was sometimes constructed as inevitably moving towards killing themselves. On the other hand, we also discussed notes in which their authors positioned themselves in the present of the situation in which they would eventually kill themselves. In other words, they constructed the situation as lasting, and they took the time to do things before they took their lives.

Such constructions were taken to the extreme of explicitly referring to the act of killing oneself, and we argued that such notes are constitutive of suicide. Such an approach, however, requires a different understanding of suicide and moving away from seeing suicide solely in terms of taking one's life. We explore this further in the conclusions below.

Conclusions

In this chapter, we have discussed definitions of suicide and offered insights into what is constructed as important and relevant in understanding suicide. We have shown that definitions of suicide construct it as an event which happens without human participation or with human participation only implied. We have argued that their linguistic form has consequences not only in how suicide is constructed but also in how it might set out dominant practices of suicidology. Backgrounding or removing the person and their actions from descriptions of suicide suggests that their experience is low in research priorities. Indeed, this is how we interpret a significant paucity of qualitative research in suicidology.

We have also shown that lived accounts of suicide, recorded in suicide notes, construct suicide in a different way. The people writing these notes represent suicide as a time-extended process. Lay representations of suicide are quite far from how it is rendered by suicidology. We have also argued for the notion of doing suicide, that is to say, engaging in a set of activities which eventually lead to the physical ending of the person's life. Time and again, writing a suicide note was positioned as part of 'doing suicide'.

One of the key issues we have touched upon here is that academic and lived definitions of suicide cannot be more different. Suicidology seems completely uninterested in the lived perspective on suicide, as it strips away from suicide all that the lived perspectives furnish it with. The reductionist academic view of suicide offers a view which removes all of the nuances which exist in its lay representations.

In this concluding section, we now turn to consider some of the consequences of our arguments. The first and probably most pressing consequence is that of how suicide should be understood and defined. If suicide is not merely a point on the timeline, then how should we understand it?

We have argued that one of the reasons why suicidology seems to understand suicide as outside any temporal or social context is that such a definition presents a largely unproblematic object of study, immediately ready for scientific inspection. Focusing on suicide as an event makes it much less contested, as researchers need only establish the occurrence of self-inflicted death. This, in turn, makes studies of suicide more readily available.

We suggest this view of suicide is oversimplified and reductionist. Suicidology should espouse the lived understanding of suicide and see it as a complex set of events. We would go as far as to argue that the word 'suicide' should refer to the entirety of the situation in which, eventually, a person's life is taken. Suicide is not only not death – it is very far from being simply death. We would also suggest that suicide should be distinguished from the act of the physical termination of life, a suicidal act, which is part of any suicide.

Thus, understanding this leads us to another key question which suicidology has not yet asked. If suicide is a process, then it makes sense and it is probably important to ask when the process starts. The question has at least two dimensions. First, it is crucial for a suicidological understanding of suicide. For example, if the differences between the so-called 'attempters' and 'completers' are enshrined in suicidological research, as researchers study them as two separate populations (Beautrais, 2001; DeJong, Overholser & Stockmeier, 2010; Silverman & Simon, 2001), with the same distinction being made in the study of suicide notes (e.g. Brevard, Lester & Yang, 1990; Callanan & Davis, 2009; Cerel et al., 2014; Haines, Williams & Lester, 2011; Joiner, 2005), and if suicide is understood as a process which starts perhaps a significant amount of time before physical death, then the distinction between the groups is on much shakier grounds than might be expected. Moreover, if the process has a start, when is it? Is it ten minutes before? Or perhaps an hour? Or could suicide begin a day before the death? As we shall show in this book, such timescales are not as improbable as it might be thought at first sight.

The second issue to be considered with regard to the beginning of suicide is that of suicide prevention. If we assume that suicide has a beginning, understanding it is crucial from the point of view of suicide prevention activities. Questions of whether suicides can be stopped and when it can be done become both more relevant and more pressing.

Seeing suicide as a small point on the timeline is likely, in our view, to misinterpret the time before the suicidal death. In other words, such an understanding of suicide constructs the time before suicidal death as a largely homogeneous time and largely uninteresting from the point of view of suicidology. And even though such models of suicide as O'Connor's integrated motivational-volitional model of suicidal behaviour (O'Connor, 2011; O'Connor & Kirtley, 2018) seem to assume that what happens before suicide happens in time, it is almost an afterthought rather than an important consideration. Incidentally, the timeline that is implied in the model ends at the stage of suicide itself, which again becomes a point in time.

This discussion is relevant from one further perspective. Suicidology, and in particular suicide prevention, has for some time been interested in discovering the so-called warning signs of suicide (Rudd, 2003, 2008; Rudd et al., 2006). They are normally described as those phenomena which indicate a rise in suicide risk in the near future, namely minutes, hours, days (Rudd et al., 2006; see also Mandrusiak et al., 2006). Despite much focus in suicidology on suicide risk factors, relatively little research has been done on warning signs.

What little research there is suggests that a warning sign should not only be seen as observable behavioural changes in a high suicide-risk person but also point to the person's state of mind. For example, Hendin and colleagues (2001) identified three signs preceding patients' suicide. They listed (1) an event which triggered the crisis; (2) an emotional state, most often depression, the loss of a relationship, feelings of rejection, hopelessness; and (3) behavioural manifestations of suicide crisis, such as communicating suicidal intent, worsening of functioning or stopping therapy. Similarly, Busch, Fawcett and Jacobs (2003) report mind-related warning signs, such as high anxiety or arousal.

A somewhat similar line of research has concerned the so-called suicidal mode (Rudd, Joiner & Rajab, 2004), which is described as a network of interconnected factors: cognitive (a suicidal system of beliefs characterized by helplessness and the absence of self-worth), emotional (characterized by negative emotional states, e.g. depression, feelings of guilt, shame), physiological (e.g. sleeplessness, lack of concentration, pain) and behavioural (related to strategies of coping with stress, substance abuse or non-lethal self-injury). All these factors are related to and with the right trigger reinforce each other and lead to suicidal crisis. The suicidal mode results in the suicidal act.

What we suggest is that such research would benefit from considering the extent to which the warning signs or the 'suicidal mode' are actually part of suicide and that they should not be seen as phenomena leading to suicide so much as phenomena which are part of the suicide process. This, in our view, would lead not only to a better understanding of suicide on the one hand and warning signs on the other but also to better and, in the process, more effective prevention strategies.

This book has arisen from the largely unasked question of what a person about to kill themselves does a day, an hour or perhaps ten minutes before taking their life. As we show throughout the volume, they do quite a lot, and understanding this will bring us closer to understanding suicide and also what exactly suicide prevention activities target.

In Chapter 3, we continue the argument we have set out here. We shall contrast how the dominant suicidological discourses position the person who kills themselves and their agency behind both the decision and the act of killing themselves. The argument we make is that once again the dominant suicidological discourse can be seen as removing the agency of the person involved in suicide. Yet those who tell the story of their suicide attempt paint a much more complex picture of themselves and their attempt to kill themselves.

Appendix

Extract 1

LIST PISAŁEM JUŻ JAKIŚ CZAS TEMU ALE W KOŃCU SIĘ NIE ZDECYDOWAŁEM NA TAKI KROK. DO DNIA [date] nic nie uległo zmianie dalej mnie oszukuje i jest niedobra dla mnie. Śmierć moja nastąpiła o godz. [time] około.

Extract 2

jestem świadom tego co robię idę do mamy bo mama czeka na mnie dłużej nie mogę, dłużej odkładać ani zwlekać chcę spędzić teraz z mamą z Ukochaną Żoną mama mówi mi żebym przyszedł do niej i będziemy razem i będzie o mnie dbała jak to robiła dla nas wszystkich też nie chciała dla nikogo źle dbała o wszystko zostawiamy wam

Extract 3

Wybaczcie mi kochane dziewczyny mój haniebny postępek ale nie mogę inaczej nie mogę nie dłużej zwlekać bo w końcu nie miałbym siły wykonać co zamierzam.

Extract 4

Ciężko cokolwiek mi napisać w tej chwili … Boję się tego co ma się stać za chwilę, bardzo się boję! Ale nie umiem żyć z tą świadomością, że tak bardzo mogłem skrzywdzić osobę, która tak bardzo mnie kocha. Jestem zerem kompletnym zerem! Nie chcę już skrzywdzić nikogo, a tym bardziej jej.

Extract 5

Trzeba kończyć trzymajcie się zdrowo i nie przejmujcie się.
Pa, pa, pa Wasz [first_name].!!!
(Na każdego przychodzi czas)
Jestem na strychu lecz już z nikim nie będę mógł porozmawiać.

Extract 6

Jesteś naprawdę wartościową osobą, każdą spędzoną z Tobą będę wspominał do końca życia:), mało czasu:/.

Extract 7

Zostało mi bardzo mało czasu żegnaj

Extract 8

Dla odwagi przybuchałam sobie i teraz jest mi fajnie. Nawet nie wiesz ile łez wylałam przy pisaniu tego listu. Wiem że będziecie cierpieć. Wiem że będziecie płakać. Ja też płaczę.

Extract 9

Kochałem Cię do ostatniej minuty

Extract 10

4,25 KONIEC

Extract 11

JEST GODZINA 2.30

Extract 12

Tak chciał Los.

Extract 13

Jest godzina 17.26. z chwili na chwilę widzę że moje życie nie ma sensu, rozmawiałem przed chwilą z [first name] i przygnębiła mnie jeszcze bardziej nic nie powiedziała ale chodzi o ton jej głosu był taki nieszczęśliwy, jakby chciała powiedzieć jaka ja jestem nieszczęśliwa z tobą.

Extract 14

Ciągle coś dopisuję bo chcę Was przekonać że życie i zdrowie to jest piękne dopóki się je ma.

Extract 15

Trochę mi się trzęsą ręce bo się boję tego co chcę zrobić. Jak będziesz czytał ten list to znaczy że jest już po wszystkim.

Extract 16

Sorka za ortografię i pismo, ale nieco zdenerwowany jestem, gdy to piszę:

Extract 17

jestem świadom tego co robię idę do mamy bo mama czeka na mnie dłużej nie mogę, dłużej odkładać ani zwlekać

Extract 18

Idę do tamtego świata.

Extract 19

Idę powinno się udać

Extract 20

WIESZAM SIĘ NIE SZUKAJ MNIE

Extract 21

[first name] idę się powiesić nie szukaj mnie

Extract 22

Odbieram życie. Zabierz proszę swą komórkę.

Extract 23

Ja [first name] się zabijam.

3

Agency in the suicidal process

In Chapter 2, we contrasted the dominant constructions of suicide with their lived counterparts. We compared how suicide is represented in suicidological definitions with how it is written about in suicide notes. It turned out that there are significant differences in how these two discourses construct suicide. While the definitions have suicide as a point outside time or social context, and as an unstructured event, suicide letters construct a very different picture. They show suicide as a set of actions which are not only time-extended but also involve considerably more than simply taking one's life.

Suicide and agency

In this chapter, we continue the argument set out in Chapter 2. Here, we contrast how the dominant suicidological discourses position the person who kills themselves and the person's agency behind both the decision and the act of killing themselves. The argument we put forward is that once again the dominant suicidological discourse can be seen as removing the agency of the person involved in suicide. On the other hand, those who tell the story of their suicide attempt paint a much more complex picture of themselves and their attempt to kill themselves.

Suicide is the result of actions taken against the self by a person with the intention of ending their own life. It assumes the knowledge and awareness that the most likely consequence of their activities will be death. In suicidal behaviour, there is an actor independently taking a decision on suicidal death; the individual is at the centre of the suicidal act and it is their intent which leads to it. As Andriessen (2006) writes, suicide is explicitly an individual decision and act (see also Jaworski, 2010). Even if we assume that the time preceding the suicide attempt is associated with an altered state of consciousness (see, e.g.,

Baumeister, 1990; Shneidman, 1993, 1996), it is still accepted that the suicidal person is intentionally pursuing suicide and is the agent of a suicidal act.

Although agency is a key element in suicidal acts, researchers pay little attention to it. According to Webb (2011), contemporary studies on suicide are not bringing us any closer to an understanding of suicidal experiences and behaviours, while understanding them goes far beyond determining the strength of the association between the variables and comparing the statistics of suicidal deaths. Indeed, by focusing on people's narratives about suicidal attempts, we argue that the constructed agency in narratives becomes much more complex than what one could assume based on definitions of suicidal behaviour.

In this chapter, we are interested in the linguistic picture of agency in narratives of suicide and, in particular, the decision to commit suicide. Our objective is to demonstrate that agency is a dynamic characteristic of narratives about suicidal experiences, subject to change in the context of telling the story. We will also show that agency in narratives about the suicide decision is distinct from the construction of agency in narratives about preparation for and the act of suicide. Narratives about thoughts and the decision to commit suicide are not agentive, and the decision about suicide is constructed as something coming from the outside, regardless of whether the study participants describe their attempt as planned or not. On the other hand, narratives about the suicide act are their opposite; in describing the suicide attempt, participants emphasize their agency by constructing an agentic story focused on the course of events.

We take the following route in this chapter. We start with another brief discussion of definitions of suicide. This time we focus on how such texts represent the person in the suicide process. We contrast these discursive constructions with those we found in farewell letters, only to make the picture more complex when we move to discussing our interview data.

In this chapter, we are interested in how those who write or speak about their suicide or suicide attempt position themselves in terms of linguistic agency. That is to say we wanted to see how 'doing things' is represented in discourse, paying attention especially to who is positioned as doing what kind of things in relation to what or whom. Our focus lay predominantly on the lexicogrammatical form rather than on the contents of what was written. In other words, it was more important to us whether the linguistic form renders the 'doer' as doing things.

Our analyses were informed particularly by the linguistics of Halliday (1994) who sees agency in terms of the linguistically represented participant and the process, namely who was involved in a particular action. It is important to remember that the linguistic agent might not necessarily be the 'sociological' one (van Leeuwen, 2008), that is to say, one who is taken to be an agent in a particular social context. What we focused on, significantly, was how reality was constructed and how our interview informants and the authors of the farewell letters chose to represent it.

The person in suicide

In this section, we explore constructions of who kills oneself in the definitions of suicide. As we indicated above, the dominant constructions of the person taking their life are that of removal of both agency and the person in general. Consider the following examples:

1. '[S]elf-induced annihilation' (Shneidman, 1985).
2. 'A fatal wilful self-inflicted life-threatening act without apparent desire to live' (Davis, 1988).
3. '[An] act inflicted upon oneself with the intention to kill oneself' (Rosenberg et al., 1988).
4. '[A] death that is caused by a self-inflicted intentional action or behaviour' (Silverman & Maris, 1995).
5. '[A] self-inflicted act led to the person's death' (Goldsmith et al., 2002).
6. 'Self-initiated, intentional death' (Ivanoff, 1989).
7. 'Fatal self-inflicted self-destructive act with explicit or inferred intent to die' (IOM, 2001).

The definitions of suicide consistently describe suicide without mentioning the persons who take their lives. A person's participation is only implied through reference to either an unattributed action (e.g. 'self-inflicted act', self-induced annihilation') or a mental state (e.g. 'intentional death', 'wilful act'). Any explicit references to persons or to their actions are removed from the texts' explicit content.

Expressions referring to mental states such as 'desire to live', 'intention to kill oneself' or 'intent to die' are also used as if they existed on their own without any person, token or type actually holding them. A classical definition takes this to the extreme:

8. 'Suicide is (1) a murder (*selbstmord*) (involving hatred or the wish-to-kill), (2) a murder by the self (often involving guilt or the wish-to-be-killed), and (3) the wish-to-die (involving hope-lessness)' (Menninger, 1938).

'Hatred', 'wish-to-kill' or 'guilt' are all used in abstraction of anyone who might feel them. Indeed, the reference to the person committing suicide is made through the ambivalent 'self', while, at the same time, it is separated from the psychological states. It is also worth noting that the linguistic constructions contained in this classical definition, potentially outdated, are in fact similar to those used in later definitions (see examples 9–11). Linguistically, not much has changed over the years, it seems.

Furthermore, it is also significant that only mental states are referred to in the definitions. This is consistent with today's dominant constructions of suicide which place it in the person (Battin, 1995; Marsh, 2010; Pridmore, 2011) and ignore the social, economic or political context which might have a significant impact upon the decision to kill oneself. This is all despite the fact that suicidology is very well aware that suicide occurs in certain social circumstances (governmental austerity measures, certain institutional contexts; see, e.g., Branas et al., 2015; Flynn et al., 2017).

Yet there are a number of definitions in which the person who took their life is referred to explicitly. What dominates, however, are definitions in which the agency of that person is removed or backgrounded. Consider the following definitions:

9. 'Death from injury, poisoning, or suffocation where there is evidence (either explicit or implicit) that the injury was self-inflicted and that decedent intended to kill himself/herself' (O'Carrol et al., 1996, 1998).
10. 'A commits suicide by performing an act x if and only if A intends that he or she kill himself or herself by performing x (under the description "I kill myself"), and this intention is fully satisfied' (Hill, 2011).
11. 'Suicide is an act [...] by means of which an individual autonomously intends and wishes to bring about his death because he wants to be dead or wants to die the death he enacts' (Fairbairn, 1995).

While suicide is death, the person involved in suicide is constructed only to have a mental state – intention to kill themselves. The focus on the intention is so strong that in example 10 the act of suicide is, quite bizarrely, we think, referred to as satisfying the intention. In contrast, the definition in example 11 does not refer to the act of killing oneself at all, only describing what kind of intention the person referred to has. Interestingly, these definitions are similar to that proposed by Shneidman, one of the founders of modern suicidology:

12. 'Suicide is a conscious act of self-induced annihilation, best understood as a multi-dimensional malaise in a needful individual who defines an issue for which suicide is perceived as the best solution' (Shneidman, 1985).

The distance Shneidman constructs between suicide and the person committing it is even larger. Suicide is conceived of as a malaise, a sort of state of illness in an individual, and thus it cannot be performed. The individual taking their life is only reduced to defining the issue which is the source of them killing themselves. Not only does suicide not have anyone who performs it but the person who actually does it is constructed only as defining things.

You could argue that the undermining of agency in Shneidman's definition is not only linguistic. If suicide is 'a malaise', presumably the person committing it can hardly be held responsible for it. Suicide becomes something that happens to the person rather than results from the person's decision to kill themselves. Although implicitly, Shneidman's definition not only removes agency from the person taking their life but also pushes it towards pathologization. Indeed, the American Psychiatric Association (APA), in its most recent edition of its manual, DSM-5, announced that suicidal behaviour would be viewed as a mental illness (APA, 2013).

So far, we have argued that definitions of suicide remove or background those who take their lives. Human participation tends to be a characteristic of the act which happens as if on its own; and, when the person taking their life is referred to explicitly, they are ascribed mental states rather than actions. We are not suggesting, however, that anyone reading those definitions will have any difficulty in understanding that the individual, for example in the Shneidman definition, is also the person who kills themselves. Rather, we focus on the way the relationship between the act of suicide and the person who commits it is constructed. Linguistically, the definitions obfuscated it and relied on the reader to supply a coherent reading constructing the relationship for themselves.

We now turn to contrasting these academic and institutional discourses with lay/lived accounts of suicide. We discuss the data in two sections, representing what tends to be seen as the two main phases of suicide: the decision to take one's own life and the suicidal act. And so, in the next section, we examine how the decision to commit suicide is represented in our two sets of data: the interviews with informants who attempted suicide and farewell letters. We then move on to discuss agency in representations of the suicidal act.

Agency in the suicide decision

The suicide decision would seem to be the most important element in the process of arriving at the suicide act. As Ringel notes, 'there is no suicide without "decision", which often is nothing but submission to the pressure which pushes with overwhelming force to death' (1987: 103). In the interview data we collected, the suicide decision is constructed as external. As such, it is represented as escaping the attempter's control and as having characteristics of a revelation. Interestingly, such a construction of the decision appears regardless of whether the participants describe their suicide attempt as planned or not.

We found three different ways in which the origin of decision is constructed; the level of agency is the differentiating factor. The first and most common is the construction of an independent and external agent – most often an enigmatic 'something' – that elicits the suicide decision. The second is the discursive separation of a part of the Self or the voice which is constructed as responsible for the decision. The third way is the construction of the decision as appearing, self-arising, without an active agent behind it. We shall discuss them in turn.

Consider first:

Extract 1

> A: do you remember the moment you made the decision?
>
> B: Well, the first decision it was when I was going to bed, I said: maybe I will get up, maybe something. I went to bed, but I woke up at five o'clock. No, it was in me, no. I can't go. I can't go there because the doctor will examine me, all my papers and it will be this and this. So I got up at five, there were medicines. I didn't have to look for them because I took a lot of them. I took the medicines, I lay down, it was kind of not thought out. As if to say impulsive, because it was not thought out. Because when I was going to bed, I didn't know that I would do it, but I woke up and I say, it's not OK. Something, something forced me to do it. Something, I don't know? (.) so I took [medicine], didn't I?

Despite the fact that the informant talks about considering suicide at bedtime and constructs it as a dialogue with himself, the decision about suicide is constructed as something coming from the outside – it is his 'something' that forced him to do it. In this way, he becomes only an executor of the decision that was made without his participation. Moreover, he uses the word 'force', which can be interpreted as further distancing himself from the decision with the implication that the decision was made against his will. It also appears to be a surprise, as he says, 'when I was going to bed, I did not know that I would do it'.

It is perhaps worth noting, however, that there is an ambiguity in erecting the external force behind the decision. While very explicitly ascribing the agency to the 'something', the informant also represents himself as an agent. He also positions himself as an agent behind killing himself. He got up, he took the medicine – there is no doubt that it is he who killed himself. And despite the fact that his agency is mediated by references to being forced, these are almost two separate stories in his account. The two storylines not only introduce ambivalence but also show the complexity behind the suicidal act.

The final point we would like to make here concerns the reference to lying down in the account in extract 1. As we shall see in Chapter 4, one of the aspects of suicide is waiting for death to happen. The informant's reference to lying down introduces the time of waiting for the medicine to take effect. Even with a narrow understanding of suicide as the act of taking one's life, some time must pass between taking medication as poison and death. This period of time is ignored by researchers. We discuss it at some length in Chapter 4.

In the narrative in extract 1, the suicide decision is constructed as something that takes the participant by surprise, and he is discursively deprived of influence over it. The informant portrays himself as merely carrying out the decision without being its author. This manner of constructing the suicide decision is typical in the data we have collected. Consider:

Extract 2

>A: can you talk about, about how you came to that decision?
>
>B: […] I can't really say how. the thought just appeared. it just, it just showed up. no rhyme or reason, I really don't know where it came from and and I just tried to go through with it.

Here, too, the informant emphasizes the external origin of the decision. Here, the suicide attempt is a consequence of a thought arriving from the outside. In speaking of a 'thought', the participant constructs that thought as a phenomenon independent from himself. It is not the participant who thinks but the 'thoughts' that act as independent agents, in this case coming to the participant and provoking the suicide attempt.

The participants have constructed an agent – an enigmatic something, a thought, an attack – which was responsible for the suicide decision. Interestingly, the informants also pointed to a certain part of the self communicating decision about suicide to another part of the self. Here, we present two typical examples.

Extract 3

> B: this is: radial nerve paralysis of the upper left limb, and the fear that: in the case of: a visit to the occupational health doctor and I'll just lose that job. and: a lot of people made me feel really optimistic that the hand would get healthy again soon, but first it was a week, then a month, then two so that suicide attempt came up. it just hatched in my head, unfortunately. because I thought I was just useless. because it was like God gave me two legs and two hands and suddenly took a part of me away, I don't know, something inside of myself told me: it's time to end this life. and, and just stop worrying about it, feel relief.

Extract 4

> B: [...] for some time I withdrew into myself, two persons arose. And I talk to these two persons. It's kind of me, but I don't know. And it was in October that the other person said do not take, you have children, fight. And now it was something like I have had enough of everything. It's pointless, all that. And the fatigue. I remember such fatigue, like it were today. And this other person said take it quickly don't look at it and so I did it. But after a while I don't know ten fifteen [minutes] I have lost control. As if I cried out for help
>
> A: I see. mhm.
>
> B: I said to my husband that I took the pills and it was like it was the other person.

In both examples, the informants refer to a voice located inside themselves, which is constructed as ordering suicide. In extract 3, the informant starts off by mentioning the spontaneous emergence of suicidal thoughts but finishes by pointing to the internal voice that convinced him to end his own life. In constructing an internal voice, he discursively puts space between himself and the suicide decision.

And while in extract 3 it is unclear to what extent the voice belongs to the informant or is merely located within him, in extract 4 the voice becomes a second person which takes part in an argument with the informant. Again, although the informant spoke of an internal debate, the construction of a debating voices situates her only as an executor of another's commands. However, the end of the interaction in extract 4 offers an interesting twist in the narrative. Describing a conversation with her husband, the informant explicitly ascribes responsibility for taking the pills to herself – the clause is unmodalized in the first person singular active voice. But she adds another clause (with the reference to another person) whose content undermined the preceding clause. Agency becomes ambivalent.

Finally, the last method of describing the suicide decision is constructing it as appearing of its own accord, without the acting agent behind it. It is, however, the rarest way to construct a decision about suicide. The following are typical narratives.

Extract 5

> B: It arises in you, grows larger. At the beginning you thought, talked to oneself: you are stupid, what are you thinking about? But the harder it is, the longer it takes, the more the scales of the decision to take my own life tips over. and at some point, it simply burst. There is no hope. Because I felt like a third wheel for the family. I imagined that my hand would work again, this rehabilitation, what will I look like in my old age? Without an efficient hand. Of course, efficiency of my hand partially returned, but not enough to work.

Extract 6

> B: and that was the situation, everything just built up and built up inside me until it finally burst. I don't know how it happened, I really don't know. I didn't even think about it. I never thought about killing myself.
>
> A: aha.
>
> B: I never had those kinds of thoughts […] I just came home from a friend's house in the evening the children were sleeping, only ((name of child)) wasn't sleeping and I asked her about something and she mouthed off to me.
>
> A: aha.
>
> B: and probably: that was it. it burst, just something automatic. I don't even remember the moment when I took those pills out.

In contrast to previous extracts, extract 5 does not contain an agent responsible for taking the decision. The decision arises. Yet the informant locates the balance of the decision as within him and, moreover, also accesses his voice in an internal debate, once again introducing ambiguity as to the decision. But then the 'scales of the decision' tip, a process over which he does not construct any control. The ambiguity continues, however, as he goes on with his account of identifying his hardship and disability as the context in which his suicide happens.

Interestingly, the informant invokes a metaphor of bursting, carrying connotations of high pressure and breaking or tearing, but also of the inability to predict the moment of bursting. Bursting is a recurring motif in the narratives of the respondents, which we interpret as a way of emphasizing the lack of control over the decision to commit suicide. Indeed, it is also evident in extract 6. The participant speaks of a bursting, which led to behaviour over which they had no control, while the comparison to a machine (through the reference to automation) underscores this. In this context, the machine can be compared to a system that neither thinks nor remembers, but merely does things.

The absence of control constructed by the informants underscores representations of suicide as only happening to them. They are not the results of thoughtful and intentional action.

Decision in suicide letters

The construction of the decision as out of the person's control and the ambivalence in which it is cushioned was, as we suggested, typical in the interview data. In contrast, suicide letters are very different – the decisions in the written corpus are anything but ambivalent. Here, we have letter authors who very explicitly represent themselves as taking the decision to kill themselves. The following are a few initial examples.

Extract 7

> I have decided to leave this life. I apologise to you [addressing many].

Extract 8

> I so wanted, I so did.

Extract 9

> This is my decision.

Extract 10

> At the beginning I would like to point out that what I am doing is my independent decision, although forced by the situation in which I have found myself.

Extract 11

> What I did was my decision. I decided that life without you makes no sense.

Extract 12

> Apologise to everyone that I have so decided. But this is my decision and I have considered it carefully.

There is no ambiguity, no lack of control. References to the decision to commit suicide are explicit, often agentive. In extracts 7 and 12, the decision is rendered through the verb 'decide' in the active voice; in extracts 8, 10, and 11, the decision is rendered through reference to the suicidal act, also in agentive terms. Only extract 9 renders the decision statically, that is to say, without reference to what the letter author did.

The suicide letters quoted above, as well as those we have not quoted, cannot be more explicit. They are very clear in ascribing the decision behind the suicide to the person who killed themselves. And this is in stark contrast to what we heard in the interviews about the decision. No informant was so explicit in taking ownership of their decision to take their own life. The decision to take one's own life was always distanced from, made ambivalent, and things were never clear.

We think there are two contextual reasons for this difference. First, we think that notes such as those quoted above could be seen as offering a sort of legal indemnity for those who are left behind. As all suicides in Poland are subject to a police investigation as to whether they were indeed suicides, a suicide note can serve as both an explanation for what happened and protection against any prosecution or other legal proceedings and against the possibility of laying the blame on those bereaved. These notes can be seen alongside letters such as:

Extract 13

> I hanged myself on my own. Please do not blame my wife.

This extract explicitly ascribes the act to the author of the letter and, at the same time, pleads that his wife not be blamed.

The second explanation for the difference is suicide's stigma and the likely unwillingness of the informants to simply take responsibility for their actions. We suggest that distancing themselves from the decision, introducing ambiguity around it, makes the act less threatening. And the narratives we have quoted make it clear who executed the act, but the decision to do so is distanced from. Furthermore, in such a, they speaking attempter can imply that the decision to die was problematic, that the wish to end their life was not total. Regardless of the psychological reality at the time, such stories may well offer a more positive outlook on the future and perhaps could be seen as therapeutic.

Incidentally, given that our informants were in hospital care at the time of their interviews, one could argue that their unwillingness to construct their decision to kill themselves in terms of their agency was strategic. After all, they were very likely to understand that they would be assessed for their risk of any future suicide attempt or, more generally, of being a threat to themselves. Distancing themselves from their decision could be seen as contributing to this.

The final point that emerges from these considerations is that stories of the decision to commit suicide are context-bound. They are told in a particular social and legal context and must be seen as such. And the question that remains is one of the extent to which such stories offer insight into suicide and thus should be taken on board in suicidology and its accounts of suicide. We defer considering these points to 'Conclusions' section of this chapter.

Agency in the suicidal act

In contrast to the suicide decision, stories of preparation for and the act of suicide are replete with agentic narratives. The participants focused primarily on describing their own acts, emphasizing through grammatical constructions their active role as performers of the suicidal act. We start with the longest description in the collected data.

Extract 14

> B: that was all going on along the ((name of a river)). because I was planning to take those drugs, drink that alcohol and drown myself in ((name of a river)). I prepared very thoroughly at home. where there was nobody. I got everything I needed ready. everything that was <u>necessary</u> about all those valuable things like the mobile some money everything of value I left at home. I got dressed in the worst rags, the worst trousers in the worst old coat but a coat that would ((takes a drag)) blend in with the trees and the brush so that

> A: (nobody would see)?

> B: yeah. so nobody would distinguish, so nobody nobody nobody would see that I'm because if I was dressed in white then maybe I'd be more visible. So I was thinking about this too. that the coat was kind of greenish-brown and I really found a coat like that old trousers, old shoes the worst I found a bag that I never used. and I packed what I absolutely needed. a jar and I already had in the jar the pills I'd squeezed out before. (because) there was a lot it was a 3-months' supply of four kinds of pills. there was a whole lot I went to the off-license. I bought

alcohol, I bought cognac. I packed some more stuff in the bag matches because I was afraid that in the night time, when I would be sitting next to the [river], there could be rats. so I wanted to frighten them off with the fire. I thought about that. I even took a small glass and some tissues from the cupboard and and another a strong bag in case any of the canvas ones tore I prepared myself by to the waist around the waste I tied a strong, wide leather belt with with a very strong clasp and a solid, strong belt I attached three can-canvas bags to it I tied them up and I put a brick inside each of them. And then I got it ready at home and I looked it over at home if it wouldn't rip. would it would it bear the weight. or how will I feel having that on me. will it really be heavy enough that when I drown that I won't float up. I thought that that that I'd probably planned everything well enough. those canvas bags would absolutely work and everything with the bricks was ok because right there they were laying some stones. so it was just a matter of making it down and I brought them home. and and I put this together with the belt the belt (even) with those canvas bags into one big bag I got on the bus and I went to ((name of river)) not far from ((name of bridge)) there I decided to do it. I didn't leave a key at home – aha. I locked the house. [...] it was really cold that night. as it turned out. it was really cold and I right after it got dark I, I, I, I remember that it star star it was really dark when I started taking the pills. [...] I remember the moment that I don't know, it must have been around midnight because the people in apartments opposite me started turning out their lights. I mean people were going to sleep. it couldn't have been later than 11, 12. I already had, I was already- uh, sort of, losing. and at that moment I simply I have to do what I have to do. Take the next step. and at that moment I just lost consciousness and fell down with my arm under my chest. and I laid there for 24 hours. some fishermen found me. someone stole, you know, stole that awful bag. from that small glass. and there wasn't any alcohol because I drank all the alcohol the ambulance came too. the police. and I was a missing person reported by my family.

The informant offers a very detailed description of the moments leading to taking her life. It began with the preparations made at home, through taking the medication by the riverside, and ending with the loss of consciousness. A characteristic trait of her story is her focus on the actions she took as she said, 'I went', 'I bought', 'I prepared', 'I packed', 'I tied', 'I closed', 'I put in', 'I went', 'I took' and so forth. From the grammatical perspective, we observe a systematic construction of the self as the subject of those clauses and in the process as an actor performing actions. In contrast to the narratives about the suicide decision, in which that decision was constructed with reference to an external source of origin, in narratives about the final moments before the act she becomes the author of the actions taken. This emphasizes her agency and active role in the events described.

It is also worth pointing out that what is likely to count as the act of suicide, taking medication, was not the end of the story. In fact, the act of taking the medication is rendered as time-extended – the informant talks about its start and does not convey it as a finite action through the past tense which could be rendered by the verb 'took'. Moreover, the beginning of taking the pills is anchored in the story of looking around, being aware of the late time it happened. In fact, the story line with the beginning of taking the medication is interrupted by an account of yet more considerations, yet more thinking about killing herself.

What we have is a story which not only is very far from reporting on a moment in time but also offers quite a detailed account of the act of killing oneself, which is cushioned in stories of agonizing, looking around, and further decisions. Quite interestingly, it is not even the loss of consciousness that ends the story of the informant's suicide attempt.

In spite of the assumptions present in the literature concerning the role of the mental state in suicidal behaviours (e.g. Shneidman, 1993), in the narrative there are no deliberations, no dilemmas, no emotions. The story is almost a technical account of what happened and the narrative consists of a set of actions performed by the informant. They are mostly what Halliday calls material processes (Halliday, 1978; Halliday and Hasan, 1985), which construct an active story, on making and changing reality, while the agentive forms underscore the account.

The materiality of the narrative can be observed in other such stories. For example:

Extract 15

A: could you? tell about it?

B: (how did it go) I just left the house ready. I left everything I didn't need and uhhh I went with my wife and her friend to to I asked them to let me out at ((names the square)) and I just went later to ((names the river)). I did it I was (in it) a bit shocked I don't remember those details [...] and I jumped off the bridge ((background conversation audible)) (it just) turned out that it wasn't very deep water, I just swam around the shore. and I I was taken in later by the police brought here to the hospital by the ambulance.

Although the participant in extract 15 does not go into such fine detail as the participant from extract 14, the narratives are nevertheless very similar. It is also a technical description of preparations for the suicide attempt. There is no discussion of life, no constructions indicating any emotional state; it is a narrative dominated by material processes of actions taken by the participant.

Interestingly, here the story does not end with the jump – the notional suicide attempt. The story continues, as if the suicide attempt had not yet finished. What changed is agency. At the beginning of the account, the informant constructs himself as the actor of the actions taken. The linguistic agency disappears, however, when the story moves to actions taking place after the informant's attempt to kill himself. He talks about being taken, being brought to the hospital. The participant goes from being an active performer of actions ('I went', 'I did', 'I jumped', 'I swam') to the object of actions taken by other people ('I was taken in […] brought').

A similar change in the construction of agency can be observed in the extracts below. In extract 16 the construction of self as the active performer of actions stops at the moment when the son uncovers the suicide attempt of the informant. In consequence, as in extract 15, the participant goes from being the actor of the described events to an object of medical interventions. The consistency of this change suggests that agentive forms in narratives about the final moments before the act are not accidental. Consider the following two extracts:

Extract 16

> A: now I'll ask probably one of the most difficult questions you don't have to answer if you don't want to uh could you just be a little more precise in describing how it went, how the day looked in the moments before the suicidal attempt?
>
> B: so it was evening, I mean somewhere around six my son ordered a pizza. I ate some pizza. (…) we were supposed to go there the next day. my wife registered me for the doctor at 9 o'clock or something and somewhere at 9 so I was waiting for that moment like because my son goes where I do but I said I was going to the loo I see the jar out of the corner of my eye over where it always was and I took that jar I went into the loo I closed the door and I swallowed those nails those screws (…) and later I put it down when I left and my son saw of course (…) he said 'did you do it' and at ((names a hospital)) they only examined me and then brought me here. that I'm a threat to myself no.

Extract 17

> A: now I'll ask probably the most difficult question. please remember you don't have to answer if it's too difficult. could you describe how the day looked in the moments before the suicidal attempt?
> (…)
>
> B: ((crying)) normal. it was just normal. nothing stood out from that normalness that I'm living in now. there wasn't nothing. I got up from the bed I washed myself. the full routine. uhh I got the wash out because the day before

I'd brought clothes from my daughter and I went up to the attic to hang the wash. I looked around. I couldn't reach that rafter. I pushed over an old washing machine standing over there by someone else's and I couldn't get up on it.

A: uhuh.

B: I looked around very precisely how to hook up that belt and tie it. and you know the rest.

As previously, the descriptions of actions undertaken by the informants are very technical. We see the details of what the informants did, without any commentary on it. No references are made to experience, to emotionality – the stories focus solely on what happened and not on what it meant.

Summing up, agentive forms are typical of utterances about the last moments before the act. In this way, the image of the last moments before the suicidal act appears as a time of doing, and not a time of thinking, feeling or talking. The participants construct themselves in these narratives as the primary actors in the events, thereby emphasizing their agentive role in the suicide attempt.

Conclusions

Agency is a definitional feature of suicide, yet it is rarely taken on board by suicidologists. Münster and Broz (2015) argue that contemporary suicidology has an ambivalent stance on agency. On the one hand, suicide is an agentive act defined as an intentional act taken by a person who is about to commit suicide. On the other hand, however, suicidologists deny this agency as resulting from the suicidal person's free will as they relate suicide to factors that are beyond the individual's control and personhood, such as illness, genetics, financial crisis or gender. So, agency is both constructed as necessary and strongly denied at the same time (Münster & Broz, 2015). Furthermore, it is agency that makes suicide a bad death, and so putting agency outside of the person who died by suicide is crucial in countering moral and legal sanctions. As an example, Münster and Broz (2015) discuss coroners' verdicts of *non compos mentis* with regard to people who committed suicide which were popular in the nineteenth century (also Hecht, 2013; Minois, 2001). This verdict implied that the person could not be held responsible for their actions; as they lacked wrongful intent, they should not suffer any official penalties. It was contrasted with the *felo de se* verdict which implied that the individual exercised free will in their suicide act and were therefore fully responsible for it.

This absence of interest in the agency of the person who takes their life is reflected in the academic/institutional discourses on suicide. In this chapter, we began our discussions by looking at how definitions of suicide construct the person who commits it. We found that either the person is removed from the definitions altogether or their agency is backgrounded. For suicidology and suicide prevention, it seems, suicides only happen rather than are done by people anchored in social and political contexts.

We contrasted those suicidological discourses with accounts of lived experience of suicide. We considered agency in such stories in three communicative contexts. We compared agency in accounts of decisions to commit suicide in interview data and in the corpus of suicide letters. It turned out that there are significant differences in such accounts. And, while our informants spoke about the decision to kill themselves in very ambivalent ways, such ambivalence disappeared in suicide letters where their authors directly and explicitly ascribed agency to decide to themselves.

We saw the difference between the accounts as coming from two sources. On the one hand, we suggested that suicide letters were given the function of an indemnity from any guilt or responsibility for the suicidal act. On the other, we suggested that the stigma attached to suicide prevented our interview informants from speaking directly about what they decided. Let us explore this some more.

The decision to commit suicide appears to be the most important element of the suicidal process (Ringel, 1987), yet suicidological literature focuses either on the properties of thinking and decision-making by suicidal people (Ackerman et al., 2015; Pollack & Williams, 2004; Williams, 2014) or on ethical and moral dilemmas associated with the decision about suicide (Fairbairn, 2003; Hecht, 2013; Szasz, 1999). We have focused on the linguistic construction of suicide decisions and shown that the decision about suicide is constructed by the participants as independent from them, as if they were not the authors of the suicidal decision. There are three ways of constructing this. First, the participants invoke independent agents who provoke the decision. In the narratives, there was, for example, an enigmatic 'something', 'attack', 'thought' or an 'impulse' which was responsible for the suicidal decision. Another way is bringing to life a part of the Self or a voice which ordered them to kill themselves. Finally, the participants constructed the suicidal decision as simply appearing, without an agent behind it.

The participants' stories about their suicide decision are full of what has been described as 'distancing' (Bavelas et al., 1990; Galasiński, 2004, 2008). Following our earlier work (Ziółkowska & Galasiński, 2017), we assume that distancing is a dissolution of the 'ownership' relationship between the speaking subject and the category they refer to. We argue that, linguistically, it includes situations where the social actor is not rendered as the linguistic one, socially, when, say, an ill person is using strategies allowing them to avoid making a direct attribution of illness to their self. And so, in the collected data distancing consists of non-direct references to taking the decision of suicide, in particular who is taking the decision. In other words, they avoided constructing themselves as decision-makers. Interestingly, distancing disappears in their narratives of the final moments before the suicidal act. In their narratives of this period of time, the informants concentrated primarily on describing their own actions and activities, using agentive forms and material processes to emphasize their active role in those actions.

Narratives about the suicide decision which are distanced from the self in the collected data can also be discussed in terms of stigma. Suicide is still one of the most stigmatizing acts, and although there is evidence that today's stigma is subtler (Feigelman, Gorman & Jordan, 2009), people who killed themselves are still rated as more blameworthy, weak, cowardly, selfish and sinful than those who died, for example, through cancer (Sand, Gordon & Bresin, 2013). As Mishara and Weisstub (2016) argue, of 192 independent countries and states, 25 still have specific laws and punishments for attempted suicide. In Poland, suicide and attempted suicide are not illegal; only encouraging or facilitating the suicide of another person is a crime. Yet, in this predominantly Catholic country, the graves of people who took their own lives are still often placed at a distance from other graves in the cemetery. Thus, maybe the constructed distance from the decision about suicide which expresses the will of an individual and therefore makes the attempters bad, weak, selfish and/or sinful, allows them to protect themselves from the stigma. If the decision to commit suicide was not mine, I cannot be responsible for what happened.

As we have suggested, such considerations are likely to be absent in those who write suicide letters. The likely placement of the letter in a semi-public and legal context creates a very different communicative situation for the communicator for whom the letter must have a different communicative and social function.

Such considerations raise an additional methodological point. As we see accounts of suicidal decisions as highly context-bound, with informants more than likely communicating about them with different representational interests (Kress & van Leeuwen, 1996) and communicative goals, the differences indicate again the impossibility of reaching the 'true' account of, or the 'real' decision to commit suicide. What we are dealing with are only stories, accounts of what happened with their context-bound and context-creating messages. A reality of suicide apparently focused on by suicidology and its attempt to reach a uniform act of suicide must be seen as much less attainable than might appear.

What is particularly interesting in the data we have analysed in this chapter is the change in linguistically constructed agency between the accounts of the decision and the accounts of the act. While the acting agents distance themselves from the decision about suicide, in narratives about the preparation and the act of suicide the informants emphasize their active role. We cannot propose any simple explanation for this result; yet, if we assume that discursive construction of agency is associated with participants' experiences, then the findings are likely to be relevant in the discussion about the suicide process and social meanings.

Having said that, what we see in the data is that agency in the process of suicide is likely to be dynamic and changes within the act. And while stories we have cannot be seen, as we indicated above, as a window onto reality, they do afford us some insight into how suicide and suicide attempts are experienced. Such experiences seem to undermine the assumptions of uniformness of suicide or suicidal behaviour.

And so, the emphasis on quantitative methodology and its focus on causation in contemporary suicidology, as well as the practical challenges associated with conducting qualitative research, limits our understanding of the suicidal process (Gordon, Stevenson & Cutcliffe, 2014; see also Aldridge, 1998).

Although such quantitative studies give us knowledge about factors that affect the duration of the process or its successive stages, they do not allow us to fully understand how the suicidal process is subjectively perceived by people with a history of suicide attempts. And so, perhaps the results of this research can be related to experiences of people who are about to kill themselves and the change in agency reflects the dynamic nature of the suicidal process. Perhaps the path to suicide is not by the accumulation of certain negative emotional states but, on the contrary, is a process that is associated with qualitative changes in experiences of the attempters, leading to different constructions of agency in narratives about the decision and those about the act. If so, then further studies are necessary to explore the linguistic picture of agency in narratives of people with suicidal experiences.

In addition, our data and analyses suggest very strongly a much more significant focus on the contextuality of suicide, its accounts and experience. And by contextuality we do not mean the typical focus on risk factors or their protective counterparts but on the subjective experiencing of suicide and its social anchoring.

There is one final point we would like to make here. Accounts constructing the process of suicide and suicide attempts as time-extended, construct the suicidal act as not ending the process. That raises another new question: is what happens after the suicidal act part of the suicide process? At present we cannot answer such a question. However, in the chapters that follow the question returns and we consider it afresh.

In Chapter 4, we continue the discussion of accounts of the time before suicidal death. We discuss how the time of committing suicide is constructed as full of activity. Suicidal death is preceded by a series of actions and, in fact, actions which are explicitly constructed as taking time. In particular, in Chapter 4 we raise the question of when suicide starts. What constitutes the beginning of suicide? And so, we discuss accounts of what we see as the three stages of suicide. We begin with constructions of the beginning of the process, move on to discussing what happens during the time of 'committing suicide' and end with constructions of the end of the process.

Appendix

Extract 1

A: a: pamięta pan moment w którym podjął pan tę decyzję?

B: no ta pierwsza decyzja to jeszcze tak jak szedłem spać to jeszcze mówię a: może wstanę może tego. (.) położyłem się ale o piątej się budzę (.) nie jednak nie bo to już we mnie było takie że: no nie mogę iść. nie mogę tam iść bo lekarz mnie przebada wszystkie te moje papiery i będzie to i to (.) no i wstałem o piątej leki były (.) nie musiałem szukać bo to brało się tego (.) zażyłem leki położyłem się to to było takie (.) nieprzemyślane takie jakieś: jakby to powiedzieć (..) impulsywne [trochę] bo to takie nie- nieprzemyślane nie? (.) bo jeszcze jak szedłem spać to nie wiedziałem że to zrobię ale obudziłem się mówię jednak nie coś tego (.) coś mnie do tego zmuszało. takie no ja wiem (.) no i wziąłem nie?

Extract 2

A: a może pan opowiedzieć o: o o: o tym jak podjął pan tę decyzję?

B: [...] nie potrafię pani odpowiedzieć jak. (.) po prostu taka taka myśl przyszła. po prostu taka taka myśl przyszła. (...) ni z tego ni z owego nawet nie wiem jak skąd się wzięła i: (.) i próbowałem to realizować po prostu.

Extract 3

B: to jest u: porażenie nerwu promieniowego kończymy górnej lewej no i w obawie przed tym że: w przypadku y: wizyty u lekarza medycyny pracy po prostu ja stracę tą pracę. i: dużo ludzi optymistycznie mnie nastawiało że ta ręka wróci szybko do zdrowia jednak minął tydzień potem minął miesiąc minęło półtora miesiąca (.) no i powstała ta próba samobójcza. to się w głowie urodziło niestety. z powodu tego że no uważałem się za nie niepotrzebnego. bo skoro: Bóg dał mi dwie nogi dwie ręce i nagle zabiera część mnie to nie wiem coś wewnątrz mnie powiedziało mi że: warto skończyć z tym życiem. i i nie przejmować się po prostu mieć ulgę.

Extract 4

B: (w mojej głowie) to ja nie wiem tak jak kiedyś mówiłam, że (.) od jakiegoś czasu jak ja zamknęłam się w sobie (..) powstały jakby dwie osoby. i z tymi dwiema osobami ja rozmawiam. niby to ja niby nie ja nie wiem (5sek.) i to właśnie tak w październiku było to że (..) ta inna osoba mówiła nie bierz. masz dzieci wal- (7sek.) o maj (..) tak a teraz było to coś takiego y: (.) mam wszystkiego dość (..) nie ma gdzie komu wierzyć. bez sensu to wszystko jest. (..) i zmęczenie.

po prostu pamiętam jak dziś zmęczenie takie. i właśnie ta () mówiło takiego weź szybko (..) nie patrz na to. i tak zrobiłam. (...) ale po jakimś czasie nie wiem dziesięć, piętnaście już kontrolę straciłam (.) tak jakbym wołała o pomoc.

A: aha. mhm.

B: powiedziałam do męża właśnie żeby coś tego że wzięłam tabletki to już było tak jakby ta druga osoba była.

Extract 5

B: no i (.) w człowieku tak się rodzi potęguje. na początku: człowiek myśli mówi do siebie c- głupi jesteś o czym ty myślisz. ale im im trudniej jest im im dłużej to trwa to tym bardziej w człowieku jakby ta szala decyzji o podjęcia śmierci tak jakby przeważa się. i w pewnym momencie to pęka po prostu. jest już nie ma nadziei. bo (bo) się tak czułem jak piąte koło u wozu. dla rodziny. że wyobrażałem sobie że ta ręka nie wróci ta rehabilitacja jak ja na starość jak ja będę wyglądał? bez tej ręki mówię sprawnej. oczywiście sprawność częściowo wróciła. ale nie na tyle satysfakcjonująco żebym żebym dalej na przykład mógł pracować.

Extract 6

B: i to taka była sytuacja to się wszystko tak we mnie kumulowało kumulowało aż w końcu pękło. nie wiem jak to się stało naprawdę nie wiem. ja nawet nie pomyślałam o tym: nigdy nie myślałam o tym o tym żeby się zabić.

A: aha.

B: nigdy nie miałam takich myśli [...] po prostu przyszłam od znajomej do domu (.) wieczorem (.) dzieciaki już spały jedynie tylko ((podaje imię córki)) y nie spała i coś tam ja jej się zapytałam i ona do mnie zapyskowała.

A: aha.

B: i chyba: wtedy. pękło po prostu jak automat. ja nawet nawet nie pamiętam (.) tego momentu jak ja wyciągałam te tabletki.

Extract 7

Postanowiłem odejść z tego życia Przepraszam Was.

Extract 8

Tak chciałem i tak zrobiłem

Extract 9

To jest moja decyzja

Extract 10

Na wstępie chciałbym zaznaczyć, że to co zrobię jest moją samodzielną decyzją, aczkolwiek wymuszoną sytuacją w jakiej się znalazłem.

Extract 11

To co zrobiłem to była moja decyzja. Stwierdziłem że życie bez Ciebie nie ma sensu

Extract 12

Przeproś wszystkich że tak postanowiłem. Ale to jest moja decyzja i uważnie ją przemyślałem.

Extract 13

Powiesiłem się sam. Proszę nie winić nie winić Żony.

Extract 14

B: y to wszystko się działo: nad ((podaje nazwę rzeki)). bo ja zamierzałam m: wziąć te leki wypić ten alkohol i: utopić się w ((podaje nazwę rzeki)). y: do tego starannie się przygotowałam w domu. gdzie nikogo nie było. przygotowałam sobie wszystkie potrzebne mi rzeczy. y: które mi będą niezbędne o wszystkich wszystkie wartościowe rzeczy typu komórka jakieś pieniądze wszystko to wartościowe zostawiłam w domu. ubrałam się w najgorsze rzeczy najgorsze spodnie (.): w najgorszą s- starą kurtkę ale kurtkę na która by ((cmoka)) zlewała się z drzewami z krzewami żeby m: żeby

A: (nikt nie zauważył)?

B: tak. żeby nie odróżniał żeby nikt nie nie nie nie zobaczył żebym: bo gdybym ubrała białą być może bardziej bym się rzucała w oczy. więc to też wzięłam pod uwagę. żeby kurtka była coś zielonkawo-brązowa i rzeczywiście znalazłam taką kurtkę stare spodnie stare buty najgorsze y: znalazłam jakąś torebkę której nigdy nie używałam. no i do tej torebki zapakowałam to co było mi zupełnie niezbędne. y: słoik w tym do tego słoika miałam już y: wyciśnięte wcześniej przygotowane tabletki. (bo) było tego BARDZO BARDZO dużo że to był zapas 3-miesięczny czterech rodzajów leków. było tego bardzo dużo. m: poszłam do: sklepu monopolowego. kupiłam alkohol kupiłam koniak. to zapakowałam do torebki zapakowałam jeszcze: (.) zapałki bo: obawiałam się że w nocy kiedy będę siedziała nad Odrą mogą m: pojawić się szczury. więc chciałam je jakby odstraszać ogniem. o tym pomyślałam. wzięłam jeszcze literatkę y: z barku jakieś chusteczki higieniczne (.) i: (.) i: y: dodatkową ym: mocną reklamówkę w razie gdyby któraś z płóciennych mi się y: urwała. m: a przygotowana byłam w ten sposób że y: do pasa m: (.) y: w okolicy pasa przywiązałam sobie y: szeroki mocny pasek skórzany z: z bardzo mocną y klamrą i bardzo <u>solidny</u> mocny pasek y: do tego przyczepiłam m: zawiązałam trzy płó- płócienne worki (.) zawiązałam je i do każdego z nich włożyłam cegłę. i tak y: m: przygotowałam to w domu i sprawdziłam y: w domu czy czy to się nie urwie. czy to y: czy to y: wytrzyma tą siłę. czy: jak ja będę się czuła mając to na sobie. czy rzeczywiście to będzie takie obciążenie żebym m: kiedy u: m: się utopię to żebym nie wypłynęła. sądziłam że y: że y (.) że chyba dobrze wszystko zaplanowałam. te płócienne worki jak najbardziej zdały rezultat. y: (.) i: z cegłami nie było problemu bo obok y: wykładali jakiś bruk. tak że kwestia była tylko zejścia na dół i: ja je przyniosłam do domu. i: i tak przygotowane razem z paskiem pasek (nawet) z tymi płóciennymi workami i z cegłami włożyłam do jednej dużej torby (.) wsiadłam w autobus i pojechałam nad ((podaje nazwę rzeki)) niedaleko ((podaje nazwę mostu)) (.) tam postanowiłam to zrobić. m: y: w domu m: nie zostawiłam żad- aha. zamknęłam dom na klucz. (.) [...] ta noc była bardzo zimna. okazało się. była bardzo zimna i: ja y: po prostu natychmiast jak zrobiło się już ciemniej y: i i i: m: m: (.) y: m pamiętam że zaczy- zaczy- już było dosyć ciemno jak zaczynałam zażywać leki. [...] wi- pamiętam y moment że: nie wiem musiało być koło północy bo u ludzi z naprzeciwka w bloku zaczęły y: gasnąć światła. czyli m: ludzie szli spać. to najpóźniej mogło być 11 12. to już miałam o już miałam- yyy taką utratę takie. i w tym momencie po prosty y: powinnam zrobić to co powinnam. czyli dalszy krok. a ja w tym momencie po prostu straciłam świadomość i upadłam z: jakąś podwiniętą ręką pod klatkę piersiową. tak przeleżałam 24 godziny. znaleźli mnie jacyś wędkarze. no wcześniej no mówię no ktoś mnie okradł z tej biednej torebki. z tej literatki. no alkoholu nie było już bo ja alkohol cały wypiłam. m: także przyjechało pogotowie. policja. i byłam osobą poszukiwaną przez rodzinę.

Extract 15

A: mógłby pan? opowiedzieć o tym?

B: (jak to było) to po prostu wyszedłem z domu już przygotowany. zostawiłem właściwie wszystkie rzeczy niepotrzebne i (.).hhh jechałem z żoną i jej koleżanką do do do (). [..] prosiłem żeby mnie wysadziły na placu ((podaje nazwę placu)) i po prostu poszedłem później na nad ((podaje nazwę rzeki)). dokonałem tej (...) byłem (w tym) lekkim szoku to nie pamiętam takich szczegółów ().. [..]

no i s:: skoczyłem z mostu (.) ((słychać rozmowy w tle)) (jakoś to się) okazało że to nie była zbyt głęboka woda, no po prostu płynąłem tam gdzieś pod brzeg. no i: zostałem zatrzymany później przez policję przez (.) przywieziony tutaj do szpitala przez ambulans.

Extract 16

A: a: zadam teraz ch- ch- chyba jedno z najtrudniejszych pytań nie musi pan na nie odpowiadać jeśli pan nie chce (.) e: czy mógłby pan jesz- jeszcze dokładniej opowiedzieć o tym jak wyglądał jaki był dzień chwile przed próbą popełnienia samobójstwa?

B: no to wieczorem znaczy się (.) gdzieś o sió- szóstej syn zamówił pizzę. zjadłem pizzę. (..) mieliśmy na drugi dzień iść. gdzieś tam na dziewiątą żona mnie zarejestrowała do lekarki (.) no i gdzieś o dziewiątej (.) tak czekałem na moment jak (.) bo syn gdzie ja to on ale mówię że idę do ubikacji kątem oka widzę słoik że tam zawsze stał no i wziąłem ten słoik (.) wszedłem do ubikacji zamknąłem się no i połknąłem te gwoździe te śruby (..) a no ale później tam odstawiłem jak wyszedłem no i syn zobaczył (.) oczywiście (..) mówi co żeś zrobił tego i: na ((podaje nazwę szpitala)) (.) tam mnie tylko prześwietlili i tu przewieźli. (.) że to zagrażam sam sobie nie.

Extract 17

A: zadam teraz chyba najtrudniejsze z tych pytań. proszę pamiętać że nie musi pani na nie odpowiadać jeśli jest to zbyt trudne. czy mogłaby pani opowiedzieć o tym jak wyglądał dzień chwile przed próbą popełnienia samobójstwa?

(…)

B: ((płacze)) zwyczajnie. po prostu zwyczajnie. bez żadnych tam jakichś odstępstw tej niby normalności w której teraz tkwię. nie było (.) nic. wstałam z łóżka umyłam się. pełna rutyna..hhh wyjęłam pranie bo dzień wcześniej przyniosłam pranie od córki i poszłam na strych powiesić to pranie. rozejrzałam się. nie mogłam dosięgnąć do tej krokwi. przewróciłam taką starą pralkę tam stoi koło czyjaś (.) tak nie mogłam na nią wejść.

A: mhm.

B: obejrzałam bardzo dokładnie jak zahaczyć ten pasek go zawiązać. no a dalej już pani wie jak.

4

Suicide activities

In the previous two chapters, we have discussed a conflict between the institutional/academic discourses of suicide, embodied in definitions of suicide, and lay accounts of killing oneself. We have found significant differences between them. First, we have shown that definitions of suicide represent it as an event outside time and social context. Suicide is shown to be a point in time, often equated with death. Yet accounts of suicide in suicide notes suggest that suicide is anything but a point on a timeline. It is a time-extended set of actions for which taking one's life is only one stage.

Second, we have also shown that definitions of suicide largely remove references to the person who kills themselves as well as their agency. In the definitions, suicides happen, while human participation is only implied. On the other hand, our interview data suggest a very complex picture of agency constructed in the narratives of suicide, one which we have argued should be acknowledged and studied in suicidology.

In this chapter, we continue the discussion of representations of time before suicidal death. We want to discuss in detail how the time of suicide is constructed as full of activity. Suicidal death is preceded by a series of actions and, in fact, such actions are constructed as taking time, sometimes significant time. In particular, in this chapter we raise the question of when suicide starts. What constitutes the beginning of suicide?

In what follows, we discuss accounts of what we see as three stages of suicide. We begin with constructions of the beginning of the process, move on to discussing what happens during the time of 'committing suicide' and end with constructions of the end of the process.

The beginning

In this section, we focus on how authors of suicide letters construct the beginning of the process of suicide. Consider first the following extracts:

Extract 1

I am going. It should work out.

Extract 2

I am going to get the dog-lead. Farewell.

Extract 3

I do not feel like living. I have taken tablets.

The first two extracts use the verb 'idę' (literally, 'I'm going'). In such a form, the verb can be used to mark a starting point, a journey, not necessarily a literal one. And this is the important aspect of the notes. By using the verb in the first person singular, the letter writers explicitly indicate not that they are about to kill themselves but that they are starting to go about doing so. These are notes that indicate the beginning of a process, not only an event, let alone one action.

Extract 3 is different. While linguistically the writer does not suggest the commencement of the process, this is how the note can be interpreted. By saying that she took the tablets, the woman also implies that the process of waiting for her death had started. In other words, the note does not tell us about the end; it tells of a beginning of waiting.

There is, in fact, something quite fascinating about the note. The information about taking the tablets is almost redundant. Whoever will find her body, with a note that she does not feel like living, will presumably be able to guess what has happened. And yet, she decided to write it. Incidentally, the question of redundancy of the message can be asked also of extracts 1 and 2. The phrase 'Idę' is more than likely to be used in situations when someone is, here and now, communicating to an addressee that they are starting to do something. In the situation of writing a suicide note, this is unlikely. It is difficult to see the note as serving a clear communicative purpose.

When the note is read, the message of starting the process will be long since overdue, while the information about the tablets will no longer be necessary. Such phrases seem to violate Grice's Cooperative Principle (Grice, 1975), which is postulated as the foundation of communication. Basically, they state the obvious, what the addressee already knows. The explanation, however, might be that phrases such as these are not directed at the addressee of the letter. They might well be made for the benefit of the author of the note; the author writes a letter which will be read in a diametrically different reality from the one they know, a reality in which they no longer exist. The phrases such as those above might well be expressions that anchor the decision, that is to say, they 'remind' the person what exactly they are writing. They might also help them face the reality before it actually happens. Thus, they set the scene in which the letter will be read and, crucially, for which the letter is written. It is perhaps not so much a phrase that helps them cope with the new reality but, rather, one that helps them face it. In such a way, such notes are also a way of acknowledging the situation in which the man who killed himself has put those close to him.

We could continue this argument by pointing out the varied social practices of recording important things. From diaries, letters or chronicles all the way to news bulletins or, today, Twitter posts, important or significant events have been recorded, and perhaps suicide notes are part of this complex and long-standing practice. We shall come back to this in the 'Conclusions' section of this chapter.

But there is another avenue of interpretation here, not necessarily exclusive of the others. We would like to borrow the idea of 'long suicide' (Galasiński, 2017), the notion that suicide is not something which happens when life is terminated. Rather, that it is a set of actions which in one way or another lead to the person's death. It might well be that the notes also serve the function of starting the suicide. They are a way for the author to adopt a reality in which they are either already dead or about to die. In other words, their suicide is happening, the process is starting, the act of life-termination is only the physical realization of the acceptance that suicide has commenced, and for all intents and purposes one is already either dead or about to become dead. Such a note therefore can be seen as the non-physical part of the process of suicide; they have not yet physically extinguished their life.

Intent

While extracts 1 to 3 announce the beginning of suicide, in other letters their authors can be considerably less direct. Their notes announce intent rather than action. Consider:

Extract 4

> I have had the intention to commit suicide for some time. Since 16 March when I caught [name] with her lover.

Extract 5

> Today is [date], 13.40 hours. I have decided to take my life for the reason that my wife, [first name], married me in a civil ceremony, we had a child, but she has never loved me and she has hidden everything from me.

Extract 6

> I was writing this letter some time ago, but finally I have decided to take this step. Up till the day of [date] nothing has changed, she is still cheating on me and she is nasty towards me. My death happened at [time]. Approximately.

Extract 7

> Forgive me, my beloved girls, for my disgraceful act, but I cannot differently, I cannot put it off any more, because in the end I would not have the strength to do what I want to do.

Extracts 4 and 5 announce the decision to commit suicide. Even though the two letters describe a different timescale – extract 4 talks about days, extract 5 talks about a decision taken minutes before the moment of writing – linguistically they are much the same. One could argue that the extracts are ambivalent with reference to whether they indicate the beginning of the suicide process; yet, commonsensically, the length of the period between the decision and the death would suggest that the process could not have started yet. Indeed, when we consider extract 6, it extends the process to its author's death. The chronicler records the entire process, including the death.

It is letters such as extract 6 which lead us to argue that accounts of the decision to kill oneself recorded in the letter may well suggest the beginning of the suicidal process. The letters presumably serve to inform their addressees of what 'really' happened, and, while explaining the reasons for the decision, they also presumably serve to apportion blame. For the discussion here, however, the important point about them is that it is quite likely that they mark the beginning of a period of time which ends with suicidal death.

Extract 7 is quite different. While it refers to the intent, it positions it as something that has existed for some time but that the letter writer had resisted it. The note, interestingly, marks the moment when resistance is no longer possible. The letter records the tipping point, so to speak. Whatever happened before writing the letter had not yet been 'suicide proper'; it starts only now.

The final point we would like to make about the letters is that those quoted above suggest that the process is quite flexible: one can decide, go back on the decision, wait some more, only to come back to it. It is unclear whether such accounts should be thought of as describing a single process or perhaps several; it is clear, however, that the time before suicidal death is full of actions, decisions or, indeed, accounts thereof.

The final two extracts refer to intentions that also warrant further discussion:

Extract 8

I hope I will effectively take my life.

Extract 9

I have a feeling that I am too fucking clever to end my miserable life. I think I shall try.

There are two points we would like to make with regard to these extracts. First, it is unclear who they are addressed to. In fact, we would argue that they are unlikely to be addressing anyone. It is unlikely that information about one writer's hope that he would be successful (extract 8) and the other's statement on her cleverness (extract 9) is information that is expected in a suicide note. Rather, the notes are records, perhaps records of reflections, much like one would write in a diary or perhaps in a blog. These little snippets seem to be aimed at reflecting the situation in which the person has found themselves as well as their state of mind.

It is unclear what the point of these letters is. Perhaps they are a way to face what is about to happen, perhaps they are a way of leaving a note. We shall come back to this in the 'Conclusions' section of the chapter. A note of caution is needed here, though. We do not wish to claim that the notes give us insight into the person's state of mind, a suicidal mind, as much suicidology claims (Bauer et al., 1997; Ioannou & Debowska, 2014; Leenaars, 1988; Lester, 2015; Sinyor et al., 2015); rather, we suggest that the notes are textual devices through which their authors render a particular perspective on how they feel or what they think. We are interested in the reality which is constructed by the writers of farewell letters rather than in 'what really happened'.

The other point we would like to make is that both notes record that something starts. In extract 8, the reference to the hope of effectively killing oneself implies the beginning of the process; in extract 9, the reference to trying is an indication of the beginning of the process. Moreover, the context, the fact that both letter writers did kill themselves, makes the implications and the reading thereof stronger.

To end the discussion, we would like to consider one final note:

Extract 10

> I have considered my life and I know that there is no way out for me and I have to leave this world because I have no one to live for. I am sorry for everything that I have done badly and well. Today at night my life will have run its course. I cannot live without you.

The note predicts the suicidal death of its writer. The problem, however, is to what extent we could see it as the commencement of the suicidal process. We have no information about when the note in extract 10 was written, but it is possible to surmise that it was written before the evening or the night, otherwise the reference to time would have probably been different. Can it be taken to record the starting of the process? If not, what does it do? We do not have good answers for such questions. We return to this issue in the 'Conclusions' section of the chapter.

In this section, we have discussed suicide notes which record the beginning of suicide or the process which ends in the death of those who wrote the letters. The beginning of the process is marked by the decision to kill oneself, both explicitly and, as in extracts 8 and 9, implicitly. In the next section, we discuss letters which describe the preparations for committing suicide.

Preparations for suicide

In this section, we discuss preparations for suicide. We quoted stories of preparations for suicide in the previous chapter when we discussed agency in suicide. We showed that the stories were in what could be seen as technical language, focusing solely on preparatory actions. Here, we focus on suicide notes which construct preparations as one of the stages in the series of actions leading to suicide. We argue that preparations are represented as part of the suicidal process. In other words, they are not activities that happen before or alongside suicide, but are part of it.

In the first set of extracts, we discuss suicide notes in which the authors position certain activities as necessary conditions for their suicidal death. Consider:

Extract 11

> Everyone probably thinks that I hanged myself because I was drunk. Nothing further from the truth. I did do a bottle for the courage, because I think I would not have done it sober.

Extract 12

> Forgive [addressing many] me, I had to have a drink for courage, because I am a coward.

Extract 13

> The blue towel, it is [first name]'s and the little sponge too. I have taken a bath, bury me in [town].

The three extracts describe preparations for killing oneself: two of them refer to drinking alcohol, one to taking a bath. The first two, moreover, explicitly position drinking alcohol as preparation for suicidal death; the third only implies it. Our argument is that extracts 11 and 12 explicitly show alcohol as part and parcel of taking the letter writer's life. The authors of the suicide letters position it explicitly as the condition *sine qua non* of killing oneself. In other words, there is no killing yourself without having a drink. The reference to taking a bath is different. We are both aware of understanding taking a bath as a stage in the preparations for important events, both institutional or private, which could be seen in terms of a purification ritual (Smith, 2007). Water and a bath can be seen as symbols of transition and renewal, in both secular (e.g. admission into the military or a prison) and sacred (e.g. baptism) settings (Twigg, 2000). And so, being bathed means being ready for something. Indeed, this is how we see the reference to having taken a bath in extract 13, though it is unclear what exactly the author of the letter was ready for. It might be both dying or being buried.

Just as the three extracts show drinking and having a bath as necessary conditions for suicide, suicide notes show different kinds of preparations. The following extracts show certain activities as preparations for the aftermath of the letter author's death.

Extract 14

> I shall be finishing, my nerves do not let me write. I am putting my ring in for you, so give it to your friend, but best have it made into a ring for you.

Extract 15

I have put my ring into mum's envelope, so ask her to take it a goldsmith and have it made it into a ring. I do not know if she lets you read her letter, but if you watch [television series], there is something like that at the beginning. I wanted to share my sorrow, but I have no one to do it to.

The two extracts offer a scene from the moments before suicidal death. It is a scene of a person preparing themselves to take their own life. It is much like a person is going through a to-do list, making a record of the things they need to do or crossing off those they already have done. Presumably, here, the note is also a personal diary, as it probably offers important information to whoever is meant to read it. The note-chronicle is meant not only to be read but also to tell the addressee(s) what they might want to know.

There are another two interesting aspects of the notes. First, in extract 14, the note's author uses the present tense to refer to the act of putting in the wedding ring (it is unclear where he puts it). The man records the action as it happens. We suggest that such a record makes the action more real – that is to say, we witness the action as it happens. It also offers insight into what the person was doing at the time – the note dramatizes the time. In such a way, the man offers us a snapshot of the time just before his death. Note that we are not suggesting that the note is a feel-good one. If anything, it is the opposite, as it offers an insight into how the man spent the time just before his death, and it is through this it becomes more tragic. The reference to passing the wedding ring on makes it even more poignant.

What is interesting in extract 15 is the last sentence which we translate as 'I wanted to share my sorrow, but I have no one to do it to.'[1] Similarly to extract 14, the sentence offers a snapshot of the note's author before his death. It renders the author as attempting to contact someone but having no success. The note carries connotations of solitude, of a forlorn person who has no one to turn to. What is crucial for our argument in this book is that both notes construct the time before taking one's life as the present. As we have suggested, the notes paint a picture of someone doing something, whether it be putting a ring somewhere or just sitting and thinking. The notes offer us a picture of the suicide the two men are 'doing'. Soon after, presumably, they killed themselves.

The final two extracts we want to discuss here refer to preparations which are shown to last days rather than hours. Consider:

Extract 16

> Today it is Tuesday, [date], and I am performing it tomorrow, that is [date] because today I still need to attend to a matter.

Extract 17

> I have finally managed to hang the dog-lead. I will go for a walk the day after tomorrow and I am going to my death.

The notes offer a record of a process which takes days. On the one hand, in extract 16, the note's author talks about 'an errand', a matter to deal with before he can take his life. The note indicates that things were put in motion, but there are things to be done before the suicidal death. Extract 17 is perhaps even more surprising. After the successful preparation of the suicide method, the author informs us that he will take a walk 'the day after tomorrow' and then he will kill himself.

Both letters are written in the present tense. Things are happening, the authors seem to suggest a certain urgency in what is about to happen. The present tense, just as we suggested in Chapter 3, constructs the suicide as happening. In such a way, the notes become diaries, perhaps even micro-blogs in which the writers record what is happening to them. Indeed, as we both have accounts on Twitter, the systemic question that Twitter asks in the tweet dialogue box is 'What's happening?' The above suicide notes seem to answer such a question.

Such an argument, even if made tentatively, raises several significant issues for how suicide notes and their function should be understood. As Galasiński (2017) stresses, the assumption that farewell letters should be seen as offering insight into the 'suicidal mind' is untenable. Suicide notes are acts of communication, and there is no reason to assume that they are devoid of a variety of communicative functions and do not serve a variety of communicative goals just as any other act of communication.

The time perspective the two notes construct makes our argument somewhat problematic, however. Admittedly, it is hard to assume that a suicide lasts a few days. And yet, we do not believe we should rethink the argument. Rather, we suggest that what is needed is a rethinking of the notion of suicide in terms of a person's death. We discuss this further in the 'Conclusions' section of the chapter.

Passing the time

In this section, we discuss constructions of the time when a person is engaged in committing suicide. It turns out that authors of suicide notes also construct this period of time as filled with activity, sometimes directly related to taking their own life, sometimes not. But one of the most poignant aspects of the notes is the construction of time passing and waiting for death. And while it is fairly obvious that, particularly after taking poison, death does not happen immediately, the insight into the waiting can be quite dramatic.

Let us start with the most striking letter we found:

Extract 18

> I didn't go to school today. I decided to commit suicide. I tried to cut my veins, but I was not very successful. I overdosed on [medication] I think and I am waiting for what will happen. I have done it because I do not want to go to school. Otherwise I would have to go tomorrow and I would not bear it.

The note describes a teenager's suicide: from the decision, through an ineffective first attempt/method, to taking medication, which resulted in the person's death. It raises a number of issues. First, it shows suicide as a set of actions, some of which were ineffective and only some effective. We see a struggle to take one's own life effectively, a process which, to our knowledge, has not been described in the literature. Suicide here consists of trials and errors, a process which is inevitably extended in time. Moreover, the suicide note raises again the issue of what constitutes a suicide attempt. In her account of trying to cut her veins, is the letter's author describing a suicide attempt? Or is she simply telling the story of her suicide, which took more time and effort than she had expected? In other words, is the failed attempt from the beginning of the note part of her suicide?

Incidentally, our linguistic sensitivity is heightened with the use of the phrase *nie bardzo* ('not very'). It tends to be used as a phrase to describe failure, usually as either relatively unimportant or perhaps jocular. The initial attempt is rendered as banal, something not worthy of much attention. In the context of a suicide note, this is surprising to say the least. The only explanation for the use of the phrase is that its lack of importance is cancelled out by the fact that the letter writer had already made another attempt. In such a way, the initial one does not count, so to speak.

Now, the most interesting aspect of the note is that it is written after the eighteen-year-old took the medication. She describes herself as waiting for 'what will happen'. There is an ambivalence in the construction of the waiting. Because of the *chyba* (normally rendered as 'I think') inserted into the sentence of overdosing, the waiting is shown as the time to wait and see the result of her action, which is uncertain at the time of writing. But, because of the beginning of the extract, the waiting is also constructed as the time to see whether the teenager was successful.

In either case, suicide is shown not as death; rather, it is shown as a time in which death needs to be made sure of. Put differently, suicide is constructed as the time in which one waits to die, as the person who intends to kill themselves must wait for the result of what they did. The writing of the note can be seen both as recording what happened and as just passing the time while awaiting suicide.

Consider now extracts in which the notes' authors construct their activities with the use of forms suggesting either iteration or process:

Extract 19

> I keep writing some more, because I want to persuade you that life and health are beautiful until one has them.

Extract 20

> It's 17.26. From one moment to another I can see that my life makes no sense. I have talked to [first name] a moment ago and she has depressed me even more. She said nothing, but I mean the tone of her voice. It was so unhappy, as if she had wanted to say I am so unhappy with you.

Extract 21

> Right. Dear sister, end of feeling sorry for myself and I am sorry that I turn to you the most, but I had to talk to someone.

Extract 22

> I am crying like a child as I am writing this. Please apologise to everyone, [names], so they will not think badly about me.

All four notes describe their author as engaged in activity. Extract 19 is perhaps the most interesting as the writer constructs himself as going back to writing, as if not wanting or not being able to finish. We can almost see the man leaving the desk and immediately changing his mind and going back to it. Indeed, as the note is described as having the aim to persuade, it is thereby constructed as important and needing to be written carefully. And so, we see the note's author as engaged in an activity before his suicidal death, taking the time to get the note written. As he seems not to be in a hurry, he can spend the time getting it right.

Extract 20 is somewhat similar as the author constructs himself as continually realizing that his life makes no sense. The expression 'from one moment to another' not only suggests the passing of time but also underscores the repetitive nature of the activity. This, on the other hand, is rendered in extract 21 through the use of the iterative form of the verb *użalać się* ('complain', 'moan'). This time, however, the note records the end of moaning. Interestingly, the note also suggests that the moaning was not in solitude but in an interaction with the note writer's sister.

This reference to interacting with another person makes extract 21 a particularly interesting case (and similar to extract 13 in Chapter 2). Here, suicide, which is often assumed to be private and solitary (Salem, 1999), is rendered as anything but. Here a conversation is constructed as at the very least something significant enough to note it in the suicide note and as something very likely to have taken place quite close to the man's death.

Having said this, we cannot, of course, determine the extent to which the end of moaning was meant as the beginning of suicide, or perhaps part of its course; still, the author for one reason or another records its end in the note. And so, even though we do not know whether the man's death happened immediately after writing his note or perhaps whether some time elapsed, the writer decided that it was that particular event that should be recorded in his farewell letter. As such, therefore, the moaning can be seen as part of the situation in which the note's author was going to take his life (and actually he did). Moreover, given the particular context in which the letter was written, we would suggest that the reference to the end of the moaning marks the moment in which the person moved on to take her life. We pick up this issue again later in this section.

Finally, extract 22 is simpler in that it records crying and writing. There is no further context offered, only the fact that the person is engaged in the activity. Such references to writing have been relatively frequent. Consider:

Extract 23

> I am writing this letter because my heart tells me that this is what I should decide. Writing this, a tear is rolling down my cheek on its own.

Extract 24

> Writing this letter, I had tears in my eyes, but I knew it would be for the best.

Extract 25

> I am writing this letter after latest considerations and I have reached the conclusion that this is the way it will be best for us all.

Extract 26

> I am writing this letter with the thought that I love you very much. Only when you read it, I will probably not be in this world.

All these notes serve as metacommunicative phrases, presumably to contextualize the letter, to introduce it as important or significant. But they also render the writer as engaged in the activity of writing. As before, they serve to record the action of writing, as if telling the addressees what the person who killed themselves was doing before taking their own life. Indeed, writing is by far the most referred to activity in the suicide notes we have. Interestingly, it is also described as something that cannot be done, as in the following extracts:

Extract 27

> I will write no more, because somehow I have no inspiration and my eyes have welled up a little when I think that I will lose you.

Extract 28

> It is hard writing at the moment because at the moment I am very scared. I am experiencing a brain storm. I am sending you a picture of [place] with the letter. As you guess, this is where I am going.

Extract 29

> I do not know what I should write to you. It is hard to leave people one loves. And my heart is breaking at this moment. I am looking at a picture of the little one and saliva is choking me, tears are flowing from my eyes, but I know that this is the way it must be. And I must do it in order that it will be better for you.

We would like to finish this section by exploring extracts in which their authors write about the end of writing. Consistently, the end of writing is rendered as the introduction to dying. Consider:

Extract 30

> My dear beloved, this is all I wanted to write. Do not forget me, remember me, bury me.

Extract 31

> I have finished writing: Wednesday, 1 o'clock.

Extract 30 is the most explicit account of positioning the end of writing as the end of life. The directive sentence pleads that the addressees should not forget the writer after his death. The end of writing seems to mark the end of the period before taking one's life. This is, incidentally, how we see the phrase in extract 31.

What is worth noting is that, as the end of writing is implied to be the end of the 'suicide preparations', the rest of what happens is backgrounded. Only very few notes referred to the moments of the physical taking of one's life. However, this observation is not meant to suggest that the stage of killing oneself is not important for the people who engage in it. Rather, we suggest that the act of writing is likely to precede it and therefore it is only rarely recorded in the notes.

In this section, we have discussed how suicide notes constructed the activities of the note writers as they were engaged in 'doing suicide'. After discussing the note which explicitly constructed its author as waiting for death, we also explored notes in which such activities were described. We have argued that suicide notes represent their authors as doing things, engaged in activities both related and unrelated to taking one's own life. We have also suggested that such constructions offer a complex view of suicide, making it perhaps less useful for suicidology than, say, the concept of suicidal death. We shall discuss this in the 'Conclusions' section of the chapter.

The end

We planned the last section of this chapter as one that explores the end of the process of suicide. We assumed that the constructions of the beginning of the process should be mirrored by such constructions of the end. To our surprise, writers of farewell letters did not construct the end as the resolution of the process they were involved with. We found only one extract which implies such a resolution. Consider:

Extract 32

> I am still deceiving myself that something which will stop me will happen. There is still a spark of hope left, to be sure, a fleeting one, but still. Perhaps someone will ask me why here, in this place. The reason is simple. I do not want anyone to interrupt me and here it will almost certainly not happen.

The extract implies that its author is engaged in a process. First, this is done through the reference to being stopped and, second, through the reference to being interrupted. But the latter reference also implies that the process has an end. If the writer is interrupted, the end will not be realized. And so, the extract that constructs an end to the process of killing oneself does it through the reference that it might not happen.

Even though the suicide letters we have do not refer to the end-as-resolution of the suicidal process, there are many indirect references to the end of the process. The most frequent and interesting of those are letters which are written from the future perspective (for a detailed discussion, see Galasiński, 2017). By this, we mean that the notes represent the world as if the writer were positioned in the future, which makes the 'objective' present in the past. And by 'objective' present, to reiterate, we mean the actual time of writing the note. Put differently, these notes represent the world in which the writer is already dead and their death has happened in the past. Consider the following extracts:

Extract 33

> If you are reading this, I am already gone. Know that it was not because of you that I killed myself.

Extract 34

> [First name], if you are reading this, it means I am not longer by your side. What I wrote here was sprinkled with tears of my despair.

Extract 35

> To [first name].
>
> [First name], I apologise to you for everything. I love you more than life, but I could not live without you. I love you even though I am already gone.

Extract 36

> I would like to apologise to you again for the date of my demise. A week before the A-level exams is not a felicitous moment, but I could not [bear it] any more.

The future perspective is clear. The authors refer to their death (more or less directly) as something that has already happened in the past, linguistically using the past tense. Except, importantly, we know that the past tense is used to refer to something that cannot have happened at the time of writing.

There are two points we would like to make about these extracts. First, we would like to second Galasiński's (2017) argument that such extracts are indicative of what he called 'long suicide'. That is to say, in order to write notes from the future perspective, the writers must think themselves dead. The suicide is ongoing and the only part of it that has not happened is the physical termination of life. By adopting a reality in which the writer is already dead, much like in the notes that take a future perspective, one must also assume that suicide is happening, the act of killing could be seen only as the physical realization of the acceptance that one is already dead. In other words, the note can be seen as the non-physical part of the process of suicide, a time in which one assumes that one is already dead but one has not yet physically extinguished life.

The second point we would like to make is that, while the beginning of the suicidal process tends to be constructed in a direct way, the references to the end of the process tend to be quite indirect. In extracts 33 and 35, the writers talk about being gone; in extract 34, the writer talks about not being by the addressee's side. Only extract 36 contains a direct reference to death, except the word *zgon* ('death', 'demise') is formal and has clear connotations of being used in an institutional setting. It refers to the termination of life. As such, the note positions the writer's death as a biological fact and thereby removes it from the social context of suicide.

That said, this does not mean, of course, that the authors of the letters written from the future perspective are exempt from the social dimensions of death. In fact, such letters suggest the opposite. Letters written from the future perspective could be seen as engaging with death as a social phenomenon as much as others. By constructing themselves as dead, the authors could be seen as coping with what they are about to do. By discursively removing themselves from the world, they implicitly acknowledge the significance of what they are doing.

There are two aspects of the extracts then. On the one hand, they present the end of the process from the future perspective, a perspective when the note writer is no longer; on the other hand, they euphemize suicide. We would like to argue that the two strategies complement each other. And so, as euphemizing suicide serves to soften it and its stigma, it could be argued that the future perspective is an attempt to remove the suicide from the person who kills themselves. In other words, by shifting the perspective of viewing the end of the process into the future, note writers are able to remove the violence of the act from themselves. At the same time, they are also constructed to stand with the addressees and empathize with them in their time of grief, much like in the following extract where the author constructs himself as sympathizing with the person finding out about his death:

Extract 37

I feel like crying when I see your face and reaction.

In this section, we were interested in exploring constructions of the end of the suicidal process. Interestingly, such constructions are typically written from the future perspective. In other words, the notes' authors write about the end of the suicidal process as if it has already happened. We argue that, for the writers, such a perspective serves to remove the end of killing oneself from the reality of doing so.

Conclusions

In this chapter, we have continued the discussion of representations of time before suicidal death. We have discussed how the time of suicide is constructed as full of activity. In farewell letters, suicidal death does not happen in a vacuum; it is, in fact, constructed as preceded by much activity. Thus, we have discussed accounts of the three stages of suicide: constructions of the beginning of the process, of what happens during the time of 'committing suicide' and of the end of the process.

And so, we have suggested that the notes marked the beginning of the suicide process by referring to the decision to engage with it or the intent to do so. But what is particularly interesting in such texts is that they seem to run against the foundation of communication. In other words, such notes contain information which is, from the point of view of the addressee, irrelevant, too late. This, in turn, raises the issue of the communicative function of suicide notes.

In suicidological research, farewell letters are rarely problematized. Little has changed since the initial study of suicide notes in the late 1950s. Shneidman and Farberow (1957) did not consider what they might be and, more importantly, what they might say. As Galasiński (2017) points out, the simplicity of the assumptions that suicide notes only offer insight into the suicidal mind means that they have been seen largely as communicatively transparent. Indeed, apart from his recent study there is practically no other research looking at suicide notes as acts of communication. He continues his argument that there is no reason to assume that suicide notes are honest and sincere. Just as in any act of communication, writers of suicide notes can be strategic, manipulative or, indeed, deceptive. A suicide note might be the last opportunity to settle a score, take revenge or get one's own back. In other words, just because a person is about to take their life, does not mean ulterior motives disappear.

Galasiński's second point is that he takes issue with the assumption that suicide notes are 'ultrapersonal' (e.g. Leenaars, 2004). Suicide notes (can) have addressees – they are written to be read. The problem with this assumption is that as acts of communication they are not and cannot be seen as personal, let alone ultrapersonal (regardless of what that might mean). First, this is because suicide notes have addressees. They are written to be read, often with an explicit addressee. It is highly unlikely that the suicide note is written for the sake of it, never to be found and, if found, never to be read. Moreover, they are also more than likely to be read in institutional contexts, by people they are not addressed to. Some notes are addressed to the police and/or the prosecutor's office, while other statements of intent can be seen as indemnities protecting the family members of the person who killed themselves.

These two points help us understand what happens in the notes which offer seemingly irrelevant information about the intent or the point at which the person is starting to 'do suicide'. Such notes could be seen precisely as a semi-public record of important moments in the life of the person writing the note and those who read it.

Rather than suggesting that the notes are a window to the mind, they perhaps should be seen as records. In today's world, we would see them as private blogs, or perhaps protected tweets, with only some people allowed to read them. As such, the letter-records are likely to have a multitude of functions, some of them rendered by their linguistic form and some of them perhaps never to be understood or interpreted in an academic analysis. In other words, while the declarative sentences are likely to be intended as statements conveying some information, they are also likely to convey an emotional load which will be understood by those with access to particular contexts. Suicide notes should never be seen as transparent texts with no communicative functions. In fact, they should be seen as the exact opposite of that. They should be seen as a site of complex, multipurpose acts of communication whose reception will depend on the level of access to the context shared with their author.

Our discussion of the period of 'doing suicide' has shown that there is a significant amount of activity in that stretch of time. Perhaps the most surprising notes were those of the writers constructed as waiting for death. We see, in particular, those notes as problematizing suicide. The question of what happens between, say, taking medicines and death is not only important from the point of view of understanding the experience of suicide but also crucial from the point of view of what suicide is. In other words, has the person who took a lethal dose of medicines already committed suicide?

Such a question is likely to be answered in the negative, but then the question of the interpretive framework of such a person remains unanswered. How do we describe the person after the act which will result, but has not yet done so, in their death? Such considerations, in our view, are particularly important for extending the notion of suicide from death into a longer series of actions.

And so, for us the question we have just posed should be answered with a statement that the person is 'doing suicide', and their death will be the end of that doing. Incidentally, we offer this answer with the understanding that it blurs one of the crucial distinctions between the so-called attempters and completers.[2] We realize that such a position puts a question mark over whether suicide (as opposed to a suicide attempt) can be defined solely by its effect, that is to say, by the death of the person engaged in it.

There is, however, one further issue resulting from our considerations. It is the timescale over which suicide can happen. As we have pointed out during the discussion in this chapter, at least two suicide notes suggested that such a timescale could run into days. Indeed, the longest suicide note in our possession is around ten pages with explicit references suggesting that it was written over the course of more than a week. The questions of whether suicide had started are pertinent but very difficult to answer. We would suggest, however, that, if it is the intent to kill oneself that is a crucial defining aspect of suicide, the notion that suicide could last more than a few hours, or perhaps even more than a day, should not be rejected off hand. Rather, such possibilities should be explored, particularly from the point of view of suicide prevention. Can the person who is 'doing suicide' for an extended period of time be stopped? How can interventions respond to such eventualities?

However, what is crucial in the above points is not so much whether we are right to suggest that suicide can be significantly long but rather that suicide should be seen as much more complex than has been assumed hitherto. And perhaps there is need for a discussion on the fuzziness of the concept, while the only relatively clear concept is that of suicidal death.

Instead of the discussion on the absence of records of the end of the suicidal process, we would like to offer one last extract which refers not so much to the end of the process but to the process beyond the biological death. Consider the following extract referring to the preparations for the author's funeral and, in particular, the headstone on the person's grave:

Extract 38

> For me, in large lettering the inscription: Life is beautiful – death is a cold kiss. Lettering and the cross painted in silver. Give only the record and my little book,

the rest leave as has been. This will be done by a stone mason's shop. Make sure you tell them before the funeral, so they will give it away.

We see this letter as constructing the suicide process as going well beyond the suicidal death. In fact, it seems that the suicidal act is part of a plan extending well into the romanticized end in the form of the funeral. The detailed plans for the headstone and the author's book, presumably to be given away at the funeral (it is unclear), seem like setting up an event in which the writer of the note will (finally?) take centre stage. Suicide is a means of making sure that the end of the author's life is beautiful and poetic. The funeral seems to be the crowning moment of the person's life.

Extract 38 is not the only note of the sort. We encountered a small group of letters in which the writers more or less explicitly expressed the wish to plan and, crucially, see their funeral. Suicide, it seems, was not the end of the process they engaged in. Suicide was a means to a further social end, the nature of which cannot be certain.

Crucially, however, such letters make suicide even more complex. They show it not as an end but as a stage in the person's plan, shall we even say, the person's life. If we are right in our interpretations here, this raises further and significant issues for suicide prevention activities.

In Chapter 5, we are interested in how the informants who had attempted to take their lives talked about the act of killing themselves. We discuss two kinds of constructions. First, we discuss stories in which the informants spoke about the instructions they gave themselves; these were stories of making sure that they do things effectively. Second, we explore stories in which the informants talked about the act itself. Suicidology sees suicidal death in terms of a particular cognitive state, what we would like to show is that stories of suicide attempt to construct it as a process.

Appendix

Extract 1

Idę powinno się udać

Extract 2

Idę po smycz i żegnajcie.

Extract 3

Nie chce mi się żyć Wzięłam tabletki.

Extract 4

Z zamiarem popełnienia samobójstwa noszę się od jakiegoś czasu po 16 marca gdy [first name] złapałem z jej kochankiem.

Extract 5

Mamy dzisiaj [date] godz.13.40 postanowiłem odebrać sobie życie z tego powodu ponieważ moja żona [first name] wzięła ze mną ślub mieliśmy dziecko [first name] a ona nigdy mnie nie kochała ukrywała wszystko przede mną przede mną.

Extract 6

LIST PISAŁEM JUŻ JAKIŚ CZAS TEMU ALE W KOŃCU SIĘ NIE ZDECYDOWAŁEM NA TAKI KROK. DO DNIA [date] nic nie uległo zmianie dalej mnie oszukuje i jest niedobra dla mnie. Śmierć moja nastąpiła o godz. 1300 około

Extract 7

Wybaczcie mi kochane dziewczyny mój haniebny postępek ale nie mogę inaczej nie mogę nie dłużej zwlekać bo w końcu nie miałbym siły wykonać co zamierzam.

Extract 8

Mam nadzieję że ja skutecznie odbiorę sobie życie.

Extract 9

Mam przeczucie, że jestem KURWA zbyt mądra, żeby zakończyć moje marne życie.
Spróbuję chyba

Extract 10

Przemyślałem swoje życie i wiem że nie dla nie ma wyjścia muszę odejść z tego świata bo już nie mam dla kogo żyć. Przepraszam za wszystko co zrobiłem źle oraz dobrze. Dzisiaj w nocy mój żywot dobiegnie końca nie umiem bez Ciebie żyć!

Extract 11

Wszyscy pewnie myślą, że się powiesiłem dlatego, że byłem pijany. Otóż nic bardziej mylnego. Strzeliłem sobie flaszeczkę na odwagę, bo na trzeźwo bym chyba tego nie zrobił.

Extract 12

Wybaczcie musiałem wypić dla odwagi bo ze mnie jest tchórz.

Extract 13

Ten niebieski ręcznik to jest [first name] i gąbka mała też. Jestem wykąpany. pochowajcie mnie w [town].

Extract 14

Będę kończył bo mi nerwy nie dadzą pisać. Wkładam ci moją obrączkę to daj ją przyjacielowi, ale najlepiej zrób sobie pierścionek.

Extract 15

Włożyłem do koperty mamy moją obrączkę to poproś ją żeby zawiozła do złotnika i przerobiła tobie na pierścionek. nie wiem czy da ci przeczytać jej list ale jak oglądasz [television series] to na początku jest takie coś. Chciałbym się pożalić, ale nie mam do kogo.

Extract 16

Dzisiaj jest wtorek [date] a ja wykonuję to jutro czyli [date] ponieważ mam jeszcze załatwić jedną sprawę.

Extract 17

Udało w końcu zawiesić mi się smycz jeszcze przejdę popojutrze i idę na śmierć.

Extract 18

Nie poszłam więc dzisiaj do szkoły. Postanowiłam popełnić samobójstwo. Próbowałam podciąć sobie żyły ale nie bardzo mi to wyszło. Przedawkowałam jakiś lek chyba [medication] i czekam na to co będzie. Zrobiłam to ponieważ nie chcę nigdy więcej iść do szkoły. W przeciwnym razie musiałabym iść jutro a tego bym nie zniosła.

Extract 19

Ciągle coś dopisuję bo chcę Was przekonać że życie i zdrowie to jest piękne dopóki się je ma.

Extract 20

Jest godzina 17.26. z chwili na chwilę widzę że moje życie nie ma sensu, rozmawiałem przed chwilą z [first name] i przygnębiła mnie jeszcze bardziej nic nie powiedziała ale chodzi o ton jej głosu był taki nieszczęśliwy, jakby chciała powiedzieć jaka ja jestem nieszczęśliwa z tobą.

Extract 21

Dobra. Kochana Siostro koniec użalania się nad sobą i przepraszam że najwięcej zwracam się do Ciebie ale musiałem z kimś porozmawiać.

Extract 22

Płaczę jak dziecko gdy to piszę przeproś wszystkich [names], niech źle o mnie nie myślą.

Extract 23

Piszę ten list bo serce podpowiada mi, że tak powinieniem postanowić. Pisząc to, łza sama cieknie mi z oczu.

Extract 24

Pisząc ten list miałem łzy w oczach ale wiedziałem że tak będzie najlepiej.

Extract 25

Piszę ten list po ostatnich przemyśleniach i doszedłem do wniosku że tak będzie najlepiej dla nas wszystkich

Extract 26

Piszę ten list z myślą że bardzo cię kocham, tylko jak go będziesz czytać pewnie mnie już nie będzie na tym świecie.

Extract 27

Więcej pisał nie będę, bo jakoś weny nie mam i oczy mi się trochę załzawiły, gdy pomyślę, że Ciebie stracę.

Extract 28

Ciężko mi pisać bo w obecnej chwili bardzo się boję, przeżywam burzę mózgu. Przesyłam Ci wraz z listem zdjęcie [place], jak się domyślasz, tam się wybieram.

Extract 29

Nie wiem co mam Wam więcej napisać bo trudno jest zostawić ludzi których się kocha i serce mi w tym momencie pęka patrzę na zdjęcie małego i ślina staje mi w gardle łzy leją się z oczu ale wiem że tak musi być i muszę to zrobić żebyście Wy wszyscy mieli lepiej.

Extract 30

Drodzy kochani to już wszystko co chciałem napisać. Nie zapomnijcie mnie, pamiętajcie o mnie, pochowajcie

Extract 31

Skończyłem pisać: środa godzina 1

Extract 32

Ciągle jeszcze łudzę się, że wydarzy się coś co mnie zatrzyma. Została jeszcze iskierka nadziei, co prawda ulotna, ale jednak. Ktoś może zapyta dlaczego właśnie tu, w tym miejscu. Powód jest prosty – nie chcę, aby mi ktoś przeszkodził, a tu raczej na pewno tak się nie stanie.

Extract 33

Jeżeli to czytasz to już mnie nie ma wiedz że to nie przez Ciebie się zabiłem to

Extract 34

[first_name] jeśli to czytasz to znaczy że mnie przy Tobie nie ma. To co tu napisałem zostało skropione łzami mej rozpaczy

Extract 35

DLA [first name]
[first name] PRZEPRASZAM CIĘ ZA WSZYSTKO. KOCHAM SIĘ PONAD ŻYCIE ALE BEZ CIEBIE NIE POTRAFIŁEM ŻYĆ. **KOCHAM CIĘ CHOĆ JUŻ MNIE NIE MA.**

Extract 36

Chciałbym Cię jeszcze raz przeprosić za termin mojego zgonu. Tydzień przed maturą to niezbyt odpowiedni moment, ale ja już dłużej nie mogłem

Extract 37

Płakać mi się chce jak zobaczę Twoją minę i reakcję ...

Extract 39

Dla mnie w powiększeniu koniecznie napis. ŻYCIE JEST PIĘKNE – ŚMIERĆ ZIMNYM POCAŁUNKIEM. Litery i krzyż pomalowane srebrzanką. Dać tylko płytę i moją książeczkę – resztę zostawić jak było. To wykona zakład kamieniarski pod cmentarzem firma. Zgłosić przed pogrzebem aby to rozdali.

5

Killing oneself

In Chapter 4, we discussed the construction of the suicide process in suicide letters. We argued that authors of the letters represented it as a complex set of activities which more or less directly were constructed to lead to the person's death. The notes constructed the beginning of the process, the time represented as committing suicide. Interestingly, however, there were no constructions of the end of the process. What we did find were references to the note authors' death.

In this chapter, we go back to discussing the interviews. We are interested in how the informants who had attempted to take their lives talked about the act of killing themselves. We realize, of course, that they were not successful in killing themselves, but we assume that their stories are about how they went about killing themselves in earnest; the effectiveness of their actions, as we also argued in Chapter 4, is secondary in our view.

And so, in this chapter we discuss two kinds of constructions. First, we discuss stories in which the informants spoke about the instructions they gave themselves; these were stories about making sure that they do things effectively. Second, we explore stories in which the informants talked about the act itself. Suicidology sees suicidal death in terms of a particular cognitive state, most frequently pointing to psychache, ambivalence, lowered mood or anxiety. What we would like to show is that stories of suicide attempts construct them as a time-extended process, a set of actions which need to be performed.

The act

Before we explore the data, we would like to briefly discuss how the act of suicide and suicidal death are seen in the literature. The best-known explanation for suicide is that offered by Shneidman (1985, 1993; see also Joiner, 2005) who focuses on pain and suggests an instrumental character of suicide. He says that:

I.	The common purpose of suicide is to seek a solution.
II.	The common goal of suicide is cessation of consciousness.
III.	The common stimulus in suicide is intolerable psychological pain.
IV.	The common stressor in suicide is frustrated psychological needs.
V.	The common emotion in suicide is hopelessness-helplessness.
VI.	The common cognitive state in suicide is ambivalence.
VII.	The common perceptual state in suicide is constriction.
VIII.	The common action in suicide is egression.
IX.	The common interpersonal act in suicide is communication of intention.
X.	The common consistency in suicide is with lifelong coping patterns.

In Shneidman's model, someone who is about to kill themselves is constructed as barely in touch with reality; they are almost entirely focused on their emotions and the ways to escape them (Shneidman, 1993). They are in the thrall of the psychache, an overwhelming pain that torments the person who is about to kill themselves and which includes shame, guilt, anxiety, fear and uncertainty, amongst others. Shneidman (1985) argues that, even though suicidologists point to external causes of suicide, such as illness, loss, breakup or bereavement, it is always the intolerable pain which is behind every suicide.

Shneidman made a connection between psychache and the cognitive deficits that result from it. He paid particular attention to cognitive constriction which consists of the individual's difficulty in perceiving solutions to their crisis and focusing on suicide. Shneidman comments on the word 'only' which comes with the danger that only suicide is an available option. This was reinforced by Ringel (1987) who argued that all suicidal acts were performed in a similar psychological state, which he calls presuicidal syndrome, with the multidimensional constriction and increased aggression towards the self as well as suicidal fantasies.

Contemporary models of suicidal behaviours reinforce the importance of emotional and cognitive factors. Rudd, Joiner and Rajab (2004) speak of the suicidal mode, which they describe as a network of cognitive, emotional, physiological and behavioural factors. After a particular trigger, they reinforce each other leading to suicide. The end stage of the suicidal mode is the suicidal act (see also Rudd, 2000).

This conceptualization of suicide has been transferred to research into suicide notes. Shneidman (1993, 1996) proposes that suicide notes are 'barren' because they reflect the mind of the person about to kill themselves. Shneidman proposes that such a person is in a 'special state of mind', characterized by close-mindedness and a fixation on the purpose. Antoon Leenaars sees suicide notes as invaluable in understanding the suicidal mind and the 'special' characteristic of people who take their lives (Leenaars, 2002a). And so, Leenaars (1988; see also 1986, 1992; Leenaars et al., 2001; Leenaars & Balance, 1984) analyses suicide notes looking for:

1. Unbearable psychological pain
2. Interpersonal relations
3. Rejection – aggression
4. Inability to adjust
5. Indirect expressions
6. Identification – eggression
7. Ego
8. Cognitive constriction

Not only are suicide notes seen as leading to the uncovering of 'the suicidal mind' but, more importantly for us here, they suggest again that the suicidal mind is overwhelmed with negative emotions underpinning cognitive deficits of the person about to kill themselves. Moreover, Leenaars, in his *Suicide Notes* (1988), proposes that authors of suicide notes communicate flight from such things as pain, threat of helplessness and anticipated rejection, amongst others. He adds that emotions such as pitiful forlornness or deprivation are evident, together with contradictory feelings.

In our discussion, we follow Ziółkowska (2016) who challenges the assumptions behind such ideas. After making the assumption that narratives of the last moments before the suicidal act would be focused on what informants thought or felt, she found that this was not the case. In contrast, the informants focused more on what they did rather than on what they felt. We continue this analysis, focusing on the construction of the suicidal act as a process, consisting of a set of actions.

Making sure

One of the most striking kinds of stories our informants offered were accounts of the ways in which they tried to make sure that their suicide attempt would be successful. These were stories of what instructions they gave themselves, what they were thinking or telling themselves. What is particularly interesting in these narratives is that they offer lucid and detailed accounts of what was happening or about to happen.

There are two aspects to these stories. First, there are stories in which the informants speak of a sort of mental dry run. The informants speak of thinking about what they needed to do to make the attempt successful. Second, there are stories in which the informants recount the instructions they gave themselves during the act. We discuss them in turn.

Consider first the following two extracts:

Extract 1

> P: And just the thought, all in all whether you make a mistake doing it. So, you do not forget something important, not overlook something. So, observe closely what you do. Get dressed. See whether you are completely dressed. Whether you do not miss anything. Get ready for it. So, put this belt on with linen bags loaded with bricks, [make sure] it does not snap.

Extract 2

> P: As I say, first of all I was thinking about not missing something important. So, like step by step observe what I was doing at a given day, as I would be leaving. So, whether I will take, and not miss something important, because I know that the only thing I need to take from home and what I cannot do is to leave the flat door unlocked.

In extract 1, the informant dramatizes her account by accessing her voice (on accessed voices, see Hartley, 1988). She invokes it in order to offer a version of what had happened in which she puts herself in a position of a witness, thus making the accounts more authentic (Hutchby, 2001). Significantly, the narrated dialogue is directive. The informant uses the imperative mood, without mitigation, when she speaks to herself; these are instructions which must be followed. Interestingly, she also uses the '*żebyś* + conditional mood',[1] which is often used on its own (i.e. without the conditional antecedent) as a strong imperative form. The difference between the simple imperative mood and the '*żebyś* + conditional mood' is such that the latter implies negative consequences if the person addressed does not comply with the instruction. Our joint linguistic competence suggests that the phrase can only be used in situations with significant asymmetry of power and, in particular, when an adult addresses a child.

Also, the instructions construct suicide as a set of activities, starting from getting dressed and choosing a particular belt. We see someone who does not just 'commit suicide'. The informant is fully aware of the complexity of the tasks ahead and mentally prepares herself for them. In other words, preparations for suicide consist of a set of mental (or verbal) instructions of what to do. This is because suicide is not merely an event. It is a complex process.

Extract 2 is also an account of 'mental' preparations. This time, however, the informant switches the perspectives, starting the story from the time perspective of the interview and then switching to the perspective of the time before her suicide attempt. Here, however, the informant is also recounting her suicide journey, which she repeated for herself.

Extract 3 takes the story even further, though:

Extract 3

I: I shall ask the most difficult of the questions. Could you tell me what the day and moments before the attempt to commit suicide looked like?

P: I was just trying to more or less say things like that I will first drink three beers, then I will be sitting and do something, listen to music, for example. It was the last day as it happened, but the day before I was saying like that, like meeting people. But above all going out somewhere. Despite that I had a normal social life, but as it happened I had less time for those people, so I decided that I would spend those days, devote the time to them and they will to me. And this is what it looked like later that the place was planned, I was looking around whether there was concrete down there, so there was no sand. It is strange when I think about it now, some mania.

Here, too, the informant accesses her voice of the time of the attempt, but what is particularly interesting is that the story begins with three beers, listening to music and meeting people. No doubt it is unclear whether the informant's story is one of her, to use the term again, suicide journey; still, her narrative is part of her response to questions about the time before attempting to kill herself. As the story moves forward, it goes on to an account of confirming the place of the attempt.

In all three accounts, we witness stories of mental preparations for a suicide attempt. The preparations are rendered as self-instructions of what to do, of what steps to take before the act. Most importantly for the argument we present here, in the stories we quote above and others not quoted here, the informants construct themselves as fully aware of the process they engage in.

We accept, of course, that it is unclear whether the stories are indeed stories of a suicide attempt or perhaps of preparations for the act, as a separate process. We also understand that the stories we heard were told from the perspective of the present. We do not get insight into 'what really happened', but only a story told in another context and for another purpose. It is important to note that there are no other data which could be drawn on to gain an account of what happened around the time of suicide. As we offer a polemic with the common assumptions of suicidology, it is important to understand that the data we have are the only data possible.

And so, we would argue that the ambivalence of such stories might suggest that the distinction between different processes (such as preparations and the suicidal act) might be something that is imposed on the stories externally, either by the conceptual framework or by the interpretations of the researchers. And distinctions might not be important to the informants whose stories are processed in research. Thus, our argument, similarly to the one in Chapter 4, is that the narrative evidence suggests fluidity in the suicide process. People who take their lives tend not to offer stories of when their suicide began, and, if they do, we have no access to them. What they do construct, however, is that suicide, which is a complex process, involves planning, mental rehearsals and sometimes significant logistics.

Before we move on to discuss narratives of the act itself, we would like to discuss two more extracts in which the informants who offered stories go back to considering the method of killing themselves. Such stories are similar to those we quoted above. Consider first:

Extract 4

> P: I was analysing a lot, it may sound strange, but I was analysing ways to end life and what I was also taking into consideration was also poisoning myself or drowning. But I chose the third method. I wanted to do it at home, at my place. To say goodbye to the world. I was thinking that this would be the simplest was. That there would be the least trouble. Later I thought that if I had drowned for example, my family would not have known where I was, that I was lost or went away. They would have picked me up from the water 10 days later, all swollen up from the water, from all those gases which gather in the person, after death. I preferred that my body should be found quickly. So that it would not be like, so I would not be bad looking, so to say. So, in the coffin I would look somehow. Because it is what I planned that in the farewell letter that I wanted to be put to rest in a coffin. On a catafalque. [This method] looked the most human to me. Well, if I had had a weapon, I would have considered it as well, but in Poland it is rather impossible.

The account begins with the story of choosing the means, only to reach the solution. The informant settles on a 'humane' way of killing himself. What is significant from our point of view is that the process of suicide seems to continue beyond the death of the informant. From the account of saying goodbye to the world, through the body being found, all the way to what he would look like in the coffin, the informant's story smoothly moves between the time before and the time after his (planned) death.

Interestingly, the entire story is told with the use of mental processes (Halliday, 1994), that is, the informant used those linguistic tools (predominantly verbs) that refer to feeling, thinking or seeing, namely the emotional and cognitive activities of a person. Indeed, the informant constructs himself through processes such as analysing, considering, thinking, preferring, wanting and so forth. The choice of methods as well as the time after death is all thought about. This time, however, as we noted, it is extended from considering the method, through choosing it, all the way to what the funeral would look like.

It is worth noting, however, that the informant does not use directive forms. Rather, his story is more one of playing things out in his mind. Indeed, he implies the potential of some graphic scenery if he were to be found floating in the river. We think it is through such imagery that the informant is telling us a story of his making sure of what would and would not happen. It is similar to the story in the next extract, where the informant is speaking about playing out the scenario of his suicide. Consider:

Extract 5

> P: It had been on my mind for some time. Somehow something interrupted me. Once, on Sunday, at home, I was lying sober at home and I am thinking what are the solutions. There is this solution, this solution. Throw myself under a train, right? So, this is what I dreaming about at night. Nights are the worst. And I was thinking like that, but at the time, on Sunday morning, I was ready. […] I still thought so many people in the world hanged themselves and managed, and in war people died and still die and I said one man does not matter, it will pass. They will talk a little and that will be it, they will talk elsewhere and that will be, the world will forget. I was not successful. Maybe, maybe it is better that I did not succeed. I do not know.

The informant is again talking about the aftermath of his suicide. Even though he is likely to talk about himself, he shifts the story to a general level. He becomes an insignificant part of what always happens. Such a recasting of the story into generalities is probably aimed at softening the reference to himself. What always happens will also happen to him and he will be forgotten. The second point is that we see the narrative of the aftermath as a way of constructing the suicide process as continuing after the person's death. It seems it is only forgetting that puts an end to it.

In this section, we have discussed stories of preparing oneself for suicide. These are stories of self-directions and playing out scenarios in one's mind. What is crucial for our argument here, however, is that none of these stories positioned suicide as a homogeneous event. Rather, just as in suicide notes, the informants constructed suicide in terms of a process, the process as it was imagined before the act. In the next section, we consider stories in which the informants spoke about the suicidal act.

The act

The stories we look at in this section are about the act of taking one's own life. Here, too, suicide becomes a process, sometimes very technical and physically difficult. Consider first the following extracts:

Extract 6

> P: I did not feel pain at all. I was doing it with glass. Broken. So, these were not, shall I say, sterile conditions or something. To be honest the only thing I was thinking was that I could have prepared better for this. I mean take a knife or scalpel. So, I could do it more effectively, because I was gouging for quite long. But I did not feel any pain. That is what it was, I do not know, perhaps adrenaline did its thing. And as it took long, blood was gushing out of me. I was no sorry then. At that very moment. Later I fainted, I was unconscious for a good few hours. I woke up in the middle of the night.

Extract 7

> P: So, I was squeezing [blood] out and I was drinking and swallowing. I say to myself, how much will I swallow, I think about 26, I can't remember. 26 pills I swallowed I think. I do not know if it is little or a lot.

Extract 8

> P: Right, when the water was hot, well, kind of warm. I started feeling cold. So, I am thinking, right, I already have little blood and it does not warm the body up. So, I turned the tap with warm water with my foot, because the shower was on all the time. And I drained three bathtubs of water. No, two bathtubs of water. When the blood, when it was red.

Before we consider the linguistic working of the extracts, let us point out the physicality of suicide constructed by the extracts. References to gouging, squeezing, turning, drinking and swallowing all construct suicide in terms of material processes, representing the person behind them as an agent. We see suicide as something that is done, physically. But what is more important here is that suicide also takes time.

In extract 6, the use of iterative forms *robiłam* ('I was doing'), *dłubałam* ('I was gouging') and *wylewała* ('[it] was pouring out'), as well as adverbials of time such as *dosyć długo* ('quite long') and *parę ładnych godzin* ('a few good hours'), all construct the informant's suicide as taking a significant amount of time. Importantly, the informant does not refer to preparations or other activities; rather, she talks about the time in which she engages in taking her own life. Extract 7 is very similar – the informant uses iterative forms of verbs, explicitly constructing killing himself as taking time.

Extract 8 is different, though. Here, the informant is talking about the situation in which his suicidal act is taking place. We do not so much hear about how he is killing himself as about how he is getting cold. The informant's narrative constructs a set of activities which happen alongside his attempt to take his life. We could even say that the story is quite absurd in the sense that a person taking their own life is worried about getting cold. This narrative and others like it, we would argue, show how problematic pronouncements about a 'tunnel vision', which allows the person about to kill themselves to focus entirely on the task, are (Shneidman, 1996). In fact, such a person can still care about being cold and take action to remedy this.

The three extracts, and others like them, underpin the main argument we make in this book. Suicide and the suicidal act are not events without structure. They are not about 'simply' killing oneself, as a single and single-minded act. The question we posed at the beginning of this book, What happens ten minutes before the suicidal act and death itself?, is beginning to find an answer. The person is likely to be busy doing all sorts of things, from preparing themselves to actually being in the process of killing themselves.

However, the stories presented here have another dimension. Suicide is not only a process that involves a number of complex actions which lead to the eventual death of the person engaging in them. The stories also show that the very act of killing oneself is not just a dot on the timescale. It is as poignant as it is frightening to think of the process of cutting your veins, making sure that the blood flows, that it does not clot. The above stories show suicide not only as a process that takes time; they also show suicide as an embodied and physical action. At least some suicides mean that you have breached the barrier of your body.

Incidentally, what struck us about these stories was that what is seemingly a very violent event of cutting, gouging and ripping into the body is rendered as anything but. The violence of the physical act of taking one's life has all but disappeared from the stories of suicide. The physical actions are rendered as a means to an end. In other words, we see stories of actions taken with the goal of killing oneself and perhaps because of this they are devoid of the violence they are likely to be perceived with. This action-oriented representation of suicide can perhaps best be seen in the following extracts:

Extract 9

> P: So, no one could tell, so no one could see, because if I had put a white [garment] I would have been noticeable more. So, I did take it into account. So, it would be a green-brown coat, and, indeed, I did find a coat like that. Old trousers, old shoes, worst. I found some bag which I had never used. I packed all that was completely necessary for me, a jar, and I had prepared tablets for the jar which I had taken out of the wrapping. There was a lot of it, it was a three-month supply of four kinds of medication. There was a lot of it. I went to a liquor shop. I bought alcohol, cognac. All that I packed into the bag. Also matches because I was afraid that during the night when I would sit by the [river] rats could appear, so I wanted to scare them off with fire. I thought about that. I took a little glass from the bar, some tissues and an additional carrier bag in case one of the linen ones would snap. I was prepared in such a way that that I strapped a strong leather belt around the waist with a very strong buckle and a very strong belt. And I attached three linen sacks to it, I tied them off and put a brick into each of them. I prepared it at home and checked if they would not break off, if it would stand the force, if I would feel the it when I wore it. If it really would be the weight for me to drown, so that I would not float up to the surface. I thought that I had planned everything well. The linen sacks worked very well. There were no problems with the bricks, because nearby they were laying pavement down. So, I just had to go downstairs and take some home. And prepared like that, the belt, with the linen sacks and bricks, I put into one big bag. I got on the bus and went to the [river], not far from the [bridge]. I decided to do it over there. I did not leave any at home. I locked home. The night was cold, it turned out. It was very cold. And I simply immediately as it got darker, I remember, it was already quite dark, I was beginning to take the medications. I remember the moment, I do not know, it must have been around midnight, that in the block of flats opposite me, lights were beginning to go off. So, people were going to bed. It may have been eleven, twelve at the latest. So, I had this loss of time. And at that moment simply I should do what I should. The next step. Instead I simply lost consciousness at that moment and fell down with my arm somehow twisted under my chest. This is how I was lying for 24 hours. Some anglers found me. Earlier, as I say, someone had robbed me of that poor bag. And the little glass. There was no alcohol, I had drunk all the alcohol. And so, an ambulance came, police. I was a person looked for by the family.

Extract 10

> P: I put the beer away. And the second round. And you know, I put it around my neck, because, I am thinking, it will hurt me, right? And I am a coward because I think it will hurt me, so I took a shirt. It will not cut into the skin so much with the shirt on. I put a crate down, I took a second rope so that I could jerk it, so I would lose the grip. And so, I did it like that and the plasterboard broke and fell down. And I fell off. And nothing of it [...] I did not manage. At that time, I completely broke down. I am thinking I am such a piece of shit[2], such a piece of shit that I cannot even hang myself. I am thinking, I am sitting, sitting, sitting, sitting, thinking. I drank a beer and I am thinking, right? Shit, such thoughts overcame me. I am thinking – am I going to hang myself? Man, fuck, go sober up, get up normally and go home. What if someone beats you up? Your wife will kill you, so you will die anyway. Get up and go home. But I have drunk the beer and still cannot. If I go home, what will I say, what will I say? What will I say at home, what will I tell my children, I have a grandson.

Extract 9 is an extraordinary account of the last moments before the suicidal act. The informant focuses entirely on her actions: 'I went', 'I bought', 'I prepared', 'I packed', 'I took'. The speaker consistently positions herself as the actor of the series of actions she talks about. The narrative allows us to follow the informant in the process of both preparing to kill herself and doing so. The focus on actions makes the narrative very technical. There is no psychache in it, there are no emotions, there are no dilemmas, only a detailed account of what the informant did. The narrative contains mainly material processes (Halliday & Hasan, 1985), underscoring the action-orientedness of the account. It is a narrative about doing and impacting reality (Halliday, 1978).

It is perhaps worth noting that the informant uses the phrase *zażywać leki* ('take medicine'), a phrase which has strong medical connotations. In other words, what was an attempt to poison herself is recast as using medication for medicinal purposes. Such a phrase, it seems, underscores the dispassionate account, introducing a rational action.

This long story also takes us on a journey through the process and the suicidal act. The story begins at home. But, as we said in Chapter 3, the process does not end with losing consciousness. It goes on. Just as in the previous extracts, the narrative offers a post hoc account of the entire journey of suicide, but what is particularly interesting in this story is that the narrative does not end with the availability of the informant's experience. In other words, the informant tells a story which she is likely to have heard from others. Still, the story, it seems, must continue to its end, which happens after the suicidal act.

Extract 10 is similar in its focus on material processes. Here, too, the informant refers to himself in terms of putting a noose around his neck, cutting, sitting, tugging and other actions. What is interesting, however, is that the informant weaves in a second account which represents his reflection on what he was doing. He is also telling a story about what he was thinking about when he was going through these actions. It is the story of an online assessment of himself and his attempts to kill himself.

We hear a story of a person who is trying to extinguish his life yet cannot do it. And so, he sits and thinks about what to do. In fact, he constructs himself in terms of rational consideration – he thinks and thinks some more. Even though he talks about breaking down, which we interpret as a common way of referring to disappointment rather than referring to an actual and strong emotional state, it is followed by the picture of a thinking figure. The final argument he has with himself is a story of scenarios that cannot happen.

The final point we would like to make here is that the narrative is also one of failure. The informant tells a story of his clumsiness, ineffectiveness and coping with it. The failure ends with his 'And nothing of it', yet another disappointment with himself. But, as much as the story is about failed attempts to kill himself, it is also a story of the logistics of his suicide attempt. This is a story of a process which goes to and fro, as the informant tries to kill himself, fails, thinks, drinks and thinks some more. Moreover, extract 10 starts with the explicit reference to the second round of the attempt (the initial attempt had been interrupted by a friend). In fact, one could easily argue that the story is of two attempts which get combined into one, due to one hospitalization. We will come back to this point in the 'Conclusions' section of the chapter.

Incidentally, at the end of both extracts the agency of the informants dissipates and they became objects of others' actions. This is particularly prominent in extract 9, where in the last part of the account it shifts onto others: anglers, robbers, family. The informant no longer does things; she only recounts what others did to her. Also in extract 10 the story of the end of the suicide attempt is the moment when the account moves to talk about others, about the informant's wife. Not only can they do things but also they become a circumstance – he will need to account for what he did.

We think of this shift in agency as supporting the argument of the focus on action. Suicide seems to be a task to do rather than something to be emotional about. And so, when it (or the attempt, to be exact) ends, the informant's agency also ends. It is others that take over the scene or the consideration, as in extract 10.

Stories of reflection about what the person is doing in their attempt to kill themselves, as in extract 10, can also be found in other accounts. Here are two other extracts in which the informants offer a story of their reflection on what they were doing.

Extract 11

> P: And in this case, as I say, this is what it was like. Do not look at this, because I poured it out, something like from this side, like do not look at this. This will be the moment and indeed I chucked it all in.

Extract 12

> P: I spent the night on the square, wandering a little, wandering around in [city] and I got the [name] bridge. And I said: so, now it is time. I took the backpack, put loaded it with stones, climbed the span and hop.

The two extracts contain different narratives of self-reflection. In extract 11, which is as unclear in Polish as it is in the translation, the informant is speaking of warning herself about looking at what she was doing. In extract 12, on the other hand, the informant is telling a story of considering the time of performing the act. It is also done in the form of a directive act, though here it is the linguistically ambivalent 'it is time'.

Extract 12 is particularly interesting for considering the boundaries of suicide. Note that the suicidal act is reduced to the onomatopoeic *hop*,[3] the only narrative we found that represents suicide literally as a point in time.

Conclusions

This chapter is about stories of the act of killing oneself. First, we discussed stories in which the informants spoke about the instructions they gave themselves; these were stories about making sure that they did things effectively. Second, we explored stories in which the informants talked about the act itself. Suicidology sees suicidal death in terms of a particular cognitive state, most frequently pointing to psychache, ambivalence, lowered mood or anxiety. In contrast, we presented stories in which the suicide attempt was constructed as a set of actions which had to be performed. Suicide was more of a physical and logistical problem rather than an emotional one. In this concluding section, we would like to explore some of the issues that are raised by such arguments.

The first issue we would like to raise is rationality of suicide. In suicidology, rational suicide tends to be associated with old age or with illness or disability, and, more generally, with the issue of having the 'right to die' (Mayo, 1986; Richards, 2017; Werth, 1999). The opposition between rational suicide and the other type, shall we say, normal suicide, makes it irrational. And indeed, as we pointed out at the beginning of the chapter, 'normal suicide' is associated with emotionality, cognitive constriction and, more generally, with a person's inability to think straight.

Our data suggest that things are not as straightforward as the assumption of irrational suicide might suggest. The data show not only clarity about what must be done but also clarity as to what would be involved. In our interview data, suicide became a project to carry out successfully rather than an act of emotional despair. It is important to stress that we do not wish to argue that our data could speak for all suicides or all suicide attempts. Rather, we see them as putting a question mark over the assumptions of the commonly assumed nature of suicide as involving cognitive deficits. Our data suggest that this may not be the case.

But there is another, probably more controversial, issue – that of suicide prevention tactics. It is more and more commonly accepted that suicide is something negative, to be stopped, possibly by talking a person out of suicide. Our data suggest that not all people see suicide in such a way. As a logistical project, suicide becomes something to be done rather than be emotional about. Once again, we of course realize that our interviews are post factum accounts, done with today's concerns, yet the way suicide is constructed cannot be easily dismissed.

And so, the recent campaigns such as 'It's OK to talk' or 'It's OK not to be OK' seem not to respond at all to the concerns of people preparing to kill themselves. Again, we do not wish to suggest we have found a foolproof way to create a suicide prevention campaign, yet it would seem sensible to us to create such campaigns bearing in mind how a person engaging in suicide perceives it. If suicide is a logistical project, arguments referring to emotions or communication seem to miss the point.

The second issue that is raised by our discussion is the physicality of suicide – as at least some suicides suggest significant violence to one's body. Indeed, the accounts we have suggest that such violence is a difficult and effortful task. Stories of difficulties with cutting one's veins or putting a noose around one's neck were both very poignant and frightening. Together with those about fighting the clotting of the blood, they show suicide as a thoroughly embodied process. Through this we can begin to understand the relationship between the suicide method and the body of the person who implements it in their attempt to kill themselves. It is through the method that one breaches the body and suffers its consequences. Moreover, physicality of suicide also suggests duration. This, in turn, suggests that the process can, or at least potentially could, be stopped.

This last point, we think, has significant potential for suicide prevention. Prevention strategies for suicide seen as a timeless event outside a context can only be seen in terms of the event not happening. The moment we understand suicide as also being an embodied process which is extended in time, we potentially add the strategies of stopping or interrupting suicide. In other words, we do not only tell people not to do it, we also tell people that they can stop, they don't have to go through with it, and so forth.

Such an understanding of suicide seems to be important precisely because what seems like significant violence done to the body is rendered as a task consisting of a number of actions which must be taken. Our informants' stories turn the violence into a mechanical or quasi-medical task that must be accomplished before the suicidal death can take place. In the process, the absence of violence underscores suicide as a task, making it considerably less dramatic than might be assumed. And that is perhaps one of the most crucial aspects of the argument which we have made in this chapter. In the stories of the act of taking one's own life, suicide is not dramatic. Suicide is hard, it takes effort, it takes strength and preparation, but it is not dramatic.

A reservation is needed here. By making the above point, we do not wish to suggest that suicide is something easy, with no emotional component. The opposite is the case. Both suicide letters and interviews with persons who attempted suicide suggest that people who did or attempted to kill themselves were in a lot pain and anguish. The stories in both kinds of data show much suffering and pain which cannot and should not be ignored and done away with. However, the stories of the acts of self-killing were very different. The anguish was gone from the narratives, and suicide became a task to be dealt with. That does not mean that the pain was gone at all. It does suggest, however, that pain should not be imposed on suicide and its interpretations because of the research perspective taken to study suicidal behaviour. We would also suggest that the paradox we see in the data, between stories of much pain and stories of the act where the pain and suffering are gone, offers a deeper insight into how suicide is experienced. And even though we are unclear at the moment as to how to make sense of it, we are sure that the paradox is significant and must not be ignored for the social consistency of the picture of suicide. In fact, we think that the paradox should be engaged with both by research suicidology and by the suicide prevention field.

We would like to end this argument with one last extract, an answer to the question about what one thinks about when one makes preparations for suicide:

Extract 13

> P: Will it hurt, will I suffer long? Because I knew that there would be pain and in my thoughts, I was with what was lying ahead. Because I believe in god, will I be in heaven or in hell, or wherever else. Or what it is like over there in the other world and I was one hundred per cent sure that I would kill myself. I simply did not hesitate, I told my parents that I was going out to kill myself. I mean that I was going out to hang myself, and my father says, go then. I say in two days' time you must bury me and remember that I will not be burying myself. I will do it not far away, this is what I told him and went out of the house. I took a line of sorts, I used to go to the mountains with it, to [town name] and I had a line, like a professional line, and I knew the line would not break, and that the bough would not break. It took literally, I do not know, a minute, the matter of putting the line up, making a noose. Well, something cracked, I wheezed a little at first. That is what I remember, twenty seconds and I floated away, I cannot remember any more.

We quote this extract as yet another account of the practicalities of committing suicide and another story with no mention of anything resembling what is normally conveyed as psychache or the suicidal mode, let alone the loss of consciousness, an escape from reality. There are two aspects of the fragment that we would like to focus on in particular. First, the informant focuses on the pain which he suspected he would experience. But the brief mention of pain is replaced by 'spiritual' concerns of what happens afterward, heaven, hell or something else. What is fascinating in this account is that these still are questions of the practicalities of suicide. These are not questions of emotionality but those of what is involved, much as you would ask when taking a test.

The second issue is that suicide is made into something very normal. Regardless of what the conversation with the informant's father looked like, what is quite extraordinary is that the informant's story involves an exchange about him going out to commit suicide. The story suggests that the informant, who lived with his parents, was basically accounting for his departure, much as one would when, say, going to the cinema. In such a way, the informant renders his departure 'to hang himself' as very ordinary, something you just inform your parents about in passing. Indeed, his account of his father's account suggests a very similar attitude. Of course, it is more than likely that the father's 'Go then' stems from not believing his son; still, the way it was told by the informant suggests a minimal, largely uninterested response.

It is only then that the informant adds something that leaves the realm of the utterly ordinary. Yet we do not hear any more of the conversation; we do not know what the father's response was. But even here the informant's message to his parents is that of logistics. There is still no explanation, no pain, no emotions. The informant simply informs his parents about what is awaiting them. Such stories drag suicide into ordinariness, something that, we think, is very significant.

This ordinariness is significant as it has been observed that suicide has become more acceptable. In a recent article, the sociologist Julie Phillips (2019) raises the issue of the change in acceptability of suicide. Her argument is that taboos around suicide have lessened and, in the process, it has become more socially available. Phillips says that in the United States suicide has become more acceptable, for example, as a reaction to terminal illness but also to life setbacks. The share of Americans who accept the right to kill oneself in the case of incurable disease has risen from 46.9 per cent to 61.4 per cent in the last thirty years or so. It is perhaps more troubling that the acceptance of suicide in the case of being 'tired of living and ready to die' has also risen from 13.7 per cent to 19.1 per cent.

Phillips continues her argument by linking the rising acceptability of suicide with its destigmatization. She argues that reducing stigma is a double-edged sword. While positive for the people who need help and seek it because of the destigmatization of suicide, it is negative when reducing the stigma makes suicide more available; then one needs to stop and wonder.

Of course, we cannot claim that our data, different by time and culture, are indicative of the same phenomenon. And yet, one must wonder to what extent making suicide more of a practical task at the same time makes it more available.

So far, in this book we have explored the suicide process as the time which we have understood as the time before the suicidal act. In Chapter 6, we would like to change the perspective. And so, we shall be looking at how the future is constructed both in the suicide notes and in the interviews with people who had attempted to kill themselves.

Appendix

Extract 1

P: tylko ta myśl y: w sumie (.) czy nie popełnisz jakiegoś błędu robiąc to. [...] żebyś o czymś ważnym nie zapomniała nie przegapiła czegoś. czyli śledź po kolei to co będziesz robiła. ubierz się. zobacz czy jesteś kompletnie ubrana. czy niczego ci nie brakuje. y: przygotuj się do tego. więc załóż ten pasek z tymi płóciennymi workami obciążonymi cegłami czy on się nie urwie

Extract 2

P: a mówię przede wszystkim myślałam o tym żeby niczego ważnego nie przeoczyć. y: czyli czyli tak jakby po kolei (po) śledzić y: co y: ja zrobię w dany dzień jak już będę wychodziła. czy y: czy po prostu zabiorę i przy/i czy czegoś ważnego nie przeoczę. m: bo wiem że jedyną rzeczą którą muszę zabrać z domu i czego nie mogę to zostawić otwartego mieszkania.

Extract 3

I: zadam teraz chyba najtrudniejsze pytanie. Czy mogłaby Pani opowiedzieć o tym jak wyglądał dzień chwile przed próbą popełnienia samobójstwa.

P: tak sobie próbowałam to mniej więcej mówić no i to takie rzeczy. że najpierw wypije sobie te trzy piwa później posiedzę coś tam porobię posłucham muzyki na przykład. to był ostatni dzień akurat ale w dzień wcześniej to mówiłam tak spotykanie z ludźmi się przede wszystkim y: wyjścia jakieś gdzieś coś tam no mimo tego że ja wcześniej ogólnie prowadziłam normalnie życie towarzyskie tylko akurat być może miałam mniej czasu akurat dla tych osób to stwierdziłam że (.) akurat te dni spę/poświęcę im czas a oni poświęcą mnie i: i to tak na na tej zasadzie wyglądało później też że że miejsce to też było rozplanowane. miejsce rozglądałam się czy tam dobrze jest beton żeby to nie była ziemia dziwne to takie sobie teraz myślę (laughs) jakaś mania (laughs).

Extract 4

P: (.) długo właśnie analizowałem też (.) to trochę może dziwnie zabrzmieć ale analizowałem sposoby właśnie zakończenia życie i wchodziło w rachubę jeszcze otrucie się albo: albo y: utopienie się. ale jednak wybrałem tą trzecią metodę chciałem to zrobić w domu u siebie (.) pożegnać się z tym światem. (..) uważałem że (.) że tak będzie najprościej. że najmniej kłopotu będzie bo: też potem pomyślałem że na przykład jakbym się utopił to rodzina by nie wiedziała gdzie jestem czy może zaginąłem czy może gdzieś wyjechałem m: potem by mnie wyłowili za 10 dni takiego pełnego nabrzmiałego od tej wody od tych od tych wszystkich y: gazów co się w człowieku zbierają pośmiertnych. i wolałem żeby właśnie szybko moje ciało znaleźli. i żeby nie było w miarę jakiś sposób że tak powiem z:/bardzo źle wyglądający żebym jakoś w trumnie wyglądał bo to też se zaplanowałem że to w tym liście pożegnalnym że ja chciałbym jednak w trumnie spocząć. na katafalku (i) (.) wydawał mi się ten sposób taki najbardziej ludzki. no gdybym miał jeszcze broń to: to to by wchodziło w rachubę też ale w Polsce to raczej jest y: niemożliwe. (no.)(..)

Extract 5

P: a to mi chodziło od dłuższego czasu tylko tak (.) jakoś mi to przechodzi:ło tak (.) raz w niedzielę w domu gdzieś tak leżałem trzeźwy w domu i tak myślę tak (..) jakie są wyjścia takie jest wyjście takie (.) pod pociąg się rzucić nie: ten tak to no tak tak mi się śni:ło mi się takie te tak w nocy naj/najgorsze noce są. (..) i tak myślałem (.) ale wtenczas f: w nie/niedzielę rano to już byłem przygotowany.

I: mhm

P: to se jeszcze pomyślałem (ku:ra) tyle ludzi na świecie powiesili i jakoś to i na wojnie zginęło gi/giną ludzie i teraz giną i (powiedziałem) co to jeden człowiek (.) y to tam minie ale to troszku pogadają i na tym temat gdzie indziej pogadają i na tym i zapomni świat o tym no (..) nie udało mi się. może może lepiej że mi się nie udało (.) nie wiem

Extract 6

P: w ogóle bólu nie czułam a robiłam to szkłem. rozbitym. więc nie było nie były to warunki że tak powiem ani ani sterylne ani ani nic. szczerze mówiąc właśnie jedyne co to y: no miałam taką myśl że mogłam się do tego jakoś lepiej przygotować w sensie wziąć jakiś nóż skalpel cokolwiek. (.) żeby to zrobić po prostu skuteczniej bo dosyć długo się dłubałam z tym. żeby to zrobić. ale bólu w ogóle nie czułam. jakoś tak się nie wiem chyba adrenalina zrobiła swoje.(..) i że to trwało dosyć długo samo samo samo to jak ta krew się ze mnie wylewała. i wtedy no nie czułam żalu. w: tym momencie takim samym. potem zemdlałam parę parę ładnych godzin byłam nieprzytomna obudziłam się w środku nocy.

Extract 7

P: tak sobie wyciskałem i ten (…) tak sobie popijałem i tak sobie łykałem i tak mówię ile łykne nie i chyba dwadzieścia sześć nie pamiętam. dwadzieścia sześć tabletek chyba łykłem (..) nie wiem czy to było za mało czy za dużo.

Extract 8

P: czyli już/bo jak miałem gorącą wodę [cmoka] no średnio ciepłą. i zaczęło mi być zimno. i już teraz se myślę o już mam mało krwi już mi (organizm) nie dogrzewa. to sobie nogą kurek odkręciłem z ciepłą wodą bo cały czas prysznic mi leciał. i: (.) wypuściłem trzy wanny wody. nie. dwie wanny wody. kiedy krew y: już kiedy była czerwona.

Extract 9

P: tak. żeby nie odróżniał żeby nikt nie nie nie nie zobaczył żebym: bo gdybym ubrała białą być może bardziej bym się rzucała w oczy. więc to też wzięłam pod uwagę. żeby kurtka była coś zielonkawo-brązowa i rzeczywiście znalazłam taką kurtkę stare spodnie stare buty najgorsze y: znalazłam jakąś torebkę której nigdy nie używałam. no i do tej torebki zapakowałam to co było mi zupełnie niezbędne. y: słoik w tym do tego słoika miałam już y: wyciśnięte wcześniej przygotowane tabletki. (bo) było tego BARDZO BARDZO dużo że to był zapas 3-miesięczny czterech rodzajów leków. było tego bardzo dużo. m: poszłam do: sklepu monopolowego. kupiłam alkohol kupiłam koniak. to zapakowałam do torebki zapakowałam jeszcze: (.) zapałki bo: obawiałam się że w nocy kiedy będę siedziała nad [river] mogą m: pojawić się szczury. więc chciałam je jakby odstraszać ogniem. o tym pomyślałam. wzięłam jeszcze literatkę y: z barku jakieś chusteczki higieniczne (.) i: (.) i: y: dodatkową ym: mocną reklamówkę w razie gdyby któraś z płóciennych mi się y: urwała. m: a przygotowana byłam w ten sposób że y: do pasa m: (.) y: w okolicy pasa przywiązałam sobie y: szeroki mocny pasek skórzany z: z bardzo mocną y klamrą i bardzo <u>solidny</u> mocny pasek y: do tego przyczepiłam m: zawiązałam trzy płó- płócienne worki (.) zawiązałam je i do każdego z nich włożyłam cegłę. i tak y: m: przygotowałam to w domu i sprawdziłam y: w domu czy czy to się nie urwie. czy y: czy to y: wytrzyma tą siłę. czy: jak ja będę się czuła mając to na sobie. czy rzeczywiście to będzie takie obciążenie żebym m: kiedy u: m: się utopię to żebym nie wypłynęła. sądziłam że y: że y (.) że chyba dobrze wszystko zaplanowałam. te płócienne worki jak najbardziej zdały rezultat. y: (.) i: z cegłami nie było problemu bo obok y: wykładali jakiś bruk. tak że kwestia była tylko zejścia na dół i: ja je przyniosłam do domu. i: i tak przygotowane razem z paskiem pasek (nawet) z tymi płóciennymi workami i z cegłami włożyłam do jednej dużej torby (.) wsiadłam w autobus i pojechałam nad ((podaje nazwę rzeki)) niedaleko ((podaje nazwę mostu)) (.) tam postanowiłam to zrobić. m: y: w domu m: nie zostawiłam żad- aha. zamknęłam dom na klucz. (.) […] ta noc była bardzo zimna. okazało się. była bardzo zimna i: ja y: po prostu natychmiast jak zrobiło się już ciemniej y: i i i: m: m: (.) y: m pamiętam że zaczy- zaczy- już było dosyć ciemno jak zaczynałam zażywać leki. [...] wi- pamiętam y moment że: nie wiem musiało być koło północy bo u ludzi z naprzeciwka w bloku zaczęły y: gasnąć światła. czyli m: ludzie szli spać. to najpóźniej mogło być 11 12. to już miałam o już miałam- yyy taką utratę takie. i w tym momencie po prosty y: powinnam zrobić to co powinnam. czyli dalszy krok. a ja w tym momencie po prostu straciłam świadomość i upadłam z: jakąś podwiniętą ręką pod klatkę piersiową. tak przeleżałam 24 godziny. znaleźli mnie jacyś wędkarze. no wcześniej no mówię no ktoś mnie okradł z tej biednej torebki. z tej literatki. no alkoholu nie było już bo ja alkohol cały wypiłam. m: także przyjechało pogotowie. policja. i byłam osobą poszukiwaną przez rodzinę.

Extract 10

P: to piwo tak odłożyłem (.) i i druga tura. i wie pani co założyłem se to na szyję bo jeszcze myślę będzie mnie bolało co nie a tchórzem jestem bo myślę będzie mnie bolało to se wziąłem koszulę. że bez koszule że nie będzie tyle (.) cięło mnie. (.) podłożyłem sobie skrzynkę (.) drugi sznurek jak wziąłem żebym mógł se szarpnąć żeby mi (niejasne) wyślizgło (.) no i zrobiłem tak i te te ten regips się urwał spadł. i spadłem i nic z tego

I: mhm

P: nie wyszło mi. (.) no to wtenczas się już całkiem załamałem (.) myślę to jest taka szmata ze mnie taka szmata ze mnie że ja nawet się nie umie powiesić. (.) myślę t/tak sie/siedzę siedzę siedzę myślę. (..) wypiłem to piwo i tak myślę nie (.) kurde (..) takie myśli mnie naszły. myślę sobie tak (..) ja się będę wieszał? człowieku kurwa no przecież ty weź wytrzeźwiej (.) normalnie wstań idź do domu co jeżeli cię ktoś pobije żona cię zabije to tak samo zginiesz. t/(.) i wstań i idź do domu. (..) ale to wypiłem piwo no nie no nie mogę cho/jak pójdę tam do domu no co powiem będę no co co ja powiem. (.) co ja powiem w domu no co ja powiem dzieciom mam wnuka

Extract 11

P: no ja w tym przypadku tak jak mówię tak było tak nie patrz na to, bo to tak wysypałam i coś tak z tej strony jakby nie patrz na to, bo to będzie moment rzeczywiście tak szybko wrzuciłam tego

Extract 12

P: tą noc spędziłem na rynku (.) trochę tak wałęsając się: wałęsając się po [city] i doszedłem na most [bridge name] powiedziałem no to teraz jest pora (.) wziąłem do plecaka naładowałem kamieni wszedłem (...) na przęsło no i: hop (4 sek.)

Extract 13

P: czy będzie bolało czy: długo będę y: cierpiał bo to wiedziałem że będzie ból. wiedziałem że: no i po prostu już byłem myślami co mnie czeka bo ja wierze w Boga.czy będę w niebie czy będę w piekle czy będę gdzieś tam czy jak to jest na tym drugim świecie no i już byłem na sto procent przekonany że: się zabije. byłem pewny siebie po prostu no nie zawahałem się powiedziałem rodzicom że idę zabić się znaczy/że idę się powiesić ojciec mówi no to idź. ja mówię za dwa dni masz mnie pochować pamiętaj ja nie będę się chował. bo ja zrobię to niedaleko zobaczysz tak mu powiedziałem i wyszedłem z domu. wziąłem linkę taką w: bo ja z nią w góry jeździłem do [nazwa miejscowości] i miałem taką linkę jakby no taką profesjonalną no i wiedziałem że linka nie pęknie że gałąź nie pęknie no (.) trwało to dosłownie no ja wiem minutę. kwestia założenia linki pętli zrobienia no i szczykło trochę poharczałem z początku to co pamiętam no i dwadzieścia sekund już odpłynęłem już nie pamiętam po prostu.

6

Future

So far, we have explored the suicide process as the time before the suicidal act. In other words, we have talked about all those things that happen in the past looking from the perspective of taking one's life. In this chapter, we would like to change the perspective. Here, we would like to look at how the future is constructed both in the suicide notes and in the interviews with people who have attempted to kill themselves.

Future in suicidology

Suicidology is not much interested in the future. Researchers occasionally point out that people with a history of suicidal ideation or attempts describe the future in terms of something that is impossible to imagine (Shneidman, 1993), as associated with emptiness and the absence of hope (Jamison, 2004) or the absence of anything positive (Williams, 2014). Negative attitudes towards the future can be translated into fewer reasons to stay alive for such people (MacLeod, Rose & Williams, 1993). Researchers hypothesize that, in the experience of people with a history of suicidal ideation or attempts, time flows slowly, which means that the present is experienced as unchanging and the future appears as very distant (Neuringer, Levenson & Kaplan, 1972).

The mainstream of the suicidological research on the future focuses on the relationship between expectations of the future and the risk of suicide. Research focuses on the assessment of psychological and environmental variables related to suicidal behaviour, also defined through feeling helpless and pessimistic about the future (e.g. Wenzel & Spokas, 2014). Initially, researchers wanted to see whether people experiencing helplessness have negative expectations of the future, do not have positive expectations of the future, or both. This is why MacLeod and Byrne (1996) constructed the *Future Thinking Task* (FTT), which consists of generating as many expected positive future experiences within a minute and, in the following minute, as many expected negative future experiences. Participants provide responses within three time frames: next week, next year and in five to ten years.

The results of the study consistently show that, in comparison with the control group comprising persons in psychiatric care and healthy persons, people with a history of suicidal ideation or attempts have difficulty in generating positive experiences but do not differ in terms of generating negative experiences of the future (Conaghan & Davidson, 2002; MacLeod et al., 1997). On this basis, researchers conclude that it is the low levels of positive thoughts rather than the presence of negative ones that is related to feelings of helplessness and suicide ideation (e.g. O'Connor et al., 2004). The relationship between the low level of positive thoughts and suicide potential is independent of the diagnosis of depression, verbal fluency or even attribution style (Hunter & O'Connor, 2003; O'Connor, Connery & Cheyne, 2000; Williams et al., 2008). Research also indicates that difficulty in positive thinking about the future also relates to generating positive expectations of oneself (MacLeod & Conway, 2007).

It was only in 2015 that the content of positive expectations of the future was studied (O'Connor, Smyth & Williams, 2015). Researchers classified their participants' expectations of the future into one of the following categories: social-interpersonal, achievements, intrapersonal, leisure, health, financial and other. It transpired that not only the content of the positive expectations of the future influences the strength and direction of the relationship, but, surprisingly, a high level of intrapersonal expectations (i.e. those which focus on oneself) explained future suicidal behaviour.

In this chapter, we focus on the future in a different way. We are interested in how people who attempted to or did kill themselves construct their own or others' future. We start by exploring suicide notes and show that accounts of the future are rendered in very certain terms. We then turn to interviews and ask the question of what suicide is constructed to end. If suicide, commonsensically, puts an end to life, to everything, one could say, we were interested in how our informants put it. It turns out that in their narratives suicide is not constructed to put an end to life; rather, we argue, it ends a particular kind of living. We end the chapter with a discussion of how our informants saw their own future. What we found particularly interesting was that the future in the informants' stories was entirely out of their control.

Certainty of the future

In this section, we are interested in exploring those suicide notes which could be seen as predictions of the future. In other words, some authors of suicide notes wrote about what would happen after their death. And what is particularly interesting about these predictions is that they are all made at the highest level of certainty.

Before we discuss this, we need to offer a very brief account of epistemic modality. Modality in language is to do with the expression of the speaker's attitude towards the proposition they render in their utterance: to what extent the speaker commits to or distances themselves from what they say. The concepts that modality deals with are truth and, related to it, necessity and possibility as well as obligation and permission. In the case at hand, we are dealing with epistemic modality, the capacity of clauses to express the speaker's certainty as to what happened (or, indeed, will happen) or the certainty that what they say is true, this certainty ranging from very low to very high (Halliday, 1994). At the most certain, the language is a simple statement in the third person, plural or singular, without any qualifications. Statements such as 'God exists' or 'There are lions in Africa' convey the speaker's certainty at its highest. Modalization, in contrast, introduces an aspect of degree, thus making propositions weaker or stronger. And so, sentences such as 'There might be alien civilizations' or 'Aliens have probably visited the Earth' through 'might' and 'probably' render the writer's uncertainty. In the data at hand, we focus on all those aspects which are to do with the differences between what will happen, might happen or will not happen as well as a spectrum of shades of certainty between them.

Consider first the following extracts:

Extract 1

In time you will see it was a good choice.

Extract 2

I have much doubt, but I know that it will be for the best for everybody this way.

Extract 3

Doing it, I do not regret [it], it will be better for you. I was stealing from my mum and my brother, with you I do not know what I was doing. I was like trash for them, I was stealing from them, and they were right.

Extract 4

> Nothing came off for me. I was lying to you and generally I have been a bad son. It is better I am already gone. You will live better, me too. I have only been a burden for you.

All four extracts from suicide notes contain clauses in the future tense. Linguistically, they are statements about the future; however, we think that it is fairly safe to think of such statements as predictions. Despite the minimal context, we would argue that this is the main communicative goal of such statements, regardless of whether there might be others.

In all of these statements the future is rendered with much certainty. What is particularly interesting about them is that they are predictions which do not refer to extralinguistic reality over which they might have some control. Rather, they are likely to be predictions of what those who are left behind will think or how they will feel. And so, in extract 1 we read that the addressees will see something, in extracts 2 and 3 the letter author's death will be for the best and in extract 4 the addressees will live better lives. In all these cases, the suicide notes betray no hesitation. There is little doubt that the suicide of the authors of the letters we quote above and others alike will produce the future it aims to do. Note, however, that in extract 2 the prediction is introduced through the superordinate clause 'I know'. We decided to include it here, as the verb 'know' is probably the most certain of verbs rendering mental processes.

Apart from predictions of the suicide resulting in improvement or general betterment, the suicide letters also contain references to more specific future outcomes. Consider:

Extract 5

> Good bye. I apologise to you, my mum, that this is how it turned out. You will no longer get upset.

Extract 6

> But there is much life in front of you. You are not so old, so ugly, you will make your life one way or the other.

Extract 7

> I want to see how you are making new life, how you give birth to children, how you bring them up. I have a request. If you had a son, give him my name, simply as a memento of my person. I want to see how you enjoy life.

Extract 8

   Mum, I am sorry for this act. I know it will be hard for you.

In extract 5, the author predicts that his mother will no longer get upset. In extract 6, the addressee is predicted to make a new life for herself. Incidentally, this extract contains the adverb *jakoś*, which we translated as 'one way or the other'. It is not used, however, as a means to modalize the prediction – the new life will happen. What is uncertain is what the quality of that life will be, given that the addressee is not 'that' old and ugly.

In extracts 7 and 8, in contrast, the prediction of the future is mediated via superordinate clauses with a mental process. But here, too, it seems, the future is rendered as quite certain. In extract 7, the author has put the future into the presupposition (an implied statement which is necessary for the sentence to make sense) of the 'I want to see' clause. In such a way, what is only a prediction becomes a condition for the sensibility of the two clauses. The future is not predicted so much as it is made obvious. As we explained in reference to extract 2, while extract 8 introduces modalization, the verb *wiem* (first person singular of 'know') carries with it as much certainty as is possible with a verb referring to a mental process.

We see such constructions of the future as rendering the choice of suicide as making sense. In other words, it only makes sense to commit suicide if the future that it brings about is certain. And so, references to what will happen, without hesitation, make suicide more rational and, in the process, more available. These constructions are parallel to those representing suicide as a rational choice (see the discussion in Chapter 5), one which seems to be based on evidence rather than a whim, a feeling or similar. Suicide is based on calculation; it cannot be construed as resulting from anything else but the care for the people for whom the gift is given. In addition to that, the future it will achieve is certain.

A second and complementary interpretation of such constructions of the future might also be related to making suicide more acceptable for those who stay behind. After all, if what it aims to achieve is certain, it is perhaps more understandable. In such a way, suicide is an act of caring rather than of selfishness. Such an interpretation is in tandem with Galasiński's (2017) discussion of unwavering promises of love and its certain and eternal presence. Constructing a certain future could therefore be seen as part of communicating closeness, however non-physical it is. In a way, the notes' references to the future are perhaps assurances or consolations for those who remain alive.

Now, even though the construction of a future certain to come was typical of the corpus, there were a few notes in which the future was rendered with some hesitation. Consider the following two extracts:

Extract 9

> How will you look people in the eye, when they learn the truth?
> I hope you will suffer more than I have.

Extract 10

> My dear son, I hope that when you grow up you will understand certain matters and you will forgive me. I am sorry that I will not be at your side when you go to first communion, when you go to school, that I will not watch you grow up. I want you to know that I love you very much and part of me will always be with you.

In both cases, the statement about the future is mediated by the modalizing clause 'I hope', which cancels the predicting force of the clause that follows. As Wierzbicka (2003) suggests, superordinate clauses such as 'I hope' imply that the speaker does not want to assert anything; rather, they are expressing their thoughts. Such a phrase serves as a disclaimer, continues Wierzbicka, and so, one could argue, it undermines any potential certainty with which the future is spoken of.

It is hard to say why the authors of the above notes decided to introduce the reference to the future through the modalizing 'I hope'. In the case of extract 9, it might be related to the negativity of the prediction. Perhaps the taboo of wishing someone ill does not allow the writer to simply assert the future suffering of the addressee. Extract 10 is different, and perhaps the remoteness of the future and emotional investment in it allow it to be expressed so tentatively. Such an explanation could also be made with regard to the note in extract 9.

To sum up, in this section we have talked about constructions of the future in suicide notes. Interestingly, the future is constructed as certain in such notes. The certainty of the future, we argued, could be seen as constructing the suicide as making sense. Only the future which is certain to happen as a result of the suicidal act makes the act rational.

Very few notes constructed the future tentatively. We have suggested that it was the emotional investment, possibly underpinned by the acceptability of wishing a particular future in some cases, that made it less certain. In the next two sections, we shift our attention to how the future is represented in the stories of the informants who attempted to commit suicide. Our discussion is divided into two parts. On the one hand, we explore accounts of suicide as an end to a variety of things in life. On the other, we are interested in stories of what the future holds for our informants.

What suicide ends

At least commonsensically suicide puts an end to life, at least in its physical form; one could probably say that it puts an end to much more. As it ends life the suicidal act also offers a future without it, both for those who commit it and for those left behind, though in very different ways. In this section, we are interested in what it is that suicide ends and for whom it is done. What we found particularly interesting in these accounts was that the end brought by suicide was not final. Consider first the following extracts:

Extract 11

> P: You know, what, for example, I did not think, in this case about some kind of financial question. The only thing I thought was how bad it is for me in life, so not good, that I have no support from anyone and that when I finish myself, I will have peace and quiet.

Extract 12

> P: You know, it was something like I thought that if I took my life, then I will have peace and quiet with everything.

Extract 13

> P: God gave me two legs, two hands and suddenly, he takes away a part of me, then, I do not know, something inside me told me that it was worth being done with this life, not care, simply feel relief. Because without my hand nowadays, one gets tired, because you have a problem with tying your shoes, with eating your dinner, with using knife and fork or even putting the thread through the needle's eye.

What is quite fascinating in these narratives is that suicide leads to a future in which things will be different. In extracts 11 and 12, suicide, rendered as ending with oneself and taking one's life, leads to peace and quiet. Significantly, the linguistic form, especially in extract 12, explicitly constructs the informant as having peace in the future. Suicide is not constructed as leading to the achievement of peace but rather to a future in which the informants will have it.

Moreover, the use of the complex future tense, that is to say through the use of the verb *być* ('be') and another verb, in this case *mieć* ('have'), is suggestive of the progressiveness of the construction. This is because the complex future tense in Polish tends to be used with imperfective verbs (those which suggest continuation of the action rather than its end). It must be noted, however, that Polish *mieć* is not changeable through aspect and so, linguistically, the construction remains ambivalent.

Extract 13 is similar. The very tentative reference to ending life ('it was worth being done with this life') is followed by a reference to not caring. The reference to not worrying and then to having relief[1] is ambivalent in that neither phrase suggests temporality. However, the falling intonation after the clause referring to ending life might weakly suggest that what follows is meant to refer to a new segment of experience, perhaps one which suggests sequentiality. In other words, the informant is talking about taking his life, which will bring feelings of relief.

The most significant aspect of these fragments is that they seem to construct suicide with not as much finality as it might be expected. In other words, suicide is explicitly said to be taking their life but it is also offering a future without care or worry. Whether the care-free future is to do with spirituality or seen in some other way is unclear; still, suicide is constructed to offer a future.

The ambivalence as to the future after the suicidal act disappears in the following extract:

Extract 14

> P: I mean, I can say that there is no problem, right? For example, I myself, I feel like I was looking for some freedom, right? But I know that if I do jump, I will care about nothing, I will be free and I will [care] about nothing. I will not have any legal problems or trouble. No one will torment me and I will not bother anyone. The voices will stop to exist, won't they? Everything will be all right. But in fact, this is not true. One will be tormented more when he jumps and suicide will occur than when one is alive. Because life cannot be given back, but when one is alive things can be mended, can't they?

Although the account is about generalities, a hypothetical suicide, the informant clearly constructs what will, or perhaps will not, happen after suicide. There is a clear construction of the future. References to not worrying, being free, not having legal problems, all rendered in the future tense, all construct a new and better future. This is reinforced by the future in which no one and nothing would bother the informant. However, this account is then undermined in the latter part of the story. The conjunction *ale* ('but') explicitly juxtaposes the first account with what comes next. But what quite fascinating is that the undermining argument is that the future after suicide is not going to be better but worse. One will be in more torment after jumping.

The narrative offers yet another turn when the informant starts constructing suicide in terms of finality. It is unclear, however, how these final comments relate to the previous ones, especially that the finality of suicide is used in reference to one's ability to repair things rather than in reference to death.

And here we come to a more general point that the stories we heard were not so much about death but rather about a different future. They construct suicide as remedying their unwillingness to live but, crucially, to live in a particular way. Suicide seems to offer a way in which to change the informants' way of living rather than cause death and cancel any possible future. And the future consists of being in peace, not worrying, rather than not being at all.

This perspective of switching life as it is, is underscored in extract 15 in which suicide is explicitly positioned not as a means to die but as a means to kill illness. Consider:

Extract 15

> P: I lost the sense of life. And practically it is the next thing that my illness is taking from me. First my work, my house, my family, my husband, everything I loved I lost. Because of the illness. And I could not come to terms at all with the decision that the illness takes everything away from me. I hated myself in this illness. I could not live with it. I simply wanted to kill it.

And so, after an attempt on her life someone is explicitly talking not about killing herself, taking her own life, but killing 'it', most likely referring to her illness. Suicide is an act of killing something rather than oneself. We want to make sure that it is clear that we are not suggesting at all that the informant was not aware that her act would end her life. There is no evidence of that at all. Rather, our argument is based on how the informant (and others) renders their suicide attempt. As throughout the book, we are only interested in their narratively constructed experience.

We would like to end this section with one final extract which brings ambiguity:

Extract 16

> P: I did not think, it did not cross my mind at all that I would not be successful. Or that there might be consequences, that I might be paralysed or something, a stroke, various things. Or coma, right? No. Not this. I simply thought that I would drink it […]
>
> I: and the end?
>
> P: and that would be the end. This was the only thing I thought. And later, indeed, when I poured it into the coffee, and there were some crumbs of the tablet in the glass, I am saying, I think it is too little and I put tea to those remains of the tablets and I swirled the glass and drank it. It was very bitter and went down my throat and this caused retching. Vomiting. I vomited all of it. And I was right in the middle of vomiting in the bathroom, at that moment, my daughter arrived.

At first sight, the informant is talking about not managing to kill herself and about not thinking about any other possible consequences. Yet things are a bit more complicated. The extract is ambivalent linguistically as to what the point of the attempt was. The interviewee refers to an 'it' which she thought she would be able to attain. In the second part of the extract, the informant follows the interviewer and talks about an end, yet it is still unclear what the end refers to. It is very likely that the interviewer means to talk about the end in terms of the informant's death; there is no explicit evidence, however, that would suggest that she shared this understanding with the interviewee. Consequently, while the extract is explicitly referring to a suicidal act and the process of taking poison in particular, what exactly the informant wanted to achieve is ambiguous.

As a digression, we would like to point out the use of the word *udać* which can be translated as 'succeed'. There are frequent calls not to use the word "success" when referring to the completed act of suicide, calls which are supported by the Centers for Disease Control and Prevention (CDC) (see also Crosby, Ortega & Melanson, 2011; Posner et al., 2007). Such prescriptive language policing tends to be counter useful at least insofar as people who do use such language are concerned. And language policies demanding that suicide be spoken about only in ways defined by either suicidologists or activists tend to alienate those whose way of speaking happens not to be aligned with the directives. We shall come back to this point in the concluding chapter.

In this section, we have discussed constructions of suicide as putting an end to something. Interestingly, along the lines suggested by Shneidman (1985, 1993; see also Joiner, 2005), suicide is not constructed as putting an end to life. This is because the informants' stories construct a future for the informant after performing the suicidal act. However, in contrast to Shneidman, we suggest suicide is not so much an end to consciousness but rather an end to a particular kind of living. We return to this in the 'Conclusions' section of this chapter.

Is there a future?

In this section, we are interested in how our informants construct their future. Interestingly, the responses we received to a considerable extent focused on the possibility of future suicide attempts. Significantly, the potential future suicide is constructed as outside the informant's control. Consider first the following extract:

Extract 17

> I: and now, as I understand it, you do not go out into the future in your thoughts?
>
> P: No. I live in the today. I am trying not to make any difficulties here, I take my medications. I have never been against pharmacological treatment, so I have taken up treatment. I am now trying like commit to, engage with the treatment, for the next time give myself a chance. But I do not know if again, this time for the last time, if a night will not come, an evening which will cause the return of memories and the wish to commit suicide. I do not know. I do not know that. Those thoughts return unexpectedly. What happened to me now also had come unexpectedly. I did not think at all that something would start changing so quickly. This is very good, for me it is motivating that I had had so little part in it. But something happened and in the right direction.

The story told by the informant could not be more tentative. She starts by constructing her activities not in terms of doing things but in terms of trying to do things. She tries not to cause trouble, she tries to follow the treatment, to engage with it, and to give herself another chance. The only committal statement is the one about taking up treatment; however, it follows her statement that she had not been against it.

What follows this is quite a non-agentive account, a story of suicide which is not in the informant's control. It is the night and the evening that are constructed in agentive terms. In other words, it is the time of day which will cause the return of suicidal thoughts and the will to commit suicide. The speaker constructs herself as having no power over either the thoughts or the act itself. Their construction as out of the informant's control is underpinned by representing them as coming unexpectedly. Moreover, the participant returns to what is likely to be her earlier suicide attempt and represents it as something that happened to her, again a construction which backgrounds her agency. This is followed by an explicit denial of having anything to do with what had happened. She finishes her account with a statement that something happened.[2]

This picture of the future was typical in the corpus we collected – the informants consistently painted a picture of an uncertain future, out of their control, laced with the possibility of a future suicide. Consider the following extracts:

Extract 18

> P: Well, I must get treatment so that something like that would not happen. Because, damn it, I am scared of myself. I have a family, haven't I? So, I need to get better and positively. I am a young person after all, aren't I? [...] And it is particularly, it is worst when you are young, you have a family and something like that happens.

Extract 19

> P: I know that this is horrible for a person. I would not like it to happen again at all, damn it. No other attempt to happen again. I would not like that, damn it. One like that or another, there are different attempts. [...] I do not wish it for anyone.

Extract 20

> P: I think that I will not experience a second attempt, or a third, right? That I will recover somehow or perhaps get better, and I will get work, and everything will be all right. I will start my life one way or another, same trajectory as was before, before that occurrence. I think this is what it will be like, right?

In extracts 18 and 19, the suicide attempt is constructed as likely to happen again. While perhaps it is not invested with agent-like capacity, it is represented as similar to a reoccurring phenomenon, as if it appeared of its own accord, naturally. Interestingly, in extract 18 the suicide attempt is referred to as 'something like that', the nature of the 'phenomenon' is distanced from and removed from the explicit content of what is being said. In both extracts, the informants construct the attempt as outside of their agency; in extract 18, it is reinforced by the reference to the speaker's fear that it might happen.

Extract 20 is somewhat different in that the interviewee talks about his potential suicide attempt as something to be experienced. His statement is a weak prediction, as it is introduced by the hedge 'I think'. The lack of confidence in the future is reinforced by the pronoun *jakoś* ('somehow') when the informant talks about starting a new life and by the *co nie?* (similar to the English question tag, 'isn't it?', but less formulaic).

All three extracts above are also interesting in that references to suicide are mediated by the use of verbs referring to mental processes. Suicide seems to be a phenomenon only to think about or wish for (or not, as in the case with the stories above). It is not something to do or not to do.

The absence of control over suicide was also rendered through the reference to fate. Consider:

Extract 21

> P: And I am wondering whether it fits into the category of time healing wounds. And whether the time I need at the moment will be enough. I do not know how long the time will be, is it like in bereavement after a close one's death. Will it make me shake it all off and I will eventually get on my feet. If it is not written for me here, I would like to live and function well.

Extract 22

> P: One needs time, this is what I think. I have dreams, I have good dreams. As I am saying, I dream of god, he says it is not time yet. That it is necessary to wait and suffer my share. Perhaps it is a kind of penance for what I have done wrong so far, perhaps it is a trial of sorts, a challenge. Something which was taken away from me, so that I would see what disabled people feel like. Or something was taken away from me so that I would feel that I am not giving enough of me, that I should do more. That it is a challenge for the strength of will. This is how I have described it lately. How resistant I am to loss, as I say, of my physical health. And I have been given this opportunity. I have received it from my parents, from my doctors, from my family. And I hope that my health will be heading towards getting better.

In different ways, the two extracts convey suicide and suicidal death as something which is written by fate. In extract 21, in the final statement of the fragment the interviewee makes the point explicitly. If living is written[3] for the participant, it means she will live. The removal of any agency of the interviewee from her story is complete. Extract 22 is different in that fate is mentioned through reference to having good dreams and dreams about God, which suggests it is not time for the informant to die. Presumably, it is not his fate. Yet, towards the end of the fragment, the interviewee represents himself as receiving a second chance from other people. But here, too, what follows is 'recovery' over which he has no influence. He can only hope that his recovery will be going in the right direction, again constructed in a way which removes his taking part in it.

In this section, we have considered how our informants saw their future. It turned out that their stories constructed the future in very uncertain terms. Moreover, it was also a future with the risk of another suicide (attempt). What was most significant in the stories we collected was that the informants linguistically removed their agency or other influence over what might happen. Suicidal thoughts or suicide attempts were constructed to come as if on their own, appearing much like a weather phenomenon.

Conclusions

In this chapter, we have focused on constructions of the future in suicide notes and in our interview data. Our first finding was that suicide notes consistently constructed the future in very certain terms. We argued that in such a way suicide was rendered as more rational; as it made more sense, it also became more available for the authors of farewell letters. Our second discussion was about the finality of suicide. If suicide puts an end to something, we were interested in what our informants positioned as the end resulting from the suicidal act. It turned out, significantly, that for our informants, suicide did not put an end to their physical or biological life. Rather, it put an end to the life they were living. The final point we made was that, when asked about their own future, our informants saw it as uncertain and out of their control. In this section, we would like to further explore these issues.

Probably the most striking result of the analyses of our two sets of data is the diametrical difference between how the future is constructed in the suicide notes and in the interviews. As we have just noted, suicide notes construct the future in very certain terms; the interviews do just the opposite. We think that such a result has significant consequences.

Whether through suicide letters or when discussing suicides, suicidology is largely interested in accessing the suicidal mind of the person behind the suicide. And so, right from the classical study by Shneidman and Farberow (1957), suicide notes were analysed for their 'thought units' and assumed to be barren, as they reflect the close-mindedness of the person behind the suicide. Similarly, suicidology describes the suicidal mind (or a person in the suicide mode) in very similar terms. We think it is fair to say that in both its strands (suicide notes and suicides), suicidology postulates a uniform 'special state of mind' of the person who kills themselves. Needless to say, suicidology has some sort of access to such a state of mind, whether through psychological autopsy (see Cavanagh et al., 2003; Isometsä, 2001), assessment of those who attempted suicide (see DeJong, Overholser & Stockmeier, 2010) or suicide notes (Leenaars, 1991).

Our data suggest that such assumptions are at least too hasty. If there is a uniform state of the suicidal mind, then it should impose itself on the accounts of the future which should be, roughly at least, similar to each other regardless of the context in which they are made. And yet, people who for all intents and purposes engage in a similar act construct the future in very different terms. How do we explain this? Should we at least put a question mark over the assumption of the suicidal mind?

Before we offer comment, we would like to acknowledge at least one potential counterargument for the point we have just made. One could argue that we compare data which are hardly comparable. Suicide letters are written at the time of the suicide, are unsolicited and cannot therefore be compared to post hoc accounts, made in a research situation, possibly outside the 'special kind of state of the mind'. As we acknowledge the point, we continue to be sceptical of the argument of the state of mind, which, at best, is a postulation with very little direct evidence for it. The difference between the two sets of data is far better explained by the social context in which suicide letters and interviews are created and their communicative point.

We think it is more useful to argue that the difference between the two accounts of the future boils down to what the note writer and the interviewee want to achieve and the social acceptability of suicide. Suicide notes construct the future as a gift; it results from something that could almost be seen as a sacrifice. The evil, undesirable person removes themselves from reality making the future for those concerned brighter. As such, as we have suggested in this chapter that suicide notes serve as an assurance, as a claim to rationality, and possibly also as an expression of love.

These kinds of stories in a post hoc interview make no sense at all, as the person offers an account of their suicide which, they cannot possibly fail to be aware of, will be inspected. They are also likely to suspect that what they say might have clinical ramifications. Moreover, their stories will be subject to the usual face concerns (Brown & Levinson, 1987) and other social contexts when in conversation with a person who is likely to be perceived in terms of a power imbalance.

What we see therefore is not so much a suicidal mind that is reflected in the stories as a social context in which an account is made. Any postulation, as particularly research into suicide notes makes, of discovering a particular kind of mind behind the text is surely doomed to fail. If anything, our data show that suicide is a thoroughly social affair whose stories are not exempt from social concerns.

Consider now the following extract from an interview:

Extract 23

> P: I think every person has in life such moments when they simply do not want to live any more. Taking my life experiences into account, as it happens, I simply have more of such moments than others. There is no point in saying more, what is there to be said?

We quote this extract here as we want to point to its latter part where the informant is explicitly giving up on the story. The fragment consists of two clauses. The first one is a statement of a general rule – further talking about suicidal ideation and, possibly, suicide attempts make no sense. The second clause seems to be an elaboration of the former one, except it is rendered by a rhetorical question. Both clauses are ambivalent as to how to interpret them. They could be seen as an expression of frustration or a resignation regarding channels of communication on suicide.

Yet, we think that a more likely interpretation of the fragment locates it in the particular context of a research interview carried out in a hospital. The initial fragment of the extract seems to be an attempt to naturalize suicide ideation and through this, possibly, suicide. But in the research context, with the clinical context potentially invokable, such an account could be seen as risky. And so, what we have is an interviewee who is implicitly acknowledging that her story is done in a particular context and as such cannot continue. First and foremost, suicide and its accounts must be seen as part of a society and its institutions, rather than as windows to anyone's mind. And judging by extract 23, the windows can be explicitly closed.

Let us now turn to the issue of constructing the uncertain future. Informants' control over their future suicide is at best indirect and this absence of control results in constructing the future in terms of desires that suicide should not happen again. As their future lives also are constructed as an unknown, the informants remind us of actors playing their life roles, yet without having access to the script.

We think that the discursively constructed absence of control is significant not only for qualitative research but also for research that ignores the significance of the lexicogrammatical form of language. As we pointed out earlier, researchers have already noted the significance of the thematic content of participants' expectations of the future. Such research was carried out with the use of the *Future Thinking Task* (MacLeod & Byrne, 1996; MacLeod et al., 1997). We would argue that it would be interesting to take the results further and explore how participants construct themselves with regard to their expectations and, in particular, whether they see themselves as in control of the future.

Research on the future and participants' control over it would be useful in the context of suicide prevention and help for people at risk of suicide. For example, the narratively constructed absence of control over a future suicide might be important for discussions on the chronic and acute nature of suicidal ideation and behaviour (Jobes, 1995; Schwartz, 1979). Suicidal behaviour tends to be conceptualized as a consequence of the current crisis which results in ideation and often leads to suicidal behaviour. But apart from suicides which are a result of an acute crisis, researchers have also pointed to chronic suicidality where suicidal ideation is a stable feature of one's life. Schwartz (1979) calls this a suicidal character (see also Jobes, 1995; Paris, 2007). So far, assessments of the chronic nature of suicidal behaviour have been based on data on the number of attempts, a diagnosis of personality disorder, or frequency of hospitalization (Sanchez, 2010). We would argue that narratives on the future and, in particular, future suicide attempts might be a new avenue to explore in this context. We also suggest that qualitative research and, in particular, text-based discourse analysis could significantly complement existing research and, importantly, also offer new avenues of research both in suicidology and in suicide prevention.

The last point we would like to make is the constructed goal of suicide. Before we do, let us recall the classical assumptions behind why people commit suicide. Shneidman (1996) proposed that the goal of suicide is not so much death as cessation of consciousness. As Leenaars (2010) comments, Shneidman focuses on the cessation of the person's introspective life. The anguished mind, writes Shneidman (1996), sees the end of consciousness as the way to end suffering. If, further, it is the psychache, the bearable psychological pain that underpins suicide, then it is ending consciousness that resolves it.

Our data also suggest that it is not death itself that is the goal of suicide. But both our corpora suggest that such a cognitive approach to suicide might not be very helpful. And so, both suicide notes and interviews with people who attempted to kill themselves construct suicide as ending life as it is. And the addition of 'as it is' to the word 'life' is crucial in this account. Suicide is not about life in general or in abstract, suicide seems to be about life as it is at the moment.

Time and again, the accounts we analysed focused on fairly concrete outcomes of the person's suicide. Whether it be life without the person, or life without illness, or simply the peace and quiet that suicide is supposed to provide, the narratives of suicide consistently showed suicide leads to something outside the current life a person has.

To underscore this point, let us quote one last fragment, a suicide note of a sixteen-year-old boy:

Extract 24

> You must be asking yourselves the question why. So, I answer like that. Before they amputated my leg, when I was lying at home, curled up in pain, I was telling myself that when they wanted to amputate my leg I would commit suicide. A person who is healthy and is standing on the side, can only see a boy who has no leg, but cannot see that the boy cannot go with his mates and [female] friends to the swimming pool, a lake in summer. Go hiking in the mountains, skiing in winter, or just go on a trip with his class. I could not live like that. I have had enough looking at my mates playing ball, or going everywhere on a bike. I think I have managed to bear it long, thanks to [first name] and [first name] with who I could always go with for a stroll. But as regards the pain, then after the amputation it was supposed to go away. Yet, you cannot even imagine what it is like when you walk somewhere and you only wait to reach the place, or when you sit in lesson in sweat and you wait till the bell rings so you can change the position. I simply cannot live like that.

This is a dramatic note by a boy who became severely disabled. The boy describes his experience of what Bury (1982) calls biographic disruption. And it is this disruption which is the reason for his suicide. Basically, the boy did not want to continue his life as it was. His letter lists all those things that he wanted to have in life and could not. There is, in fact, a calm poignancy about the note, as he makes the case of ending his life as it was. Indeed, his final 'I simply cannot live like that' makes a resounding summary.

Thus, in contrast to Shneidman, we would suggest that it is not so much the boy's 'consciousness' that needed to be changed. And it is precisely this emotional detachment that makes the note more dramatic and poignant – it is not an account of his inner self or his suffering. The letter is constructed as a sober assessment of the situation. And suicide is represented as a solution to the situation the teenager finds himself in. Suicide ends the life as it is.

If our argument is plausible, it has significant consequences both for clinical practice and, even more so, for suicide prevention. It is particularly the strategies which suggest compassion and the simplicity of letting people speak that we suggest need to be re-evaluated on the basis of what we suggest. In other words, the help is not so much in holding the hand of someone whose life is intolerable but rather in changing that life, whether in physical reality or in the assessment thereof.

Of course, we understand that qualitative research cannot provide a sufficient evidence base for such arguments, let alone action. However, we suggest that it offers sufficient evidence to explore the possibility that such a direction of suicide prevention strategies be explored. The very popular current approach suggests simply talking to people compassionately (Connecting with People, 2015; Dickens & Guy, 2019), however there seems to be little or no evidence to support such a strategy. And while we have no doubt that compassion is a very important aspect of approaching suicidality, our data suggest a somewhat different direction. Indeed, a recent report by the British Office for National Statistics (ONS) shows that there are more suicides in deprived communities than in their non-deprived counterparts (ONS, 2019b). Such research builds on earlier studies which suggest that unemployment (which is up to four times higher in deprived communities) (Blakely, Collings & Atkinson, 2003; Mäki & Martikainen, 2012) and other economic factors such as indebtedness significantly increase the risk of suicide (Meltzer et al., 2011; Reeves et al., 2014). You could say that compassion is unlikely to offer much to an unemployed person in a lot of debt. We think that our qualitative research offers a significant complement to what is already known.

In Chapter 7, we change the perspective of the analysis again. We are interested in exploring visual representations of the suicide process by people who made a suicide attempt. In other words, rather than listen to people's stories of their suicide attempt, we want to explore their own constructions of the suicide process.

Appendix

Extract 1

Z czasem zobaczycie że to było dobre wyjście.

Extract 2

Mam duże wątpliwości, ale wiem że tak będzie najlepiej dla wszystkich.

Extract 3

Robiąc to nie żałuję będzie wam wszystkim lepiej mamę i brata okradałem, a z tobą nie wiem co zrobiłem, dla nich byłem jak śmieć okradałem ich i mieli rację!

Extract 4

Nic mi nie wychodziło. Kłamałem Was i w ogóle byłem złym synem. Lepiej że mnie już nie ma. Lepiej będzie wam żyło i mi. Byłem tylko ciężarem dla Was.

Extract 5

Do widzenia. Przepraszam cię moja mamo że tak wyszło, już, już więcej nie będziesz się denerwować.

Extract 6

Ale przed Tobą jeszcze dużo życia; nie jesteś jeszcze taka stara, brzydka, jakoś sobie życie ułożysz.

Extract 7

Chcę widzieć jak układasz sobie nowe życie jak rodzisz dzieci jak je wychowujesz Mam prośbę gdybyś miała syna daj mu moje imię tak po prostu jako wspomnienie mojej osoby. Chcę widzieć jak cieszysz się życiem

Extract 8

Mamo przepraszam Cię za ten czyn. Wiem że będzie Ci ciężko

Extract 9

Jak spojrzysz ludziom w oczy gdy poznają prawdę?
Mam nadzieję że będziesz więcej cierpieć ode mnie.

Extract 10

Kochany synku mam nadzieję że jak dorośniesz to zrozumiesz pewne sprawy i mi wybaczysz. Przepraszam że nie będzie mnie przy Twojej pierwszej komunii przy pójściu do szkoły i że nie będę mógł patrzeć jak dorastasz. Chcę żebyś wiedział że kocham Cię bardzo mocno i część mnie zawsze będzie przy Tobie.

Extract 11

P: wie pani co ja na przykład nie myślałam w tym wypadku o jakiejś tam kwestii finansowej. tylko ja myślałam że jest mi już tak w życiu źle tak niedobrze że ja nie mam żadnego wsparcia od nikogo że ja jak z sobą skończę no to wtedy już będę miała spokój wtedy.

Extract 12

P: wie pani co to było coś takiego że pomyślałam sobie że jeżeli ja na przykład sobie odbiorę życie to wtedy ja już będę miała spokój z tym wszystkim.

Extract 13

P: Bóg dał mi dwie nogi dwie ręce i nagle zabiera część mnie to nie wiem coś wewnątrz mnie powiedziało mi że: warto skończyć z tym życiem. i i nie przejmować się po prostu mieć ulgę. bo jednak bez tej ręki to do dzisiaj człowiek się męczy bo ma problem przy sznurowaniu butów przy przy jedzeniu obiadu normalnie przy użyciu noża czy widelca nawet przy przewlekaniu nitki przez igłę.

Extract 14

P: znaczy no: mó/mogę powiedzieć nie ma problemu (no nie). no ja na przykład no ja sam osobiście ja czuję że [cmoka] tak jakbym (szukał takiej) wolności (co nie?) ale wiem że już skoczę już nic mnie nie będzie obchodziło by/będę wolny i nic mnie nie będzie nie będę miał żadnych problemów prawnych ani kłopotów. nikt mnie nie będzie męczył ja nikogo nie będę gnębił te głosy przestaną istnieć nie? będzie wszystko ok. ale jednak to jest nieprawda. (.) człowiek się właśnie wtedy będzie gorzej męczył jak skoczy i: dojdzie do samobójstwa niż że żyje. bo: życia (się nie zwróci) a: a jak człowiek żyje to jeszcze idzie naprawić to. (nie?)

Extract 15

P: straciłam sens życia i że praktycznie (.) następna kolejna rzecz którą zabiera mi choroba. najpierw praca dom rodzina mąż wszystko co kochałam straciłam. przez chorobę. (.) i: nie mogłam się kompletnie pogodzić z tą decyzją że ta choroba zabiera mi wszystko. tak siebie nienawidziłam w tej chorobie (.) że nie umiałam z tym żyć. m: [łamiącym się głosem] chciałam to po prostu zabić.

Extract 16

P: ja nie nie myślałam o/w ogóle nawet mi przez myśl nie przeszło że mnie się nie uda to. (.) albo że mogą być jakieś y: inne konsekwencje że może być jakiś paraliż jakiś y: wylew przy tym czy no różne. czy zapa/zapadnięcie w śpiączkę prawda? nie. to nie. ja po prostu uwa/ja ja myślałam że ja to wypiję

I: i koniec

P: i koniec będzie. to miałam (na uwadze). i później właśnie i jak ja (.) y: wlałam to do kawy no i w tej szklance jeszcze zostały te okruszki tej tej tabletki (.) i: ja mówię no to chyba za mało i dolałam sobie herbaty do resztek tych tabletek i zamieszałam szklanką i wypiłam to. i była straszna gorycz tego i (spłynęło) mi się to w gardle i to spowodowało torsje. wymioty. I ja to wszystko zwymiotowałam. i jak byłam właśnie w trakcie (wym/wymiotów) w łazience córka (.) w tym w tym momencie przyszła.

Extract 17

I: mhm. i teraz jak rozumiem nie: nie wybiega pani w przyszłość?

P: nie. żyję dniem dzisiejszym. nie staram się nie sprawiać tu żadnych trudności przyjmuję y y: leki z- m: czyli nigdy nie nie nie byłam przeciwna jakby leczeniu farmakolo- i podjęłam leczenie więc y: (.) y: (.) m: staram się w teraz jakby y: oddać temu leczeniu zaangażować się w to leczenie i (.) kolejny (.) kolejny raz dać sobie szansę. ale nie wiem czy znowu (.) tym razem nie ostatni nie wiem czy nie przyjdzie taka noc (.) taki wieczór który spowoduje nawrót (.) wspomnień i: chęć popełnienia samobójstwa nie wiem. tego nie wiem. te myśli (.) wracają nieoczekiwanie m: to co się ze mną zadziało teraz też przyszło nieoczekiwanie w ogóle nie sądziłam że TAK SZYBKO coś zacznie się zmieniać. (.) to bardzo dobrze y: dla mnie to jest motywujące. że ja jakby niewiele miałam w tym udziału ale (.) ale coś się zadziało i: i: w dobrym kierunku.

Extract 18

P: no nic muszę się leczyć i: żeby takie coś się nie powtórzyło (..) bo to kurczę sam się boję (..) żeby mam rodzinę przecież co nie (..) żeby właśnie (..) wyleczyć się i pozytywnie żeby było wszystko żeby y: jestem młodym człowiekiem przecież nie? […] no: i tak właśnie jest (..) jest najgorsze wręcz człowiek młody jeszcze i ma rodzinę i że takie coś w ogóle.

Extract 19

P: wiem że to na pewno jest straszne dla człowieka. (..) nie chciałbym kurde (.) żeby to się powtórzyło. w ogóle. żadna próba żeby się nie powtórzyła. ((laughs)) czy taka czy jakaś inna, bo to różne są [...]ale to nikomu nie życzę tego.

Extract 20

P: myślę że ja: nie: (.) ja nie doświadczę drugiej drugiej próby ani trzeciej co nie? że jakoś (.) się wyleczę i: i przynajmniej zaleczę i pójdę do pracy i będzie wszystko okej co nie? (..) jakoś zacznę swoje życie (.) tak takim torem jak było przedtem (..) przed tym zajściem (...) myślę, że tak będzie co nie?

Extract 21

P: i i zastanawiam się czy to jest y czy to jest czy to się mieści w tej kwestii czas leczy rany. czy to y: czy ten czas który właśnie jest mi potrzebny czy on wystarczy? nie wiem jak długi to będzie tak jak po żałobie jak jest y: po śmierci kogoś bliskiego. y: czy to spowoduje że ja się z tego w/w końcu otrząsnę stanę na nogi. chciałabym żeby to zadziało się jak najszybciej. żebym: mogła stanąć na nogi (.) jeżeli jest mi pisane tutaj żyć to chciałabym y: żyć i: d/dobrze funkcjonować.

Extract 22

P: trzeba dużo czasu tak mi się wydaje. (.) miewam sny miewam dobre sny. mówię Bóg mi się śni mówi że że to jeszcze nie czas. że jeszcze trzeba poczekać (.) przeboleć swoje. może to jest jakiś rodzaj pokuty za to co dotychczas źle robiłem może to jest jakaś próba jakieś wyzwanie (.) coś co (.) zabrano mi żebym zobaczył (.) jak się czują ludzie niepełnosprawni. albo zabrano mi coś żebym się poczuł że nie daję z siebie zbyt wiele że powinienem dawać więcej. (.) taka si/próba silnej woli może. tak ostatnio to określam właśnie. jak bardzo: odporny jestem na na na utratę mówię swojego zdrowia fizycznego. (.) no i dostałem tą szansę. dostałem od rodziców od od od lekarzy od rodziny (.) no i mam nadzieję że (.) będzie to dążyło to to moje zdrowienie ku ku ku lepszemu. (.)

Extract 23

P: myślę że chyba każdy w życiu człowiek ma takie chwile kiedy po prostu nie chce już żyć. (..) biorąc y: moje doświadczenia [łamiącym się głosem] życiowe (.) (bywa) że tak po prostu tych chwil miewam więcej niż inni. (... ... .) nie ma tutaj dalej mówić no bo co tutaj dalej mówić.

Extract 24

Pewnie zadajecie sobie pytanie dlaczego? No więc odpowiem tak. Jeszcze zanim amputowali mi nogę, jak leżałem w domu i zwijałem się z bólu mówiłem sobie, że jeżeli będą chcieli mi amputować nogę to popełnię samobójstwo. Człowiek który jest zdrowy i stoi z boku widzi tylko chłopaka który nie ma nogi, ale nie widzi, że ten chłopak nie może w lecie pojechać z kumplami i z koleżankami na basen, nad jezioro, pójść w góry, w zimie pojeździć na nartach, czy pójść na wycieczkę z klasą itp. Ja nie mogłem tak żyć. Miałem dość patrzenia jak kumple idą grać w piłkę, jeżdżenia wszędzie na rowerze. Myślę, że wytrzymałem tak długo dzięki [first_name] i [first_name] z którymi zawsze mogłem się gdzieś się przejść. A jeżeli chodzi o ból, to po amputacji niby miał mi przejść. Jednak Wy sobie nawet nie wyobrażacie jak to jest jak się gdzieś idzie i czeka się tylko kiedy się tam dojdzie, albo jak się z potem siedzi na lekcji i czeka się kiedy zadzwoni dzwonek, żeby zmienić pozycję. Ja po prostu nie mogę tak żyć

7

The multimodality of suicide

In this chapter, we are interested in exploring visual representations of the suicide process by people who attempted suicide. We want to explore the participants' own constructions of the suicide process, which are prompted by researchers' questions or the interview agenda.

The rationale behind asking for visual representations of the suicide process was two-fold. First, we wanted to cede control over the agenda to the participants in order to be representative of them. As the visual representation cannot be seen as a direct response to the verbal cue, to a large extent the participants were not fettered by our own interview agenda. Their representations were as 'free' as is possible in a research interview (for use of visual material in the social sciences, see, e.g., Meinhof & Galasiński, 2005). The second aspect of the rationale to go visual is that it is more than likely that all the participants had been rehearsing their stories in clinical contexts. Time and again, patients are asked to tell their story (or at least a part of it) and there is at least anecdotal evidence that patients understand this. In other words, as their stories are likely to have been told over and over again, the patient may tell a story which they perceive as the most advantageous. By asking them to make visual representations, we circumvent this issue.

We realize, of course, that a research interview is not a clinical encounter; however, it is plausible to assume that at least some of the narrative content offered would have been intertextually related to what was said in clinical encounters. Asking for a visual representation breaks away from what might have been rehearsed narratives. In such a way, again, visual representation takes us as close to an unsolicited message as is possible. In such a way, we obtained data which construct the suicide process in a way which is uninfluenced by our questions.

Visual representation

In this chapter, we are interested in both the verbal and the visual aspects of the messages. We follow the work of Kress and van Leeuwen (e.g. Kress & van Leeuwen, 1996, 1998; Kress, Leite-García & van Leeuwen, 1997) who postulate the inclusion of the visual dimension of messages whenever it occurs. Advertisements, textbooks, newspapers and television all not only communicate by linguistic means but also have a dimensional aspect which is crucial to the message. Setting out their analysis, Kress and van Leeuwen (1996) argue that the visual aspect of books that introduce children to literacy is an indispensable quality. The verbal is in an inherent relationship with the visual and is informed by it. Just as the verbal does, the visual in the literacy primers serve as a means of introducing the world in a particular way, a way that reflects the interest of the authorized and legitimized author.

And so, like verbal discourse visual discourse also goes beyond a transparent representation of some external reality (Kress & van Leeuwen, 1996), the process of representation is guided by a complex interest in the object. It is through this object that a communicator arrives at a particular visual text which represents reality from a particular point of view. The communicator can only ever focus on what they assume (more or less consciously) to be a criterial aspect of the represented reality.

Moreover, Kress (2010) proposes that image representation requires an epistemological commitment. When you represent something visually, you must take a number of decisions as to where you put the image's parts and how you arrange them. You also, it would seem, require such a commitment from your reader. As will be clear, the timelines we asked our informants to draw are particularly apt in demanding such a commitment. Our informants had to make such decisions.

Put a different way, we assume that representation is a process subject to regimes of production and reception, which, in turn, are reflective of the ideological complexes present in society. Practices of representation, resting on more or less (un)contested sets of classifications of people and circumstances, are always part of a communicative situation, which is marked by, and indicative of, the power differentials between communicators as well as those who are the object of the representation (see, e.g., Hodge & Kress, 1988; Kress & van Leeuwen, 1996).

It is precisely this assumption that led us to ask our informants to make a visual representation of their suicide process. We wanted to see the particular perspective which our informants would adopt. We also assumed that just as the creation of a visual text cannot be an individual act, neither can its reading.

The way we create, 'read' or interpret a visual text is a social rather than a purely individual act (Burgin, 1982; Eco, 1982), invoking a common knowledge of prevailing social facts and values. Photography and other visual representations are embedded in social and cultural contexts, just like any other form of communication – in this sense, visual texts are historical rather than 'evidence' of history (Tagg, 1988).

And so, we asked our informants to create texts which are multimodal, that is to say, texts which draw upon both verbal and visual resources, and we want to explore these multimodal texts in both modalities, assuming that they complement each other, offering a complex message. It is this message that we are interested in.

Timelines

We asked the interviewees to record the process of their suicide on two timelines.[1] The two timelines presented different temporal perspectives. The first, on an A4 sheet, in a landscape position, represented a long-term process. It consisted of an arrowed line (from left to right) and the word 'past' (in Polish) to the left of the sheet. We decided not to introduce any additional information, such as division of the timeline into units (e.g. years) as we did not want to impose a particular temporal perspective on the participants. The long-term timeline was aimed at getting the participants to situate their suicide attempt in the context of their life. The other timeline represented a day and consisted only of an arrowed line, running from left to right, with no other information. The day-long timeline was aimed at getting the participants to situate their suicide attempt in the context of the day on which it happened. Here, too, we decided not to introduce any temporal units. We wanted them to come from the participants.

Both timelines were introduced by the interviewer and the participants were told they were free to make any visual representation they wished. This resulted in a variety of representations ranging from individual dots on the line all the way to written descriptions of stages of the suicide process.

The use of timelines is anchored within research in which the life course perspective is taken, which, as Nelson (2017) says, unites ecological systems theory (Bronfenbrenner, 1979; Bronfenbrenner & Morris, 2006) with a temporal approach (Elder, 1974). The individual is seen here as an active subject operating in the micro and macro context. Researchers point out the role of time, social context, process and meaning of human development and family life (Bengtson

& Allen, 2009; see also Holstein & Gubrium, 2000). Understanding the individual as a dynamic subject operating in various contexts requires tools for collecting data which will reflect the individual's agency within multiple social contexts and historical time. Thus, timelines are a family of methods whose common characteristics is the use of various forms of time-representation tools.

In quantitative research, for example, it is the life history calendar method which collects retrospective event timing and sequence data for quantitative life course studies (Freedman et al., 1988). Alternatively, van der Vaart (2004) uses timelines as a recall aid. The main advantage of such a method is the increased accuracy and greater amount of information recalled compared to questions from a standardized questionnaire (see also van der Vaart & Glasner 2007). Finally, it can also be the timeline follow-back (TLFB) interview method which is used as a clinical and research tool to obtain quantitative estimates of marijuana, cigarette and other drug use (Sobell & Sobell, 1992). In qualitative research, researchers adapt quantitative tools for their purposes (e.g. Fortune et al., 2007; Nelson, 2010) or to create their own timeline tools (Adriansen, 2012).

Timelines have already been used in research on the process preceding suicide attempts. For example, the TLFB method was adapted by Bagge and colleagues to collect quantitative data on suicide attempters. They studied negative life events and suicidal ideation leading up to the suicide attempt (Bagge, Glenn & Lee, 2013), impulsive suicide attempts (Bagge, Littlefield & Lee, 2013), suicide ideation (Bagge et al., 2014), alcohol use prior to the suicide attempt (Bagge et al., 2015) and the behaviours and affect prior to the attempt (Bagge & Borges, 2017).

On the other hand, the qualitative version of the method was used by Rimkeviciene and colleagues (2016) in research with persons after suicide attempts. They used timelines to understand the suicidal process and in particular the events, thoughts and emotional reactions leading up to the impulsive suicide attempt in the group of adults and young adults.

In our research, the timeline is an instrument supporting the interview. It serves as the initial instrument potentially structuring semi-structured interviews. The participants were asked to mark the beginning and end of their suicidal process as well as any milestones thereof. They were then asked to offer comment on what they did.

In this chapter, we have discussed the results of our analyses of the two timelines we asked our participants to produce. There are two arguments we present here. On the one hand, the timelines on which the participants were asked to record their long-term road to suicide suggest medicalization of their experience. On the other hand, the day-long timeline is the opposite. Here, the participants constructed a day as any other, one without drama or, indeed, medicalization. We conclude by discussing the significance of our findings.

Medicalization and its language

Before we discuss the narratives in which the participants' experiences were medicalized, we would like to offer a few comments on medicalization itself. Medicalization is understood as dominance of the medical view of reality over a lay one (e.g. Conrad, 1992; Ballard & Elston, 2005) or the often-explored question of medicalization of patients' experiences and their transformation into objects of interest to medicine (Cassell, 2004; Mishler, 1984; see also Foucault, 1977). Medicalization is often seen as transforming subjective experiences into an objective account for the institutional record of such an experience. Indeed, studies of clinical notes suggest that they are written in an objective way, with the use of medical jargon, both of which objectifies the patient and their experience (e.g. Barrett, 1996; Berkenkotter & Ravotas, 1997; Hak, 1992; Sarangi & Brookes-Howell, 2006). It is worth pointing out that psychiatric problems are deemed to be the largest area for medicalization (Conrad, 2007).

Conrad and Schneider (1992) have proposed a broader conceptual frame which sees medicalization on three levels: (1) conceptual, when a medical vocabulary is used to define a problem; (2) institutional, when organizations adopt a medical approach to treating a problem in which they specialize; and (3) interactional, when a problem is defined as medical and medical treatment occurs. Under the scope of medicalization are a variety of behaviours and conditions ranging from life events (e.g. birth, grief) and biological processes (e.g. appetite, menstruation) to different forms of deviance (e.g. drinking, obesity) (Conrad & Schneider, 1992).

Such claims tend to be associated with assertions that it is language that is the primary conduit of medicalization. Psychiatrists and psychologists make well-known pleas for not using the 'language of the disorder' (Kinderman et al., 2013), while Gwyn (2002) makes the point that medical vocabulary permeates everyday language.

While we agree in principle with such arguments, we are less convinced that medical vocabulary can easily be identified. For example, if you take ICD-10's (WHO, 1993) account of the depressive episode (commonly referred to as depression), you will see words such as:

confidence, self-esteem, guilt, self-reproach, thoughts, indecisiveness, change in appetite, weight change, ability to concentrate.

Such vocabulary can hardly be considered medical, and yet, quite clearly, its presence in the account of a mental disorder suggests that it pertains to medicine. Indeed, you can add words such as 'emotion', 'personality' and 'suicide' and those are also hardly medical.

And here is the first problem. We can relatively easily identify the terminology which is used in medicine; we can also identify other linguistic/discursive practices in the disciplines. But just because medicine (in the case of interest to us: psychiatry) uses a particular word and in a particular way, it does not mean that it becomes solely and exclusively 'medical language', once and forever. While no doubt there will be terminology which is unlikely to be used by a layperson, there is a huge overlap between the language used by the medic (whose language is unlikely to be the same as the language of institutional or academic medicine) and the patient. And it is worth noting that the direction of travel of such vocabulary is by no means certain, everyday use of words such as 'depression' or 'personality' makes those words' medicalness at least ambivalent.

Moreover, just commonsensically, we speak differently of the common cold, of depression and of terminal cancer. Needless to say, there are multiple social, cultural and psychological reasons why this is so. Apart from a huge variety of contexts in which we talk about such illnesses, we also have goal upon goal we want to achieve with such talk, from apologizing for not putting the rubbish out, through to reassurance, all the way to expressing love and compassion. And these are stereotypical situations just for starters. What about getting a sympathy date, self-humiliating to get an audience to laugh or making a point in a lecture? Which of these communicative acts constitute the 'language of medicine' is very far from clear.

Similarly, the assumption that the 'language of medicine' belongs only to clinicians is quite problematic. A recent language guide created by the British National Health Service (NHS) suggests not only that the 'language of medicine' is not forged in clinical interactions, physical or written, but that it is imposed on the clinical staff by its management. Moreover, the change to what is admittedly quite infantilized language (e.g. the change from 'stool' to 'poo') has now been officially declared the language of the NHS and, as such, presumably, of (British) medicine (NHS, 2019).

It is worth noting that we both remember our mothers' medicalized arguments to get us to do things or prevent us from doing things. One such situation was baking cakes which children were forbidden to eat when the cake was still warm. Apparently eating it warm would lead to catastrophic effects on the body, including death from intestinal volvulus (in Polish *skręt kiszek*). Of course, the 'language of medicine' was predominantly used to save the cake rather than make a claim about the iatrogenic effects of warm-cake eating; there is no doubt, however, that the argument was disease-oriented.

Similarly, one of us (Galasiński) has had a long-term eye condition, commonly referred to in English as a squint, while in medicine it is referred to as strabismus. When an optometrist used the word 'squint', they were asked to use the medical term. It is the medical term that does not carry all the negative connotations of colloquiality. It is the medical term which depersonalizes it and detaches it from the sometimes traumatic experience of wearing a white patch on the spectacles and all the mockery this attracted. What is supposed to be 'medical language' is turned into a useful detour of the lived experience by the patient and not by the healthcare professional.

The final point we would like to make is that medicalization, that is to say, constructing an experience within a medical framework, can be done without the use of vocabulary which is commonly associated with medicine. A doctor's question such as, Do you ever work out?, asked of an overweight person can very easily be construed as pathologizing (and at the same time rebuking) the person and their size. And yet, 'working out', which perhaps has become part of health discourse, is unlikely to be perceived as a language of medicine but it can be used as such.

Still, one could argue that doctors belong to a particular 'community of discourse' (Swales, 1990). They share the same interests and practices and, by using a specialized discourse, they seek to achieve certain goals. A particular role in acquiring the professional identity is played by the medical studies during which doctors learn specialized knowledge and practices allowing them to become community members (Atkinson, 1995). In other words, though risking some oversimplification, you could argue that doctors become doctors because they learn to speak like doctors.

So, doctors' spoken professional discourse is said to lose the patient's voice (Hydén & Mishler, 1999; Sinclair, 2000). Psychiatry's professional discourse, as evidenced by the diagnostic manuals (ICD-10 and DSM-5), textbooks and papers, is described as impersonal, formal, abstract and dry (Galasiński, 2008; Kraus, 2003; Mezzich & Berganza, 2005; Philips, 2005), as it reconstructs the individual and unique into the general and usual. In such a way, practices of objectification were shown to reframe the contextual, experiential raw material provided by the patient into decontextualized professional psychiatric categorizations (Barrett, 1988; Berkenkotter & Ravotas, 1997; Soyland, 1994, 1995).

The preference for objectifying and formalizing discourse can be seen as a local rendering of the dominant biomedical model, which tends to avoid the personal dimension (Double, 2005). And, indeed, doctors may instinctively favour a biomedical model. In addition, they may assume that the adjustment of the professional discourse to lay recipients may question their status as experts. That is, talking medicine at a lower level of abstraction demystifies their profession and does not meet the demands for precision, conciseness, objectification and passivity which are the paradigm of medical science (Zethsen & Askehave, 2006).

One could also see medical discourse at the level of the linguistic form. For example, Galasiński (2008) argues that psychiatry favours nouns over verbs, preferring to construct clear objects of medical inspection. Indeed, when one assumes that nominalization obscures human agency and its social and temporal contexts, it is arguable that doctors did not reach the important information about the patient's functioning. They focus on apersonal, atemporal and acontextual information about isolated objects.

Medicalization of the suicide process

In this section, we discuss representations of the suicide process on the timeline introduced as the long-term temporal representation. The most important characteristic of how the long-term suicide process was noted on the timelines is that, by and large, our participants' experiences were constructed as objects. The typical way to render what was happening to the participants was in terms of things, rendered by nouns. In order to facilitate our discussion, we divided the vocabulary into three groups: first, those words that refer to suicide; second, those which in one way or another refer to other medical (largely – psychiatric) issues; and, third, those which refer to social and personal issues.

Let us first focus on the first group of words (or phrases) – those that referred to suicide. Representations of the long-term process are made with no detail. Suicide or suicidal ideation were referred to with the barest minimum of lexical representation, consistently and exclusively with the use of nouns, such as 'suicide', 'suicide attempt' or 'suicide thoughts'. And so, the research participants made notes of such events as suicide attempt, sometimes preceded with an ordinal numeral (first or second suicide attempt). Similarly, suicidal ideation, its duration or beginning, was represented with no additional detail or contextual anchoring. The participants simply made note of suicidal thoughts.

We see such representations as emanations of the 'discourse of medicine'. Suicide experience was invariably put with the use of nouns, rendering it as things, presumably ones to be identified and inspected. The patients provide clinicians (or, in our case, researchers) with ready-made objects such as suicidal thoughts or suicide fantasies, and clinicians do not need to look any further.

Such nominalizations (i.e. rendering actions and processes as things) make suicidal experience more objective, almost universal, as if the suicide thought of John, a farmer in England, was like the suicide thoughts of Agnieszka, a businesswoman in Poland. Our informants took over such a way of speaking and made it their own, at least in the interaction they had with a researcher. The timelines offer no experience of distress for any patient. All that happens with the person who comes for psychiatric help after a suicide attempt is reduced to a few 'objective' categories which can easily be assessed by the clinician.

The rendering of suicidal experience in nominalized terms is similar to how a wider experience of medical problems and healthcare was recorded. Also, this group of words and phrases reduced an experience to a number of things. For example, healthcare interventions were reduced to the name of the medication (e.g. clonazepam) or type of intervention (e.g. hospital, psychotherapy) or type of problem (e.g. addiction, depression). Experiences that were both complex and extended in time were recorded with the help of a single noun.

Incidentally, in one of the timelines, the informant wrote:

Extract 1

I did not take my pills for two weeks.

Aggressive behaviour towards my parents.

We quote the extract because, in contrast to other such records, it does contain a mini-narrative account of the informant's experiences. The reference to not taking medication is conveyed in the use of a full sentence. There are two possible arguments as to why the informant is positioning the sentence outside of an objectifying medical discourse. First, you could argue that the sentence does not directly refer to a medical/psychological problem. Second, the informant is referring to non-compliance and, as such, it might be easier to render it outside of the medical context.

The other sentence, on the other hand, reframes what is likely to be a complex experience of a number of actions into an object for medical or psychological inspection. However, we acknowledge the argument that such reframing of what must have been a difficult and potentially stigmatizing situation with the informant's parents through a nominalization might also be a way of distancing the informant from it. In other words, through the nominalization the informant closes the space for any further narrative about what happened. We give precedence to the argument of medicalization because it is consistent with the remainder of the corpus. It is likely, however, that the face saving function of the record had also played a part.

We think that the explanation for representations of medical or psychological problems in reduced, nominalized ways can partly be brought from our argument about how suicidal experience was rendered. In other words, if one issue, likely to be medicalized in clinical contexts, is represented in a certain way then other issues perhaps follow. This is particularly so when references to medications or to records of other medical conditions were made. Similarly, references to self-confidence or injury could be explained in terms of the intertextual use of discourses of psychopathology.

Yet we think that there is another complementary interpretation which can be used. Before we present the argument for this interpretation, however, we would like to discuss the third and final group of nouns, those referring to social issues. Here, too, the participants drastically reduced their experience. They simply recorded phrases such as 'divorce', 'mum's death', 'relationship with (name)', 'difficult situation at home' or 'decision to study'. There was no context, no story, only a nominalized reference to complex, sometimes very difficult experiences.

These brief accounts of social relationships are complemented by very brief records referring to the informants themselves. Our informants wrote about the 'state of vegetating', 'loneliness', 'lack of courage' or 'absence of an idea for myself'. All these phrases refer again to highly complex emotional and social contexts, practically removing them entirely from their representation.

The question we would like to pose is whether we could also see these constructions as part of a 'language of medicine', and the answer we would like to argue is in the affirmative. We see these non-narrative accounts of social experience as what is expected of the patient during the so-called history-taking stage in the interview (e.g. Pridmore, 2000). We suggest that both the setting of the interview and the psychologist-interviewer are likely to be conducive to producing an account which is expected during the clinical encounter.

The argument has some qualitative evidence in the form of interviews of patients after a clinical encounter. In an account of discourse analysis's relationship with ethnography, one of us (Galasiński, 2011) quoted the following two extracts:

Extract 2

> I: you know I do make the cardinal mistake and with tenacity. Namely, I do try to say the most, in order to make a diagnosis easier for the doctor. And then I think that I talk too unnecessarily, too much and off the topic. Or that the doctor looks at me with a distance, like at a hysterical broad who is so self-centred and is completely unable to control herself and tells what needs to be told and particularly what doesn't. Without thinking. And has become verbose, and that it is unnecessary.

Extract 3

> I: I mean the doctor asked me to tell her about the whole matter, briefly tell somehow. She listened. And I tried not to expand but just say how it is, sincerely.

A communicative event which is designed for the patient to be able to tell their story (e.g. Poole & Higgo, 2017; Shea, 1998) is constructed by the two informants as one in which they should limit themselves. Talking is represented as a mistake, as the other informant attempts to be brief – only then, it seems, will the doctor listen. We suggest that it is precisely this kind of image of clinical communication that contributes to the brevity of the records.

We would like to end with two timelines on which the representations of suicidal experience were minimal. Consider Figures 1 and 2.

The experience of suicidality and suicide attempts is reduced in the first timeline to one date (Figure 1) and in the other to four dates (Figure 2). Here, too, we see the representations in terms of medicalization. The importance attached to time in the diagnostic criteria of mental illnesses is explicitly written into the diagnostic manuals (APA, 2000; WHO, 1992, 1993) and psychiatric textbooks (Black & Andreasen, 2014; Hales, Yudofsky & Weiss Roberts, 2008), which require doctors to ask questions about symptoms or illnesses and to review their onset, frequency, intensity and duration. Ziółkowska (2014) argues that, when asking about past illnesses or therapies, psychiatrists consistently asked about the timing; in fact, time was the dominant factor during interviews when the past was discussed. The doctors abandoned such questions when the current complaint was discussed.

Figure 1 Timeline 1.

Figure 2 Timeline 2.

We propose that it is the above-mentioned timelines, together with others we do not present here, that reflect such doctors' questioning practices. In other words, when consistently asked about when certain events or conditions happened, it is hardly surprising that the informants respond in such a manner. Their experience is reduced to the point on the timeline, for the perceived need of a clinician.

In this section, we have discussed representations of the suicide process on the long-term timelines. Our main argument is that those representations are medicalized. Our informants reduce their experiences to acontextual objects which are reminiscent of diagnostic criteria. In the next section, we move on to the representations on the day-long timeline – these are in great contrast to those we have explored in this section.

A day like any other

In this section, we turn to the timelines which record the suicide process on the day-long scale. In contrast to the timelines we discussed in the previous section, the short-term timelines construct the suicide process as part of a normal day, one like any other. There is little evidence of medicalization, our informants write few stories on the timelines, sometimes ignoring the timescale altogether.

Let us start with the following two timelines. Consider Figures 3 and 4.

Extract 4 (translation of Figure 3)

> We had breakfast, I wanted to go to church, there was lunch, and after lunch I decided to commit suicide.

Extract 5 (translation of Figure 4)

> Sunday
>
> I got up in the morning, coffee, I started preparing lunch, church, I finished lunch, I ate, I watched television, between 5 and 7 pm I took the pills and lay down.

These extracts tell a story of a normal day. Breakfast, lunch, church, a day like any other, suicide is just another event in an otherwise unremarkable day. What is fascinating here is that the suicide attempts are not marked in any way, including linguistically. References to them are simply put in the clauses next to

Zjedliśmy miodowie, dziś alum pójść do kościoła, potem być obiad i po obiedzie postanowiłam popełnić samobójstwo

Figure 3 Timeline 3.

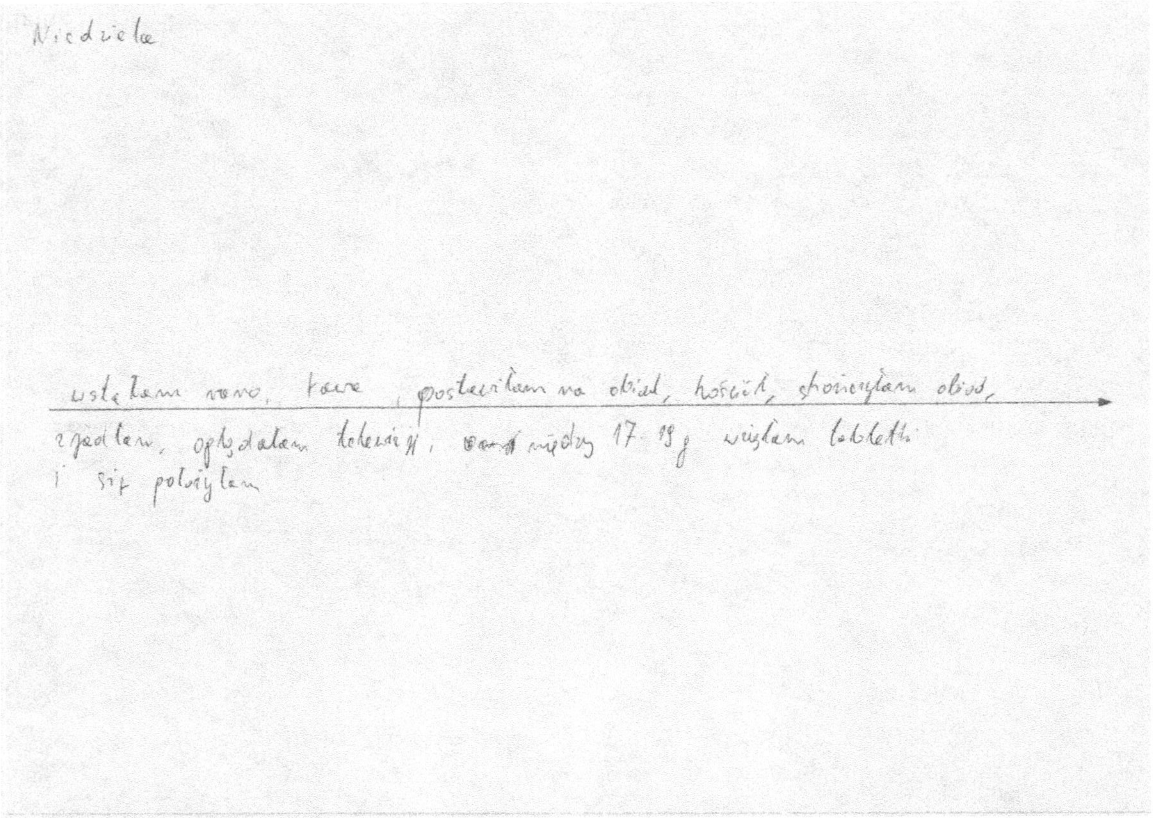

Niedziela

wstałam rano, tozn. postawiłam na obiad, hóśród schonowam obiad
zjadłam, oglądałam telewizji, Około rajóby 17-18 wzięłam tabletki
i się położyłam

Figure 4 Timeline 4.

The Multimodality of Suicide 159

the accounts of the mundane. Suicide becomes just another thing one does in a day like any other. Both the written and = visual records of the day of the attempt contain no drama, no emotion, no significance of what happened.

It is worth noting that the accounts do introduce a timeline, using both the visual representation of the passing of time and references to time in language. And so, we see the day passing by, as if nothing is about to happen, only to end in a suicide attempt. Although very brief, this is a canonical story developing a temporal structure.

Most importantly, however, these stories are in some contrast to those we discussed in the previous section. We see a significant shift from the medicalized accounts of the long-term process to the narrative of the process localized within one day. The nominalized accounts of objects-events from the long-term suicide process are replaced with representations in the narrative mode. Here, the participants actually write stories of what happened. The timelines we offered were used as a basis for the participants' accounts, and the narratives were developed alongside them. It is quite interesting, in our view, that no informants chose to represent the suicide process as dots on the line, preferring to tell a story, however brief.

This negotiation of the timeline and the narrative mode can be seen in the following two visual representations:

Extract 6 (translation of Figure 5)

> It was a day like every day, all was good,
> it was just a moment and I wanted to commit
> suicide I didn't plan it, it came
> so fast on its own

Extract 7 (translation of Figure 6)

> - Conversation
>   about their problems
> - so I no more
> - they helped
> - that they are ashamed
> - Son – how much

In Figure 5, the timeline is entirely ignored; the day is taken in its entirety. The temporality is suggested by the implication of the passing day and the coming of a particular moment. The normality of the day, interestingly, is conveyed

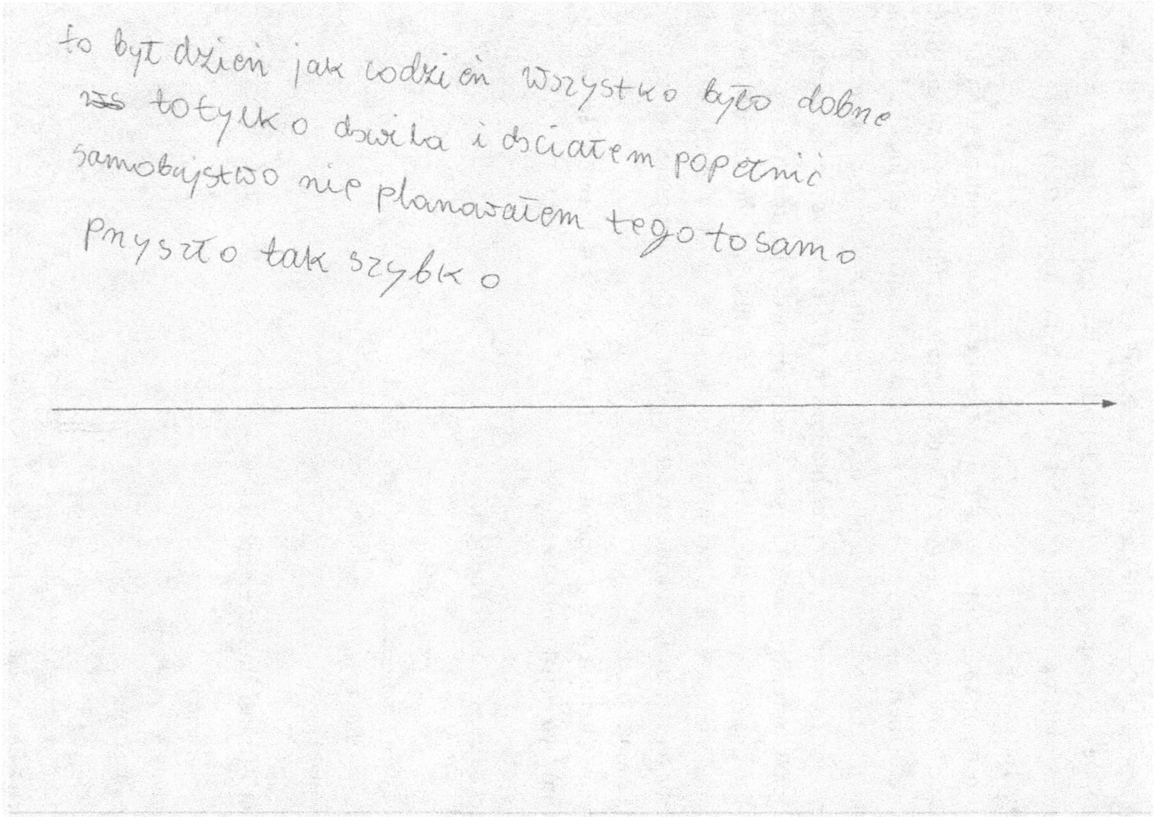

to był dzień jak codzień wszystko było dobrze
tak tylko dziwiła i ściatem popełnić
samobójstwo nie planowałem tego to samo
przyszło tak szybko

Figure 5 Timeline 5.

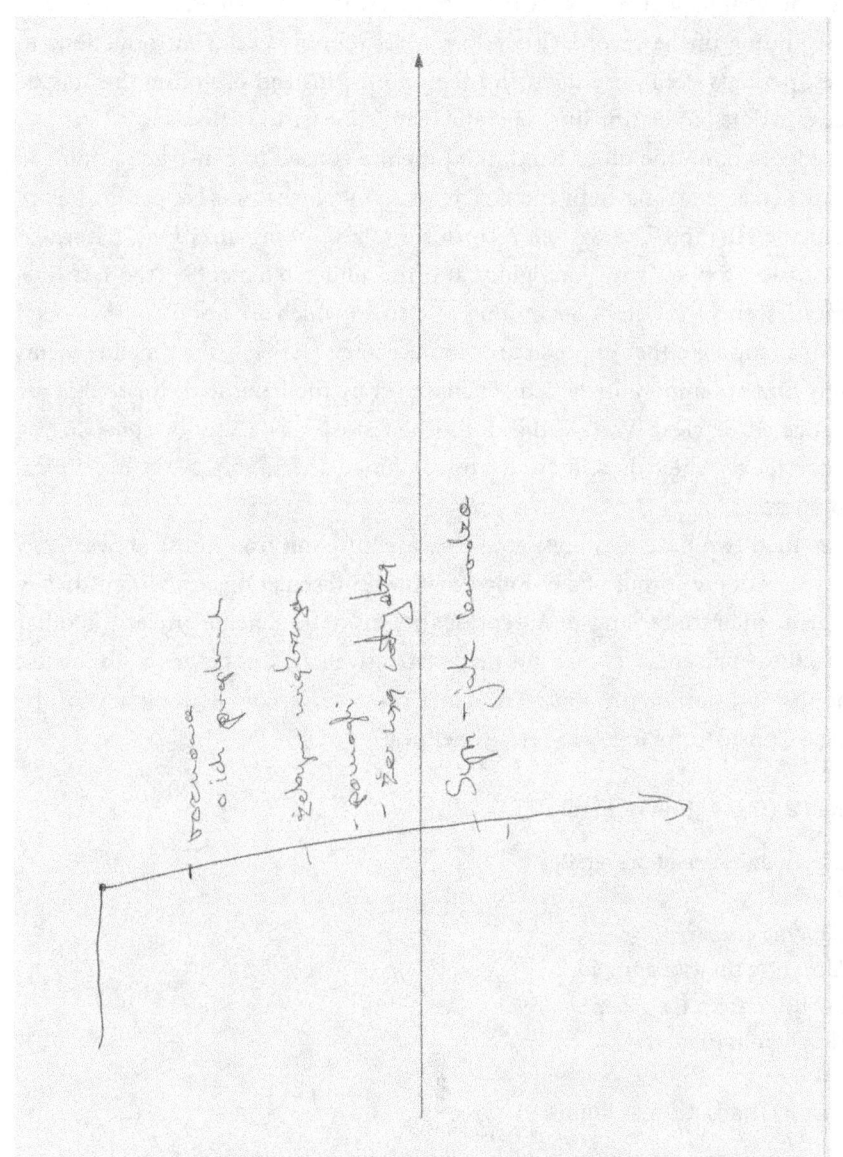

Figure 6 Timeline 6.

explicitly; it is only suicide that seems out of the ordinary, linguistically rendered as something out of the person's control. But we see ignoring the timeline not so much as constructing suicide as outside of time but rather it is a means to represent what happened in a narrative mode, with fully formed clauses. In fact, the beginning of the record, 'It was a day', is reminiscent of introductions to stories, perhaps even fairy tales. In other words, instead of noting the suicide process as dots on the timeline, the informant chooses to write a story.

In Figure 6, on the other hand, the timeline is used to construct a point in time, which is renegotiated by the sketchy account of what was happening before the suicide attempt. The written record is a mix of nominalizations, truncated mini-stories, topped with ambiguity and the understatement of the last line. Extract 7 seems to contain beginnings of clauses which are never finished, as if the explanation is either impossible or unnecessary. Here too, the timeline seems to only hint at temporality which is taken over by the truncated stories that are not finished or clear. We see the unfinished stories as a way of constructing an experience which is still fresh and untamed (Meinhof, 1997) by clinical encounters.

The final two timelines presented here are different from those above. They are atypical of the corpus of day-long timeline representations, and linguistically they are similar to the long-term representations of the suicide process. In other words, the representations are not made narratively but, as before, with the use of nouns and nominalizations. We quote them for a complete picture of the corpus. Consider the following two timelines:

Extract 8 (translation of Figure 7)

>Classes at [name of university]
>Break
>Skipping classes
>Alcohol, a tiff with a friend.
>Exclusion from the group.
>Phone from [initial]

Extract 9 (translation of Figure 8)

>Wake up
>Return home
>Visit with the psychologist
>Cutting my legs
>Painkilling tablets.

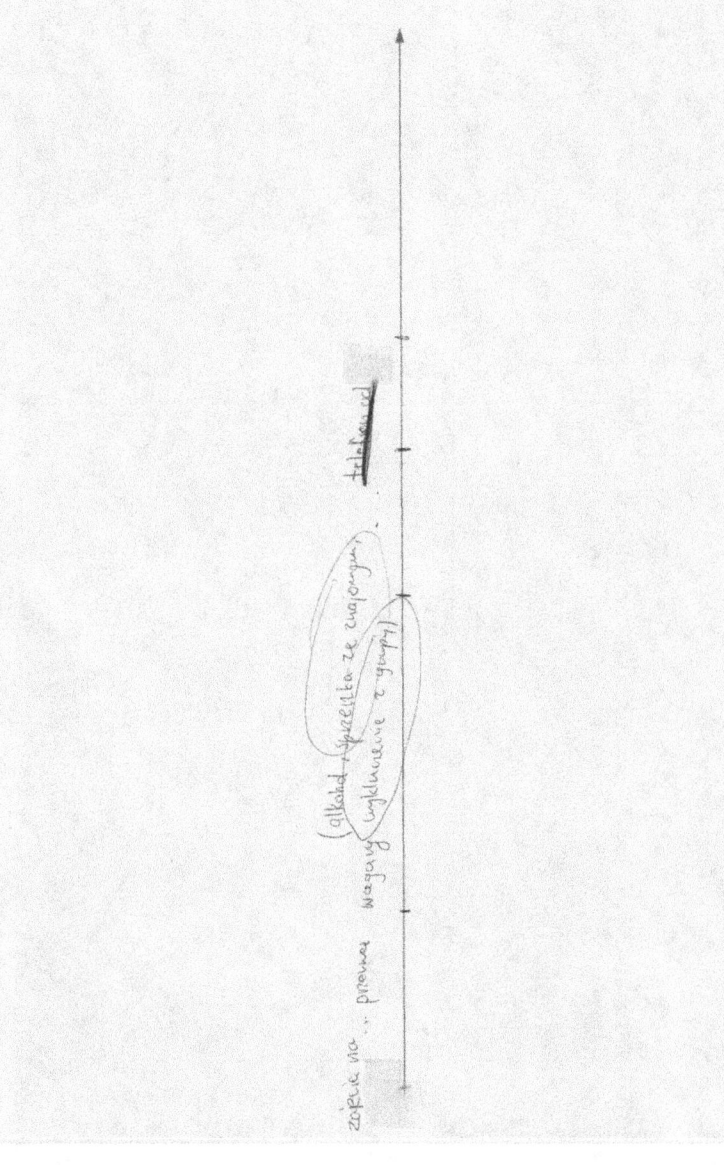

Figure 7 Timeline 7.

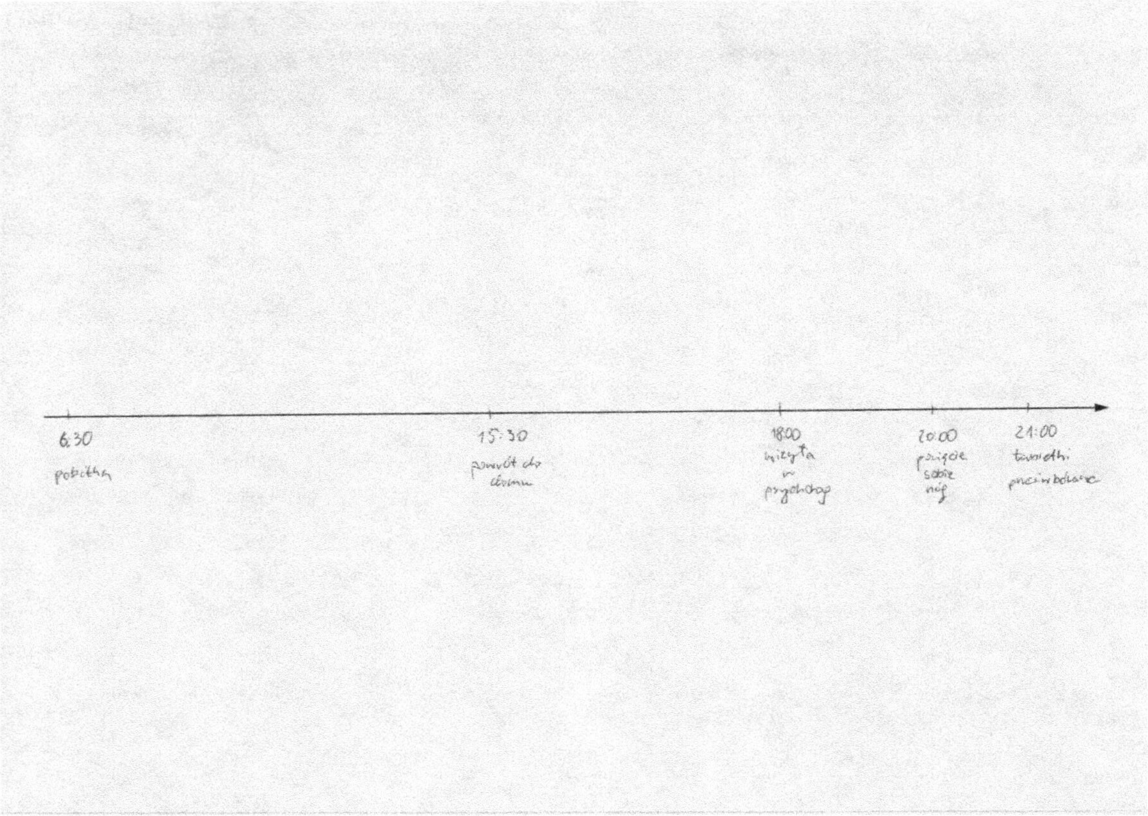

Figure 8 Timeline 8.

Even though the timeline notations are linguistically similar, there is no explicit reference to medical or psychological issues. For the most part, the two timelines also construct a normal day. On the one hand, the informant in Figure 7 shows a day consisting of university classes, skipping them and then being rejected by their friends; on the other, the informant in Figure 8 shows the timeline of getting up, going home, seeing a psychologist, only to end with a suicide attempt (cutting legs).

We do not have a good explanation for the similarity between these two timelines and the long-term ones. There are too many possibilities, including references to a clinical appointment, to taking medication, as well as social issues (exclusion). However, these two representations also construct life as normal. Suicide happens at the end of a series of unremarkable activities, perhaps as one of them. We come back to the issue in the concluding section.

In this section, we have discussed representations of the suicide process on the day-long scale. In contrast to the long-term one, the short-scale representations rendered the suicide attempt as part of an unremarkable day, perhaps as unremarkable in itself. Moreover, this short-scale suicide process was represented in narrative terms. Gone were nominalizations and the nouns referring to objects-events; the informants wrote stories about what was happening. We saw days which were like any other, the narratives constructed the normality of the passing time, suicide was constructed to have come suddenly.

Crucially, those representations were also similar to the long-term ones, that is to say, they punctuated the timelines with event-objects; they were not medicalized, and although perhaps drawing upon medical discourses they constructed suicide as part of a normal day and, ostensibly, outside of the medical realm. The second point that we would like to make is that the difference between long- and short-term timeline representations might be to do with the wish to protect and in the process background painful details. It might be that representing them visually, and through that perhaps giving them objectivity or existence, was too fresh. We return to this point in the final 'Conclusions' section of the chapter.

Conclusions

In this chapter, we have discussed verbal and visual representations of the suicide process. We asked our informants to make a record of the time leading to their suicide on two timescales, long- and short-term. The long-term timescales represented the time leading up to the suicide attempt, which extended at least beyond the day. The short-term timescale imposed the time frame of the day on which the suicide attempt had taken place.

There were significant differences between how our participants constructed their suicide attempt. On the long-term timescales, suicide and all other events were represented as event-objects, in a highly nominalized, non-narrative way. The suicide process became a punctuated series of objects. The short-term timescale, in contrast, was often ignored in order for the informants to be able to offer a narrative. Crucially, suicide became part of an ordinary day. And it is this last point that we want to take up first.

As we have just said, representations of the suicide process in the short-term of the day of the suicide were consistently weaved into the normality of the day. As the day progressed, with the informants engaged in the most mundane of things, suicide was constructed as coming along, as if on a conveyor belt. Suicide became part of those mundane things. What is crucial in these constructions is that they represent the day of suicide as an ordinary day into which suicide is written. Put differently, suicide does not define the day; had it not been for suicide, the day would have been as unremarkable as any other.

We think that such constructions pose a problem for suicide prevention. If the day of suicide is normal, is suicide itself normalized and perhaps legitimized? At the same time, the normality of the day makes suicide invisible or at the very least considerably less visible. We realize, of course, that such arguments are at odds at least with some of the points we have made in earlier chapters. The invisibility of suicide in the timelines is at odds with the explicit acknowledgement of the beginning of the suicide process in the suicide notes.

We see such differences primarily as reflecting the complexity of suicide. In contrast to dominant suicidological research, we prefer to see suicide as highly heterogeneous, context-bound and not easily uniformized.

The most interesting aspect of the comparison of the representations on the long- and short-term scale is the medicalization of the experience in the former case and the narratively constructed experience in the latter. We have argued that the nominalized linguistic forms in which the long-term representations of suicide process are constructed can be related to discourses of medicine. We think that the argument could be extended. The long-term representations could be seen as relating to medical history-taking. In other words, by telling us about suicide, suicide thoughts, taking medication or being hospitalized, the timelines provide information which would normally be sought by a clinician (e.g. Black & Andreasen, 2014; Hales, Yudofsky & Weiss Roberts, 2008; Shea, 1998). Moreover, what is deemed clinically relevant information is represented on a timeline, as if acknowledging clinicians' need to situate largely acontextual event-objects in time (Ziółkowska, 2014).

The wish to locate those event-objects on the timeline, Ziółkowka (2014) argues, disappears with the clinician's focus on the current problem/complaint. Thus, the experience of the suicide process on the short-term timescale would seem to be of no interest to a clinician, nor would the circumstances in which suicide is committed. Indeed, when we looked at constructions of suicidal thoughts in medical interviews we found that suicide ideation was only interrogated in terms of its existence (Galasiński & Ziółkowska, 2013). Psychiatrists were completely uninterested in anything that could be seen as experience of suicidal thoughts. And it is precisely the narrated experience that short-term timelines offer.

There is, however, another explanation of the difference between long- and short-term representations of the suicide process. It is plausible to argue that an interview about a very recent suicide attempt taps into an experience which has not yet been medically processed. In other words, at the time of the interview, our informants had not yet been able to incorporate that experience into the long-term construction.

The final point we would like to make about the differences between the long- and short-term timelines is that they suggest the two processes might not be the same. In other words, much as suicidology (implicitly) posits, there are two different kinds of suicide process, a long one and a short one. However, regardless of this position, suicidology investigates the two processes largely in the same way, focusing on the length of the process.

Our data show that, indeed, there are two different suicide processes, but what they also suggest is that it is unclear why it might be the case. If our arguments that the long-term process is represented in a medicalized form are plausible, then the assumption about two kinds of processes might not be tenable. Rather, the argument would be that the two processes have been created by suicidologists and reflect their own interests rather than the experiences of people who commit suicide or attempt to do so. This, in turn, raises significant questions for researchers. For example, are researchers really investigating reality or their own assumptions thereof?

This chapter ends the empirical part of our book. In Chapter 8, we offer our concluding remarks.

Appendix

Extract 1

I: wie pani, ja popełniam też kardynalny błąd i to z dużym uporem. mianowicie staram się powiedzieć jak najwięcej o tym żeby ułatwić lekarzowi diagnozę. a: a potem nagle się łapie na tym ze że gadam niepotrzebnie. za dużo i nie na temat. [...] albo że lekarz patrzy na mnie właśnie tak z dystansu jak na taka rozhisteryzowaną babę która jest tak w sobie zadurzona i tak bardzo nie jest w stanie się opanować że opowiada co trzeba i zwłaszcza co nie trzeba. bez zastanowienia. i dostała nagle słowotoku. i że to wcale niepotrzebnie.

Extract 2

I: to znaczy pani doktor no prosiła żebym tak właśnie też opowiedziała (niejasne) o całej sprawie i i pokrótce opowiedziała jakoś. wysłuchała. ja ja no starałam się nie rozwlekać tylko tak powiedzieć jak jest i i i (szczerze no).

8

Conclusions

This book is founded on our continuing astonishment with how little we know about what a person does just before either attempting to take or taking their own life. What happens a day, an hour or perhaps ten minutes before the suicidal act and death itself? We have looked at stories of the suicide process, accounts of what happens in the time leading to suicide. When does suicide start? When does it end? Who is involved? What does the act of suicide involve and mean? This book is a counterargument to seeing suicide as a singular event, a moment in time.

We start this concluding chapter by reviewing the main findings of the book and considering their consequences. And so, here are the three main points we have made in the book.

The suicide process

The first and the most important point we have made in this book is that suicide is not and should not be viewed as a homogeneous event, a moment in time. Suicide takes time, and not just the time between your first suicidal thoughts and the act of killing yourself (by whichever scale you measure it), but from the moment you start going about killing yourself. And when we say that suicide takes time, we mean that suicide is a process; it is a series of actions which in one way or another lead to or simply precede the person's self-inflicted death.

The time of suicide is constructed as full of activity. Suicide notes could be seen as constructing the beginning of the process, of what happens during the time of 'committing suicide', and of the end of the process. We suggested that engagement with suicide could usefully be seen as 'doing suicide', the time filled both with the activities preceding suicidal death and, quite surprisingly for us, waiting for death to occur. Quite astonishingly, suicide is not only about doing things but also about waiting for those things to take effect. All with time passing.

Suicide implies finality. We were therefore interested in what it is that suicide puts an end to. It turned out, significantly, that, for our informants, suicide did not put an end to their physical or biological life. Rather, it put an end to the life they were living. Suicide is not about death but, paradoxically, about changing the life one has.

But the suicide process seems not to end with suicide or the death of the person who commits it. Probably the most striking result of the analyses of our two sets of data is the diametrical difference between how the future is constructed in the suicide notes compared with the interviews. Suicide notes construct the future in very certain terms; the interviews do just the opposite.

Finally, we suggested that suicidology's understanding of suicide as outside any temporal or social context constructs it as a largely unproblematic object of study, immediately ready for scientific inspection. Focusing on suicide as an event makes it much less contested, as researchers need only establish the occurrence of self-inflicted death. We suggested this view of suicide is oversimplified and reductionist. Suicidology should espouse the lived understanding of suicide and see it as a complex set of events.

The complexity of suicide, its time-extended process, lends itself to being understood as a highly contextual set of endeavours. And this is the second point we have made in this book.

Contextuality of suicide

As we have just said, throughout the book we have argued that suicide is a series of actions which should be seen not only as time-extended but also as anchored in the social context of their doing. Time and again, we saw suicide being constructed differently in different contexts.

We contrasted the absence of interest in the agency of the person who takes their life reflected in the academic/institutional discourses on suicide with accounts of lived experience of suicide. We compared agency in accounts of the decision to commit suicide in interview data and the corpus of suicide letters, and it turned out that there are significant differences in such accounts. While our informants spoke about the decision to kill themselves in very ambivalent ways, such ambivalence disappeared in suicide letters where their authors directly and explicitly ascribed the agency to decide to themselves. We suggested that suicide letters were given the function of an indemnity from any guilt or responsibility for the suicidal act. On the other hand, we suggested that the stigma attached to suicide prevented our interview informants from speaking directly about what they had decided.

The contextuality of the accounts raise another important issue – the communicative function of the suicide note. Rather than suggesting that the notes are a window to the mind, we have argued that at least some of them should be seen as records of what happened. In today's world, we would see them as private blogs, or perhaps protected tweets, with only some people being allowed to read them. As such, the letter-records are likely to have a multitude of functions, some of them rendered by their linguistic form and some of them perhaps never to be understood or interpreted in an academic analysis. In other words, while the declarative sentences are likely to be intended as statements conveying some information, they are also likely to convey an emotional load which will be understood by those with access to particular contexts. We also reiterate the point made by Galasiński (2017) that suicide notes should never be seen as transparent texts with no communicative functions. In fact, they should be seen as the exact opposite of that. They should be seen as a site of complex, multipurpose acts of communication whose reception will depend on the level of access to the context shared by their author.

The contextuality of suicide also raised the issue of rationality of suicide for us. In contrast to the dominant suicidological view, we argued that the assumptions of irrationality or cognitive constriction in suicide are problematic to say the least. Our data show not only clarity about what must be done but also clarity as to what would be involved. In our interview data, suicide became a project to carry out successfully rather than an act of emotional despair.

The final aspect of suicide contextuality we would like to point to here are the differences between accounts of suicide on different timescales. On the long-term timescales, suicide and all other events were represented as event-objects, in a nominalized, non-narrative way. The suicide process became a punctuated series of objects. The short-term timescale, in contrast, was often ignored in order for the informants to be able to offer a narrative. Crucially, suicide became part of an ordinary day. And it is this last point that we want to take up first.

Perhaps it is the ordinariness of suicide in such accounts which is the most interesting aspect of such representations. Suicide is not dramatic; it is not extraordinary. It is one of the mundane things that one does on a mundane day. Suicide does not define the day; had it not been for suicide, the day would have been as unremarkable as any other.

Method

The final point that has been made throughout the book is our use of two corpora: semi-structured interviews and suicide notes. To our knowledge, ours is the first study that combines such sets of data, as suicidology tends to see suicide notes as a separate issue from considering suicide and, rarely, its experience.

The most important aspect of combining the two sets of data is that they offer different perspectives on suicide. The differences of perspectives are not only those we have shown throughout the book – for example, those of different constructions of the future in suicide notes and in interview data. Such differences go deeper as data differ in a number of important respects. For example, suicide notes are unsolicited; interviews are a result of interactions with researchers. Farewell letters have different addressees and therefore are likely to have different communicative goals. Crucially, the time frame is different. Suicide notes are texts preceding suicidal death and concomitant with the activities of suicide; in fact, they might be part of the activities. The interviews with people who have survived a suicide attempt offer a post hoc perspective on what happened. It is also worth pointing out that suicide notes are written, though the medium has been changing with the rise of digital notes (e.g. Ruder et al., 2011).

The juxtaposition of accounts from such different corpora has allowed us to see the suicide process from different points of view and offer a fuller picture of what it means to do suicide. Moreover, the use of the two datasets, with different representation interests (Kress & van Leeuwen, 1996) and communicative goals, suggests how futile it is to reach a 'true' account and the 'real' suicide. What we see are stories offering a context-bound glimpse of suicide without any semblance of an objective reality of suicide. Indeed, a reality of suicide apparently focused on by suicidology and its attempt to reach a uniform act of suicide must be seen as much more unattainable than might appear.

Researching suicide

Having reviewed the three main points we have made in this book, in this section we would like to offer a few final reflections on research on suicide and its process. We think that the dominant view of suicidology can be rendered as an endeavour to explore not suicide but the reality around it. In other words, suicidology is interested in two main aspects of such a reality. First, the correlates of suicide, predominantly those which can be described as risk factors; second, the warning signs of suicide. Time and again, we see a discovery of yet another, however minor, risk factor, greeted with postulations that more should be discovered. In such a way, it is argued, successful intervention and prevention strategies can be developed. Indeed, in a recent British Psychological Society (BPS) 'Position Statement' these themes are restated (BPS, 2017). In such a way, suicidology remains much the same with a research manifesto of doing more of the same. Suicide in such a research programme remains largely unexplored.

Although we do not wish to overstate it, we have sympathy with suggestions that suicidology as a discipline has reached its end (Lester, 2000). Lester argues that, after years of development, suicidology has narrowed rather than opened up its scope and methodological approaches. Similarly, Rogers (2003) suggests that a way forward is to diversify methodologically in order that suicide itself and not only its correlates can be understood. That is particularly so as suicide is still a relatively rare occurrence and suicidology is unlikely to determine all factors sufficient for suicide to occur (Lester, 1974).

The dominant research practice in suicidology can, of course, be understood. Suicide is extremely difficult to study. There is practically no way of studying suicide directly. Access to suicide as it happens is just about impossible. There are no means of 'measuring' suicide or its experience, as those involved in it are unavailable. We also think that arguments that those who attempted a serious and highly lethal suicide attempt can be accessed for experience as close to suicide as is possible (DeJong, Overholser & Stockmeier, 2010) are overstated. Their post hoc accounts must be seen as having multiple social goals which impose themselves on the account.

Arguing along the same lines, we tend to be sceptical of the multitude of models and theories of suicide, for example, Zhang's Strain Theory (Zhang et al., 2011; Zhang 2016), the Interpersonal Theory of Suicide (Joiner, 2005; van Orden et al., 2010), the Reciprocity-based Theory (Davis et al., 2009) and the existential-constructivist model of suicide (Rogers, 2001), to name just a few (see Gunn & Lester, 2014). They all seem to explain suicide in one way or another, and all are, incidentally, evidenced by suicide notes (Davis et al., 2009; Rogers et al., 2007; van Orden et al., 2010; Zhang & Lester, 2008). Yet, to our knowledge, none offers much in terms of the explanatory power of suicide as a context-bound, embodied series of actions.

We think that qualitative research offers a way forward for suicidology. The significant advantage of qualitative research is that it allows researchers to focus on the act of suicide. Whether, like ours in this book, the focus is wide and looks at the process of suicide or the focus is narrow and looks at the suicidal act itself, qualitative research offers a perspective that has been missing from the dominant view. Without understanding suicide and its meanings, effective preventive or therapeutic actions are significantly hampered, if they make sense at all (Hjelmeland, 2010; Hjelmeland & Knizek, 2010; Leenaars, 2002a; Lester, 2010).

We realize, of course, that in qualitative research, too, access to suicide itself is always indirect. Neither the ex ante (suicide notes) nor the post hoc (interviews) accounts offer anything that could be seen as the 'truth'. Qualitative research is capable only of studying stories or accounts that construct the events of which they speak. As ever, they are subject to the usual social and psychological pressures, just as in the case of communication in other settings.

You could say that such data offer only limitations, while a reflection on suicidological data and their status is, we think, overdue. For example, research into suicide notes seems not to reflect on the fact that many studies have repeatedly used two sets of suicide notes (one from Shneidman & Farberow, 1957 and the other from Leenaars, 1988). Such use of texts across time and culture seems at least problematic. Similarly, the claims that certain narratives have some epistemological advantage (e.g. through the timing of interviews with people who have attempted suicide) over others are at the very least questionable.

Qualitative research offers two advantages. First, it focuses on individual experience. It offers the possibility of looking at suicide as unique actions done by a unique individual, much as in Shneidman's (1996: 5) famous quote that 'each suicide drama occurs in the mind of a unique individual'. Albeit indirectly, in contrast to the quantitative approach, qualitative research is also capable of focusing on the very suicidal act. The second advantage is that, although narrative accounts do not offer us access to reality, they do offer us access to the meanings that such acts have, as well as, practices of the representation of suicide. We not only learn that people say something; we can also learn about the sources of such accounts.

However, we argue, qualitative research does not and should not offer a qualitative version of quantitative studies. Rather, it should offer a new agenda for suicide research, focusing on doing suicide and the suicidal act itself. In such a way, the major absence in suicidological research could be remedied.

In this section, we have discussed research into suicide. Answering claims that suicidology has run its course and has less and less to offer, we have suggested that the way forward is to focus on suicide and its experience. In other words, rather than exploring the reality around suicide, suicidology should start redressing the acute absence of research into its very central concern: suicide itself. In order to do that, we argue, suicidology needs to espouse qualitative methodologies.

As we suggest a new agenda for research, we want to complement it with a discussion of how our proposal can be translated into a new perspective on suicide prevention.

Discourse analysis and suicide prevention

At the moment, psychological strategies in suicide prevention are based on top-down theoretical models (McCabe et al., 2018) with practically no reference to what is known about experience of suicide or suicide attempts, be it through suicide notes or post hoc interviews.

The core of the problems with suicide prevention lies in the assessment of suicide risk. In a nutshell, instruments used for assessing risk do not work. In fact, their positive predictive power is as little as 5 per cent (Carter et al., 2017). This means that for every 100 people estimated to be at a high risk of suicide, only 5 will actually commit suicide. By any stretch of the imagination, this is not a sound result. Incidentally, despite this and the fact that clinical guidelines (especially in the UK) recommend that such assessments not be used, they continue to be (Quinlivan et al., 2014).

Such a poor ability to predict suicide has resulted in the development of new approaches. It seems there are three main strategies for a new approach to risk assessment. First, researchers have been suggesting new tools (e.g. Manchester Self-Harm Rule or ReACT Self-harm Rule) for assessing patients; second, neurocognitive and/or psychological functioning is being used as a marker of risk (e.g. deficits in attentional shifting, verbal fluency, poor decision-making); third, artificial intelligence and/or machine learning methods have been developed (this is used for developing statistical models or risk). In contrast, however, Kapur and Goldney (2019) suggest focusing on the needs of individual patients. They stress the importance of good-quality assessment, a safe environment and access to treatment. Suicide prevention means providing good-quality, individualized healthcare.

We suggest that our approach to understanding and researching suicide and the suicide process ties in well with what Kapur and Goldney suggest. It is the ability to elicit and understand personal narrative as a proxy for lived experience that offers both the researcher and the clinician the possibility of focusing on the individual and their experiences, and through this on their individual needs.

Our approach also acknowledges that risk is dynamic and the individual is in control of their behaviour (action) and desires. It is the narrative in a safe and supporting environment that is likely to offer the best approximation of risk. In fact, so far, the best risk assessment tool used in clinical settings was the single-item 10-point assessment scale in which the patient answers the question how likely they are to repeat self-harm within six months (Quinlivan et al., 2017). While very basic, there is no doubt that such an assessment is based on narrative evidence. We propose that extending such a method might offer better results.

The results of our research raise two other points. First, if suicide is understood as a set of actions, rather than a single act, it must have consequences for risk assessment and therefore suicide prevention. What we suggest therefore is that there is unlikely to be a uniform set of 'suicide prevention' actions. Rather, prevention strategies must take into account the fact that suicide is not a one-off, homogeneous act which can be prevented. We are aware, of course, that this complicates prevention strategies significantly.

Moreover, our data suggest that those engaging in suicide action are aware of the processual nature of suicide. In other words, their narratives show suicide as consisting of stages. If so, suicide prevention strategies should probably not only develop interventions for 'suicide' but also acknowledge its complexity and extension in time. It is very likely therefore that, just as suicide is not a homogeneous act, suicide prevention interventions must be tailored to respond to the need of the individual at risk of suicide.

The second point raised by our research is our rejection of the blanket assumption of cognitive impairment in suicide behaviour. We found no evidence of this, and, if anything, the stories we collected suggest the opposite. Not only do our informants offer complex stories of their suicide (regardless of whether they are spoken in interviews or written in suicide notes), they also construct suicide as full of parallel activities, which, if the assumption of the 'tunnel vision' were correct, should be impossible. This suggests that both suicide prevention and risk assessment and management should not be done to the individual but, importantly, with the individual.

Approaches of collaboration in the assessment and management of suicide risk already exist, most notably as the CAMS (Collaborative Assessment and Management of Suicidality) developed by Jobes (2016). We think that a deeper understanding of individual narratives afforded by discourse analysis will enhance the understanding of risk, meaning and the experience of suicide.

Furthermore, we propose that the focus on the individual narrative could represent suicide risk on a continuum without necessarily prioritizing the patients/individuals deemed to be at a high or low risk of suicide. Such prioritization has already been criticized by researchers such as Kapur and Goldney (2019). Focusing on the narrative allows such decisions to be circumvented and focuses on the individual's experience and needs.

In summary, we think that the results of our qualitative discourse analysis offer at least two new perspectives for suicide prevention. First, discourse analysis understands suicide as a more complex set of events and develops strategies to deal with them. Second, we think that suicide prevention should be focused much more on the individual's needs, underpinned by insight into individual narrated experience. Finally, we would like to stress that what we have suggested here is not revolution. Rather, it is viewing current calls for a change in suicidology and in suicide prevention in light of our research as well as the assumptions underpinning qualitative research with a discourse analytic focus.

Language and suicide

As we suggest a new agenda for research, we want to complement this with a discussion of how to speak about suicide. We want to engage with more and more common discussions about the so-called language of suicide, as they are surprisingly wide-ranging and, importantly, largely based on assumptions rather than evidence. We would like consider the question of whether policing the language of suicide is desirable and possible.

In a recent article on perceptions of words and phrases referring to suicide and suicidal behaviour (Padmanathan et al., 2019), the authors attempt to engage with the much discussed issue of how to speak of suicide in an evidence-based manner. So far, the discussion of such language has been based on assumptions and, predominantly, has referred to the meaning of the word 'commit'. It is argued both in academic discourse (Nielsen, n.d.; Sommer-Rotenberg, 1998) and more widely in activist contexts (Caruso, n.d.; Olson, n.d.) that the use of the phrase places suicide very firmly in the legal, criminalized domain. The very welcome study by Padmanathan and colleagues (2019) is the first we know of that attempts to give claims of evidential validity.

Before we continue, it is perhaps worth mentioning that claims that the verb 'commit' simply and unequivocally makes what it refers to illegal or sinful are simply fallacious. Indeed, we could say that proponents of such claims commit fallacies, which, to our knowledge, have never been illegal. To make matters worse, the verb 'commit' does not need to refer to acts which are illegal. You can as easily commit an act of bravery, an act of love, kindness, or courage, none of which are either illegal or even negative.

This possibility of the verb 'commit' to enter phrases with negative and positive connotations (though, admittedly the former are more common) results from the fact that 'commit' in such phrases can be seen as a 'light' verb. This is to say that, in a phrase, the verb carries very little or no meaning at all. Its meaning is bestowed on it by the noun it forms a phrase with (Butt, 2003; Grimshaw & Mester, 1988). And so, in phrases such as 'take a break' or 'make a request' the verbs are largely irrelevant. You could argue, of course, how light the verb 'commit' is (Nenonen et al., 2017), still the arguments made on the basis of its meaning should be made with some caution.

In their abstract, Padmanathan and colleagues (2019) argue that the study is important because of concerns that certain vocabulary could discourage help-seeking, cause distress and perpetuate stigma. Interestingly, however, in their introduction, the authors offer no previous research that would suggest there is any empirical foundation for such claims.

In what follows, we would like to briefly discuss some of the results. Let us start with the phrase 'commit suicide' which is consistently frowned upon. It turned out to be extremely controversial. What is particularly interesting is that people who 'had been affected by suicide solely through their own experiences' found it acceptable (Padmanathan et al., 2019)! Indeed, the authors quote a very poignant extract of a mother writing about her son:

> *because by the very definition of 'committed', it is EXACTLY what my son did. It has NO implications of being something unlawful or an act of crime, as many suicide 'experts' will try to tell you. Political correctness gone bat s*** crazy. Makes me SOOOOOOOOO angry. Do not tell ME what my son did! Don't you dare 'correct' me!* (8–9, italics in original)

There are multiple questions that could be raised by this written outburst, but the crucial one is how the authors see their recommendations in view of such strong emotions conveyed in the text. Probably on this basis, the authors recommend four phrases: 'attempt suicide', 'take one's own life', 'die by suicide' and 'ended one's life'; however, in our view the argument that such phrases were deemed acceptable to most people is immaterial. We find recommendations that people should change the way they speak, especially those deeply personally affected by suicide, problematic in the extreme.

The second point we would like to make here is that the authors refer to phrases outside any context. In other words, they ask for perception of a word or a phrase used in its lexical meaning rather than as used in a communicative context. This is because apart from, say, vulgarities, it is the social/communicative context which will impose itself on how language users will view lexical items. Viewing them in a dictionary, as the authors of the study did, means abstracting them from how they are likely to be used in real life. For example, words used by people we love are likely to be judged differently from those we read in a newspaper. One could take the argument even further and suggest that you can turn around just about any word commonly considered to be nice into an insult, just as you can turn around almost any word commonly considered to be not nice (or nasty) into something nice. Such is the power of context that language as we know it from the dictionary is only a mere paint to use on a canvas, on which things can appear very differently from those in the dictionary.

And so, as the researchers study phrases, they do not study how to speak. People were asked an abstract question and provided abstract answers, outside of how a word they rank as acceptable or not would be used. It is worth pointing out that the comment from the article we cited above is precisely about providing such a context. It is not about the use of a phrase; it is, actually, about a mother using a particular phrase in a story about her son's death!

The above comments make it very clear that we are rather critical of studies of phrases which are used as a foundation for policies of language use. We would like to extend this argument a little. How we speak about suicide concerns at least four groups of people:

- those who did commit suicide
- those who experienced the suicide of their close one
- those who attempted suicide
- those who are thinking about it.

In our view, arguments about the language of suicide (and its potential stigmatization) assume that they will be taken in a similar way by everyone in these groups although their relationship with suicide is likely to be significantly different from one another. In other words, all those people are unlikely to see suicide and the (potential) harm it does and, crucially here, the language in which to describe it all in a similar way, and are unlikely to follow the instructions on how to speak or not to speak accordingly.

What might be protective for the bereaved families, might not work for those with suicidal ideation. For example, research by John Oliffe and colleagues (2011) suggests that men's wish to avoid the stigma related to suicide can actually be protective. In other words, some men do not 'commit suicide' because they do not wish to cause the pain both of the act and of the stigma attached to it. It seems sensible to ask the question of whether by banning the phrase 'commit suicide', this protective factor is removed for those men.

Now, assuming that a discussion on how to speak or write about suicide makes some sense, let us then offer a few tentative suggestions as to what such discussions should include. We think that it is considerably more important to focus on communicative strategies rather than on words or phrases used to describe suicide.

There is already research to support such a stance. In a recent study, Sikveland, Kevoe-Feldman and Stokoe (2019) show how the strategy of using 'irrefutable argument' helps overcome resistance in situations of suicidal crisis. McCabe and colleagues (2017), on the other hand, show how the form of the questions in suicide risk assessment biases patients towards reporting no suicidal ideation. Our own research on suicidal thoughts (Galasiński & Ziolkowska, 2013) suggests that focusing on them as independent objects might not be useful for patients' narratives. We think that this is the most fruitful and helpful direction of research into discourses of suicide.

However, the discussions on how to speak about suicide in public contexts are likely to continue, regardless of how useful they are. Here are a few thoughts about them. We think there are at least three aspects of 'the language of suicide' that should be considered. First, how to speak about the suicidal act itself. Should suicide be euphemized out of public discourse and replaced with ever more anodyne phrases, including 'a transformative struggle', as was suggested on Twitter?[1] Second, how should a person who commits suicide be referred to? Should people who killed themselves be talked about directly or should they be written out of reports, for example, by the use of the passive voice (so, e.g., by saying 'Suicide has been committed' and not 'He committed suicide')? What identities should such persons be given? Third, for an act to be considered suicide, it must be intended as such, the person must have wanted to do it; it cannot, for example, have been an accident. Should this intention be conveyed when we talk about suicide? And so, should phrases such as 'die by suicide' be used? They clearly stress the lack of agency of the person who killed themselves. At present we do not wish to offer answers. They are very complex and might not be available at all. What we would like to suggest, however, is the following.

The first issue that any discussions of language guidance or policy raise is that, by removing a 'way of speaking', a narrative resource for those who want to use it is also removed. And while certain phrases might be undesirable or unhelpful for some people in some contexts, it is unlikely that they are so for all people in all contexts. Though Padmanathan and colleagues (2019) explicitly limit their recommendations to academic and media guidelines, mapping the boundaries or, say, academic discourse, is hardly easy. Does it, for example, mean that academics should only write in a particular way, or should they also speak in a particular way? Should speaking in a particular way be limited to formal academic events (conference presentations) or should it also involve more informal occasions?

Here, we turn to the issue of professional language. Should, for example, clinicians abide by the language policy? There is much anecdotal evidence suggesting that professionals, particularly in clinical contexts, are asked, required or forced to follow rules of language use and, in particular, eschew the use of the word 'commit'. But this might have significant consequences. A patient (or service user) who offers an account contravening a language policy will not be mirrored by a researcher or a clinician, because they are discouraged from using what can now be described as 'inappropriate language'. And persistent refusal to use 'the way of speaking' accessed by an informant or a patient must be at least disconcerting and potentially undermining. It is also at odds with the pronouncements that patients should be able to offer their own narrative.

All that brings us to the question of who has the right to police the language used. The question is particularly important in the case of policing the language of clinicians (psychiatrists, psychologists, nurses and other healthcare practitioners) and, in the process, potentially influencing the language used by people in distress. We have difficulty with people with a lot of (or at least more) symbolic capital telling other people how to speak or write. We have more difficulty when such pronouncements attempt to influence stories of people's experiences of pain and distress. In other words, at the most general level, the discussions on how to speak must include discussions on the right to speak. Or the right to have a story.

The final project

This book's ultimate project is to be useful. Our most basic argument is that accounts of suicide offering a lived perspective construct a time-extended process, a structured series of actions. These accounts are in conflict with how suicidology understands and explores suicide. We think that it is the unique perspectives of individual stories that are more useful in how we, as researchers, should understand suicide, suicidal death, and suicidal experience, and significantly, their boundaries. The question of when suicide starts becomes, we think, crucial, and it should be understood as a viable and important question to ask. And the lived perspective on suicide can, in our view, be useful in understanding and, probably, helping people who think about, plan to or want to kill themselves.

Our final contention is that text-based studies are particularly interesting when trying to tease out the discourses of people with experiences of suicide. It is the lexicogrammatical form of how people speak or write that provides researchers and clinicians not with solid evidence of social practices and beliefs around suicide but with a solid base for clinical practice. In other words, it is insight into the working of the narrative that can be the basis of clinical assessment as both representatives of narrative medicine and narrative psychology would argue (Brockmeier & Carbaugh, 2001; Charon, 2008; Greenlagh & Hurwitz, 1998a; Sarbin, 1986). And so, we argue that text-based discourse analysis can be a significant resource not merely for research into suicide and the distress of it but also for clinical and preventative practice. Discourse analysis can be a powerful toolkit in helping the practitioner (whether engaged in clinical action or suicide prevention) to unpick the experiences of those who are at their most vulnerable. This unpicking, we hope to have shown throughout this book, can lead to a more nuanced and hence better strategy for understanding suicide.

The classical 1962 film *Harakiri* tells a story of a number of deaths. One by a samurai without his sword, who is ordered to kill himself with a bamboo dagger; the other, his father's, who takes revenge. The first death takes time because of the means – the wooden blade does not cut the flesh, making the death extremely painful and the process of killing oneself very long. The other is long because it takes time to tell the story of the young samurai who had killed himself. We all know that the other samurai is on the way to death; we just need to listen to the story. As we empathize with both protagonists, we also cringe at how long it takes to take one's own life. And the film does not make it any easier – it does take time to kill oneself.

Suicide takes us to the edge of experience. Beyond it, experience ends. Perhaps this metaphor of suicide as a precipice which takes us where we are no longer offers a context in which suicide is seen as an act without structure and outside of time. From such a perspective, suicide becomes only a step off the precipice. We argue for a view of suicide that acknowledges all these experiences. We argue for acknowledging that people do not just jump off the edge. There is much to be done before they can do this. We think that understanding this will not only help understand those people and their experiences but also lead to better ways of helping them.

Notes

Chapter 1

1   The data was collected between July 2013 and October 2015 within two projects supported by the National Science Centre in Poland (SONATA 2012/05/D/HS6/02390 and OPUS 2013/09/B/HS6/02796).

Chapter 2

1   The argument in this section and part of the argument in the next chapter are an abridged version of our discussion on definitions of suicide, which will be published in the forthcoming volume *Applying Linguistics in Healthcare Contexts* (Galasiński & Ziółkowska, 2020).
2   Nominalization occurs when someone refers to actions by using nouns and not verbs. In such a way, instead of underscoring the processual (ongoing) part of actions, language is used to created objects. Normally, actions are represented by verbs, while nouns are used to refer to objects.
3   The noun 'mum' refers to the letter author's wife. This is not an unusual use, particularly in older generations and in the context of addressing children.
4   Polish *trzeba* is notoriously difficult to translate into English; it is an impersonal reference to need, necessity.
5   The use of the phrase *odbieram życie* is likely to be a mistake. The phrase misses the reflexive pronoun *sobie* (akin to English 'onself'); in other words, it should have read *odbieram sobie życie* ('I am taking my own life'). We do not know whether it is a mistake made by the author of the note or by scanning software used to create the corpus. Still, as it is, the note does not make sense in Polish, and it is more than likely that the reflexive pronoun should be read into it.

Chapter 4

1   The Polish original, *Chciałbym się pożalić, ale nie mam do kogo*, contains the verb *pożalić* which is fairly difficult to translate. It suggests both airing one's grievances, problems or sorrows and also simply having a moan.

2   We are also mindful of the fact that English offers much ease with which to create phrases such as 'do suicide'. In our native Polish, such a discussion would be considerably more difficult.

Chapter 5

1   The word *żebyś* can be translated as 'if'. However, the Polish form indicated both the type of the conditional sentence which follows (the second conditional here, i.e. 'if you were') and the grammatical person.
2   The informant uses the word *szmata* which literally means 'a rag', a piece of cloth used for wiping the floor. In Polish, the word is used as a term of abuse, mostly as an assessment of someone's moral shortcomings (when referring to a man, it usually means that he has behaved dishonourably). We chose to translate it as a 'piece of shit', to refer to the strength of the term and its generally negative tenor.
3   This is an onomatopoeic exclamation, used for marking or encouraging a jump. It is used in informal settings, often with children.

Chapter 6

1   *Mieć ulgę* (literally, 'have relief') is an odd phrase. More commonly, people would use *(od)czuć ulgę* which would be translated as feeling relief.
2   The verb *zadziać się* used by the informant is the perfective form of *dziać się* which means 'to happen'. However, the perfective aspect is often used with positive connotations. Therefore, it not only refers to something happening but also that what happened was good and perhaps successful.
3   The use of the passive participle *pisane* (written), stemming from the imperfect verb *pisać* (write), is commonly used as referring to fate. In this sense, if something is written, it means it is fate-bound to happen.

Chapter 7

1   We would like to gratefully acknowledge the assistance of Karol Strizyk who conducted the interviews in which the visual aids discussed in this chapter were used.

Chapter 8

1   Here is the link to the tweet: https://twitter.com/kennnaminh/status/987418133819543553 (accessed 23 August 2019).

References

Abrutyn, S., & A.S. Mueller. (2019). 'Toward a Robust Science of Suicide: Epistemological, Theoretical, and Methodological Considerations in Advancing Suicidology'. *Death Studies*, published online ahead of print, 10 September 2019. doi: 10.1080/07481187.2019.1660081.

Ackerman, J.P., S.M. McBee-Strayer, K. Mendoza, J. Stevens, A.H. Sheftall, J.V. Campo, & J.A. Bridge. (2015). 'Risk-Sensitive Decision-Making Deficit in Adolescent Suicide Attempters'. *Journal of Child & Adolescent Psychopharmacology*, 25 (2): 109–113.

Adriansen, H.K. (2012). 'Timeline Interviews: A Tool for Conducting Life History Research'. *Qualitative Studies*, 3 (1): 40–55.

AFSP (American Foundation for Suicide Prevention). (2019). 'Suicide Statistics'. Available online: https://afsp.org/about-suicide/suicide-statistics/ (accessed 10 February 2020).

Aldridge, D. (1998). *Suicide: The Tragedy of Hopelessness*. London: Jessica Kingsley Publishers.

Andriessen, K. (2006). 'On "Intention" in the Definition of Suicide'. *Suicide and Life-Threatening Behavior*, 36 (5): 533–538.

APA (American Psychiatric Association). (2000). *Diagnostic and Statistical Manual of Mental Disorders*, rev. 4th edn. Washington, DC: APA.

APA (American Psychiatric Association). (2013). *Diagnostic and Statistical Manual of Mental Disorders*, 5th edn. Arlington, VA: American Psychiatric Publishing.

Arsenault-Lapierre, G., C. Kim, & G. Turecki. (2004). 'Psychiatric Diagnoses in 3275 Suicides: A Meta-Analysis'. *BMC Psychiatry*, 4 (1): 4–37.

Atkinson, J.M. (1978). *Discovering Suicide. Studies in the Social Organization of Sudden Death*. Pittsburgh, PA: University of Pittsburgh Press.

Atkinson, J.M., & J. Heritage. (1984). *Structures of Social Action: Studies in Conversation Analysis*. Cambridge: Cambridge University Press.

Atkinson, P. (1995). *Medical Talk and Medical Work. The Liturgy of the Clinic*. London: Sage.

Austin, J.L. (1962). *How to Do Things with Words*. Oxford: Clarendon Press.

Bagge, C.L., & G. Borges. (2017). 'Acute Substance Use as a Warning Sign for Suicide Attempts: A Case-Crossover Examination of the 48 Hours Prior to a Recent Suicide Attempt'. *Journal of Clinical Psychiatry*, 78 (6): 691–696.

Bagge, C.L., K.R. Conner, L. Reed, M. Dawkins, & K. Murray. (2015). 'Alcohol Use to Facilitate a Suicide Attempt: An Event-Based Examination'. *Journal of Studies on Alcohol and Drugs*, 76 (3): 474–481.

Bagge, C.L., C.R. Glenn, & H.J. Lee. (2013). 'Quantifying the Impact of Recent Negative Life Events on Suicide Attempts'. *Journal of Abnormal Psychology*, 122 (2): 359–368.

Bagge, C.L., A.K. Littlefield, & H.J. Lee. (2013). 'Correlates of Proximal Premeditation Among Recently Hospitalized Suicide Attempters'. *Journal of Affective Disorders*, 150 (2): 559–564.

Bagge, C.L., A.K. Littlefield, K.R. Conner, J.A. Schumacher, & H.J. Lee. (2014). 'Near-Term Predictors of the Intensity of Suicidal Ideation: An Examination of the 24 h Prior to a Recent Suicide Attempt'. *Journal of Affective Disorders*, 165: 53–58.

Ballard, K., & M.A. Elston. (2005). 'Medicalisation'. *Social Theory & Health*, 3: 228–241.

Barbagli, M. (2015). *Farewell to the World: A History of Suicide*. Cambridge: Polity Press.

Barker, C., & D. Galasiński. (2001). *Cultural Studies and Discourse Analysis*. London: Sage.

Barrett, R.J. (1988). 'Clinical Writing and the Documentary Construction of Schizophrenia'. *Culture, Medicine and Psychiatry*, 12: 265–299.

Barrett, R.J. (1996). *The Psychiatric Team and the Social Definition of Schizophrenia*. Cambridge: Cambridge University Press.

Battin, M.P. (1995). *Ethical Issues in Suicide*. New York: Prentice-Hall.

Bauer, M.N., A.A. Leenaars, A.L. Berman, D.A. Jobes, J.F. Dixon, & J.L. Bibb. (1997). 'Late Adulthood Suicide: A Life-Span Analysis of Suicide Notes'. *Archives of Suicide Research*, 3 (2): 91–108.

Bauman, R. (1986). *Story, Performance, and Event*. Cambridge: Cambridge University Press.

Baumeister, R.F. (1990). 'Suicide as Escape from Self'. *Psychological Review*, 97 (1): 90–113.

Bavelas, J.B., A. Black, N. Chovil, & J. Mullett. (1990). 'Truths, Lies, and Equivocations: The Effects of Conflicting Goals on Discourse'. *Journal of Language and Social Psychology*, 9: 129–155.

Beautrais, A.L. (2001). 'Suicides and Serious Suicide Attempts: Two Populations or One?'. *Psychological Medicine*, 31 (5): 837–845.

Beck, A.T., H.L.P. Resnik, & D.J. Lettieri. (1974). *The Prediction of Suicide*. Bowie, MD: Charles Press Publishers.

Beck, A.T., D. Schuyler, & I. Herman. (1974). *Development of Suicidal Intent Scales*. Bowie, MD: Charles Press Publishers.

Bengtson, V.L., & K.R. Allen. (2009). 'The Life Course Perspective Applied to Families Over Time'. In P. Boss, W.J. Doherty, R. LaRossa, W.R. Schumm & S.K. Steinmetz (eds), *Sourcebook of Family Theories and Methods*, pp. 469–504. Boston, MA: Springer.

Berkenkotter, C., & D. Ravotas. (1997). 'Genre as Tool in the Transmission of Practice Over Time and Across Professional Boundaries'. *Mind, Culture, and Activity*, 4 (4): 256–274.

Bertolote, J.M., A. Fleischmann, D. De Leo, & D. Wasserman. (2003). 'Suicide and Mental Disorders: Do We Know Enough?'. *British Journal of Psychiatry*, 183 (5): 382–383.

Beskow, J. (1979). 'Suicide and Mental Disorder in Swedish Men'. *Acta Psychiatrica Scandinavica*, 277: 1–138.

Billig, M., S. Condor, D. Edwards, M. Gane, D. Middleton, & A.R. Radley. (1988). *Ideological Dilemmas*. London: Sage.

Bjerkeset, O., P. Romundstad, & D. Gunnell. (2008). 'Gender Differences in the Association of Mixed Anxiety and Depression with Suicide'. *British Journal of Psychiatry*, 192 (6): 474–475.

Black, D.W., & N.C. Andreasen. (2014). *Introductory Textbook of Psychiatry*. Washington, DC: American Psychiatric Publishing.

Blakely, T.A., S.C. Collings, & J. Atkinson. (2003). 'Unemployment and Suicide. Evidence for a Causal Association?'. *Journal of Epidemiology & Community Health*, 57 (8): 594–600.

Bloor, M. (2001). The Ethnography of Health and Medicine'. In P. Atkinson, A. Coffey, S. Delamont, J. Lofland & L. Lofland (eds), *Handbook of Ethnography*, pp. 177–187. London: Sage.

Boldt, M. (1988). 'The Meaning of Suicide: Implications for Research'. *Crisis: The Journal of Crisis Intervention and Suicide Prevention*, 9 (2): 93–108.

BPS (British Psychological Society). (2017). 'Position Statement: Understanding and Preventing Suicide: A Psychological Perspective'. Available online: https://www.bps.org.uk/sites/bps.org.uk/files/Policy/Policy%20-%20Files/Understanding%20and%20preventing%20suicide%20-%20a%20psychological%20perspective.pdf (accessed 10 February 2020).

Branas, C.C., A.E. Kastanaki, M. Michalodimitrakis, J. Tzougas, E.F. Kranioti, P.N. Theodorakis, B.G. Carr, & D.J. Wiebe. (2015). 'The Impact of Economic Austerity and Prosperity Events on Suicide in Greece'. *BMJ Open*, 5 (1): e005619.

Brevard, A., D. Lester, & B. Yang. (1990). 'A Comparison of Suicide Notes Written by Suicide Completers and Suicide Attempters'. *Crisis: The Journal of Crisis Intervention and Suicide Prevention*, 11 (1): 7–11.

Brockmeier, J., & D.A. Carbaugh (eds). (2001). *Narrative and Identity: Studies in Autobiography, Self and Culture*. Amsterdam: John Benjamins Publishing.

Bronfenbrenner, U. (1979). *The Ecology of Human Development*. Cambridge, MA: Harvard University Press.

Bronfenbrenner, U., & P. Morris. (2006). 'The Bioecological Model of Human Development'. In W. Damon & R.M. Lerner (eds), *Handbook of Child Psychology*, 6th edn, pp. 793–828. Hoboken, NJ: Wiley.

Brown, G.K., A.T. Beck, R.A. Steer, & J.R. Grisham. (2000). 'Risk Factors for Suicide in Psychiatric Outpatients: A 20-Year Prospective Study'. *Journal of Consulting and Clinical Psychology*, 68 (3): 371–377.

Brown, P., & S.C. Levinson. (1987). *Politeness: Some Universals in Language Usage*, vol. 4. Cambridge: Cambridge University Press.

Brüdern, J., T. Berger, F. Caspar, A.G. Maillart, & K. Michel. (2016). 'The Role of Self-Organization in the Suicidal Process'. *Psychological Reports*, 118 (2): 668–685.

Burgin, V. (ed.). (1982). *Thinking Photography*. London: Macmillan.
Bury, M. (1982). 'Chronic Illness as Biographical Disruption'. *Sociology of Health and Illness*, 4 (2): 167–182.
Busch, K.A., J. Fawcett, & D.G. Jacobs. (2003). 'Clinical Correlates of Inpatient Suicide'. *Journal of Clinical Psychiatry*, 64 (1): 14–19.
Butt, M. (2003). 'The Light Verb Jungle'. In G. Aygen, C. Bowern & C. Quinn (ed.), *Harvard Working Papers in Linguistics*, vol. 9, pp. 1–49, papers from the GSAS/Dudley House workshop on light verbs.
Button, M. (2016). 'Suicide and Social Justice: Toward a Political Approach to Suicide'. *Political Research Quarterly*, 69 (2): 270–280.
Callanan, V.J., & M.S. Davis. (2009). 'A Comparison of Suicide Note Writers with Suicides Who Did Not Leave Notes'. *Suicide and Life-Threatening Behavior*, 39 (5): 558–568.
Canetto, S.S., & I. Sakinofsky. (1998). 'The Gender Paradox in Suicide'. *Suicide and Life-Threatening Behavior*, 28 (1): 1–23.
Cantor, C. (2000). 'Suicide in the Western World'. In K. Hawton & K. van Heeringen (eds), *The International Handbook of Suicide and Attempted Suicide*, pp. 9–28. London: Wiley.
Carter, G., A. Milner, K. McGill, J. Pirkis, N. Kapur, & M.J. Spittal. (2017). 'Predicting Suicidal Behaviours Using Clinical Instruments: Systematic Review and Meta-Analysis of Positive Predictive Values for Risk Scales'. *British Journal of Psychiatry*, 210 (6): 387–395.
Caruso, K. (n.d.). 'Stop Saying "Committed Suicide." Say "Died by Suicide" Instead'. Available online: http://www.suicide.org/stop-saying-committed-suicide.html (accessed 10 February 2020).
Cassell, E.J. (2004). *The Nature of Suffering and the Goals of Medicine*, 2nd edn. Oxford: Oxford University Press.
Cavanagh, J.T., A.J. Carson, M. Sharpe, & S.M. Lawrie. (2003). 'Psychological Autopsy Studies of Suicide: A Systematic Review'. *Psychological Medicine*, 33 (3): 395–405.
Cerel, J., J.L. McIntosh, R.A. Neimeyer, M. Maple, & D. Marshall. (2014). 'The Continuum of "Survivorship": Definitional Issues in the Aftermath of Suicide'. *Suicide and Life-Threatening Behavior*, 44 (6): 591–600.
Charon, R. (2008). *Narrative Medicine: Honoring the Stories of Illness*. Oxford: Oxford University Press.
Chen, Y.W., & S.C. Dilsaver. (1996). 'Lifetime Rates of Suicide Attempts Among Subjects with Bipolar and Unipolar Disorders Relative to Subjects with Other Axis I Disorders'. *Biological Psychiatry*, 39 (10): 896–899.
Chouliaraki, L., & N. Fairclough. (1999). *Discourse in Late Modernity*. Edinburgh: Edinburgh University Press.
Colucci, E. (2013). 'Culture, Cultural Meaning(s), and Suicide'. In E. Colucci & D. Lester (eds), *Suicide and Culture: Understanding the Context*, pp. 25–46. Cambridge, MA: Hogrefe Publishing.

Conaghan, S., & K.M. Davidson. (2002). 'Hopelessness and the Anticipation of Positive and Negative Future Experiences in Older Parasuicidal Adults'. *British Journal of Clinical Psychology*, 41 (3): 233–242.

Connecting with People. (2015). 'NHS and Social Care Training'. Available online: connectingwithpeople.org (accessed 10 February 2020).

Conrad, P. (1992). 'Medicalization and Social Control'. *Annual Review of Sociology*, 18 (1): 209–232.

Conrad, P. (2007). *The Medicalization of Society: On the Transformation of Human Conditions into Treatable Disorders*. Baltimore, MD: Johns Hopkins University Press.

Conrad, P., & J.W. Schneider. (1992). *Deviance and Medicalization: From Badness to Sickness*, exp. edn. Philadelphia: Temple University Press.

Conwell, Y., P.R. Duberstein, C. Cox, J.H. Herrmann, N.T. Forbes, & E.D. Caine. (1996). 'Relationships of Age and Axis I Diagnoses in Victims of Completed Suicide: A Psychological Autopsy Study'. *American Journal of Psychiatry*, 153: 1001–1008.

Corrigan, P.W., A. Kerr, & L. Knudsen. (2005). 'The Stigma of Mental Illness'. *Applied and Preventive Psychology*, 11: 179–190.

Corrigan, P.W., & A.K. Matthews. (2003). 'Stigma and Disclosure'. *Journal of Mental Health*, 12: 235–248.

Costa, D.S., R. Mercieca-Bebber, S. Tesson, Z. Seidler, & A.L. Lopez. (2019). 'Patient, Client, Consumer, Survivor or Other Alternatives? A Scoping Review of Preferred Terms for Labelling Individuals Who Access Healthcare Across Settings'. *BMJ Open*, 9 (3): e025166.

Crosby, A.E., M.P. Cheltenham, & J.J. Sacks. (1999). 'Incidence of Suicidal Ideation and Behavior in the United States, 1994'. *Suicide and Life-Threatening Behavior*, 29 (2): 131–140.

Crosby, A.E., L. Ortega, & C. Melanson. (2011). *Self-Directed Violence Surveillance: Uniform Definitions and Recommended Data Elements*. Atlanta, GA: Centers for Disease Control and Prevention.

Davidson, L. (2003). *Living Outside Mental Illness*. New York: New York University Press.

Davis, J.H. (1988). 'Suicidal Investigation and Classification of Death by Coroners and Medical Examiners'. In J. Nolan (ed.), *The Suicide Case: Investigation and Trial of Insurance Claims. Tort and Insurance Practice Section*, pp. 33–50. Washington, DC: American Bar Association.

Davis, M.S., V.J. Callanan, D. Lester, & J. Haines. (2009). 'An Inquiry into Relationship Suicides and Reciprocity'. *Suicide and Life-Threatening Behavior*, 39 (5): 482–498.

De Leo, D., S. Burgis, J.M. Bertolote, A.J. Kerkhof, & U. Bille-Brahe. (2004). 'Definitions of Suicidal Behavior'. In D. De Leo, U. Bille-Brahe, A. Kerhof, & A. Schmidtke (eds), *Suicidal Behavior: Theories and Research Findings*, pp. 17–39. Washington, DC: Hogrefe & Huber.

De Leo, D., S. Burgis, J.M. Bertolote, A.J. Kerkhof, & U. Bille-Brahe. (2006). 'Definitions of Suicidal Behavior: Lessons Learned from the WHO/EURO Multicentre Study'. *Crisis*, 27 (1): 4–15.

Dear, G. (2001). 'Further Comments on the Nomenclature for Suicide-Related Thoughts and Behavior'. *Suicide and Life-Threatening Behavior*, 31 (2): 234–235.

Deisenhammer, E.A., R. Strauss, G. Kemmler, H. Hinterhuber, & E.M. Weiss. (2009). 'The Duration of the Suicidal Process: How Much Time Is Left for Intervention Between Consideration and Accomplishment of a Suicide Attempt?'. *Journal of Clinical Psychiatry*, 70 (1): 19–24.

DeJong, T.M., J.C. Overholser, & C.A. Stockmeier. (2010). 'Apples to Oranges?: A Direct Comparison Between Suicide Attempters and Suicide Completers'. *Journal of Affective Disorders*, 124 (1–2): 90–97.

Denzin, N.K. (1989). *The Research Act: A Theoretical Introduction to Social Methods*. London: Prentice Hall.

Denzin, N.K., & Y.S. Lincoln (eds). (2000). *Handbook of Qualitative Research*. London: Sage.

Dickens, C., & S. Guy. (2019). '"Three Minutes to Save a Life": Addressing Emotional Distress in Students to Mitigate the Risk of Suicide'. *Mental Health Practice*, 22 (3): 22–27.

Double, D. (2005). 'Beyond Biomedical Models: A Perspective from Critical Psychiatry'. In J. Tew (ed.), *Social Perspectives in Mental Health: Developing Social Models to Understand and Work with Mental Distress*, pp. 53–70. London: Jessica Kingsley.

Eco, U. (1982). 'Critique of the Image'. In V. Burgin (ed.), *Thinking Photography*, pp. 32–38. London: Palgrave.

Elder, G. Jr. (1974). *Children of the Great Depression: Social Change in Life Experience*. Chicago: University of Chicago Press.

Erdner, A., A. Magnusson, M. Nystro, & K. Lütze. (2005). 'Social and Existential Alienation Experienced by People with Long-Term Mental Illness'. *Scandinavian Journal of Caring Sciences*, 19: 373–380.

Fairbairn, G. (1995), 'Defining suicide'. In G. Fairbairn (ed.), *Contemplating Suicide: The Language and Ethics of Self-Harm*, pp. 68–83. New York: Psychology Press.

Fairbairn, G. (2003). *Contemplating Suicide: The Language and Ethics of Self-Harm*. London: Routledge.

Fairclough, N. (1989). *Language and Power*. London: Longman.

Fairclough, N. (1992). *Discourse and Social Change*. Oxford: Polity Press.

Fairclough, N. (1995). *Critical Discourse Analysis*. London: Longman.

Fairclough, N. (2003). *Analysing Discourse*. London: Routledge.

Fairclough, N., & R. Wodak. (1997). 'Critical Discourse Analysis'. In T.A. van Dijk (ed.), *Discourse As Social Interaction*, pp. 258–284. London: Sage.

Farberow, N.L. (ed.). (1980). *The Many Faces of Suicide: Indirect Self-Destructive Behavior*. New York: McGraw-Hill.

Feigelman, W., B.S. Gorman, & J.R. Jordan. (2009). 'Stigmatization and Suicide Bereavement'. *Death Studies*, 33 (7): 591–608.

Fergusson, D., S. Doucette, K.C. Glass, S. Shapiro, D. Healy, P. Hebert, & B. Hutton. (2005). 'Association Between Suicide Attempts and Selective Serotonin Reuptake

Inhibitors: Systematic Review of Randomised Controlled Trials'. *British Medical Journal*, 330 (7488): 396.
Fitzpatrick, S. (2011). 'Looking Beyond the Qualitative and Quantitative Divide: Narrative, Ethics and Representation in Suicidology'. *Suicidology Online*, 2: 29–37.
Fitzpatrick, S.J. (2015). 'Scientism as a Social Response to the Problem of Suicide'. *Journal of Bioethical Inquiry*, 12 (4): 613–622.
Flynn, S., T. Nyathi, S.G. Tham, A. Williams, K. Windfuhr, N. Kapur, L. Appleby, & J. Shaw. (2017). 'Suicide by Mental Health In-Patients Under Observation'. *Psychological Medicine*, 47 (13): 2238–2245. doi: 10.1017/S0033291717000630.
Fortune, S., A. Stewart, V. Yadav, & K. Hawton. (2007). 'Suicide in Adolescents: Using Life Charts to Understand the Suicidal Process'. *Journal of Affective Disorders*, 100 (1–3): 199–210.
Foucault, M. (1977). *Discipline and Punish*. London: Allen Lane.
Foucault, M. (2002). *Porządek dyskursu*. Gdańsk: słowo/obraz terytoria.
Fowler, R. (1985). 'Power'. In T.A. Van Dijk (ed.), *Handbook of Discourse Analysis*, vol. 4, pp. 61–82. London: Academic Press.
Fowler, R. (1991). *Language in the News*. London: Routledge.
Fowler, R. (1996). 'On Critical Linguistics'. In R.C. Caldas-Coulthard & M. Coulthard (eds), *Texts and Practices*, pp. 3–14. London: Routledge.
Fowler, R., B. Hodge, G. Kress, & T. Trew (eds). (1979). *Language and Control*. London: Routledge.
Freedman, D., A. Thorton, D. Camburn, D. Alwin, & L. Young-DeMarco. (1988). 'The LHC: A Technique for Collecting Retrospective Data'. *Sociological Methodology*, 18: 37–68.
Fullagar, S. (2003). 'Wasted Lives. The Social Dynamics of Shame and Youth Suicide'. *Journal of Sociology*, 39 (3): 291–307.
Fushimi, M., J. Sugawara, & S. Saito. (2006). 'Comparison of Completed and Attempted Suicide in Akita, Japan'. *Psychiatry and Clinical Neurosciences*, 60 (3): 289–295.
Galasiński, D. (2004). *Men and the Language of Emotions*. Basingstoke: Palgrave.
Galasiński, D. (2008). *Men's Discourses of Depression*. Basingstoke: Palgrave Macmillan.
Galasiński, D. (2011). 'The Patient's World: Discourse Analysis and Ethnography'. *Critical Discourse Studies*, 8 (4): 253–265.
Galasiński, D. (2013). *Fathers, Fatherhood and Mental Illness: A Discourse Analysis of Rejection*. Basingstoke: Palgrave Macmillan.
Galasiński, D. (2017). *Discourses of Men's Suicide Notes: A Qualitative Analysis*. London: Bloomsbury.
Galasiński, D., & J. Ziółkowska. (2013). 'Experience of Suicidal Thoughts: A Discourse Analytic Study'. *Communication & Medicine*, 10 (2): 117–127.
Galasiński D., & J. Ziółkowska. (2020). 'A Moment Outside Time. A Critical Discourse Analytic Perspective on Dominant Constructions of Suicide'. In Z. Demjen (ed.), *Applying Linguistics in Illness and Healthcare Contexts*. London: Bloomsbury.
Gavin, M., & A. Rogers. (2006). 'Narratives of Suicide in Psychological Autopsy: Bringing Lay Knowledge Back In'. *Journal of Mental Health*, 15 (2): 135–144.

Goldblatt, M.J., M. Schechter, J.T. Maltsberger, & E. Ronningstam. (2012). 'Comparison of Journals of Suicidology'. *Crisis*, 33 (5): 301–305.
Goldsmith, S.K., T.C. Pellmar, A.M. Kleinman, & W.E. Bunney (eds). (2002). *Reducing Suicide: A National Imperative*. Washington, DC: National Academies Press.
Goodfellow, B., K. Kõlves, & D. De Leo. (2018). 'Contemporary Nomenclatures of Suicidal Behaviors: A Systematic Literature Review'. *Suicide and Life-Threatening Behavior*, 48 (3): 353–366.
Gordon, E., C. Stevenson, & J.R. Cutcliffe. (2014). 'Transcending Suicidality: Facilitating Re-Vitalizing Worthiness'. In J.R. Cutclliffe, J.C. Santos, P.S. Links, J. Zaheer, H.G. Harder, F. Campbell, R. McCormick, K. Harder, Y. Bergmans & R. Eynan (eds), *Routledge International Handbook of Clinical Suicide Research*, pp. 39–51. New York: Routledge.
Greenlagh, T., & B. Hurwitz. (1998a). 'Why Study Narrative?'. In T. Greenlagh & B. Hurwitz (eds), *Narrative Based Medicine*, pp. 3–16. London: British Medical Journal.
Greenlagh, T., & B. Hurwitz (eds). (1998b). *Narrative Based Medicine*. London: British Medical Journal.
Grice, P. (1975). 'Logic and Conversation'. In P. Cole & J. Morgan (eds), *Syntax and Semantics, Speech Acts*, vol. 3, pp. 41–58. New York: Academic Press.
Grimshaw, J., & A. Mester. (1988). 'Light Verbs and Θ-Marking'. *Linguistic Inquiry*, 19 (2): 205–232.
Gunn, J.F., & D. Lester. (2014). *Theories of Suicide. Past, Present and Future*. Springfield: Charles C. Thomas Publisher.
Gunnell, D., J. Saperia, & D. Ashby. (2005). 'Selective Serotonin Reuptake Inhibitors (SSRIs) and Suicide in Adults: Meta-Analysis of Drug Company Data from Placebo Controlled, Randomised Controlled Trials Submitted to the MHRA's Safety Review'. *British Medical Journal*, 330 (7488): 385.
Gwyn, R. (2002). *Communicating Health and Illness*. London: Sage.
Hacking, I. (1990). *The Taming of Chance*. Cambridge: Cambridge University Press.
Haines, J., C.L. Williams, & D. Lester. (2011). 'The Characteristics of Those Who Do and Do Not Leave Suicide Notes: Is the Method of Residuals Valid?'. *OMEGA-Journal of Death and Dying*, 63 (1): 79–94.
Hak, T. (1992). 'Psychiatric Records as Transformations of Other Texts'. In G. Watson and R.M. Seiler (eds), *Text in Context: Contributions to Ethnomethodology*, pp. 138–155. Newbury Park, CA: Sage.
Hales, R.E., S.C. Yudofsky, & L. Weiss Roberts (eds). (2008). *The American Psychiatric Publishing Textbook of Psychiatry*. Washington, DC: American Psychiatric Publishing.
Hall, S. (1981). 'Encoding/Decoding'. In S. Hall, D. Hobson, A. Lowe & P. Willis (eds), *Culture, Media, Language*, pp. 128–138. London: Hutchinson.
Hall, S. (1996a). 'For Allon White: Metaphors of Transformation'. In D. Morley & D.-K. Chen (eds), *Stuart Hall*, pp. 287–307. London: Routledge.
Hall, S. (1996b). 'The Problem of Ideology'. In D. Morley & D.-K. Chen (eds), *Stuart Hall*, pp. 24–45. London: Routledge.

Hall, S. (1997). 'The Work of Representation'. In S. Hall (ed.), *Representation: Cultural Representation and Signifying Practices*, pp. 13–74. London: Sage.

Halliday, M.A.K. (1978). *Language as Social Semiotic*. London: Edward Arnold.

Halliday, M.A.K. (1994). *An Introduction to Functional Grammar*, 2nd edn. London: Edward Arnold.

Halliday, M.A.K., & R. Hasan. (1985). *Language, Context, and Text*. Oxford: Oxford University Press.

Hammersley, M. (2008). *Questioning Qualitative Inquiry: Critical Essays*. London: Sage.

Harris, E.C., & B. Barraclough. (1997). 'Suicide as an Outcome for Mental Disorders. A Meta-Analysis'. *British Journal of Psychiatry*, 170 (3): 205–228.

Hartley, J. (1988). *Understanding News*. London: Routledge.

Hayward, P., & J.A. Bright. (1997). 'Stigma and Mental Illness'. *Journal of Mental Health*, 6: 345–354.

Hecht, J.M. (2013). *Stay. A History of Suicide and the Arguments Against It*. New Haven, CT: Yale University Press.

Hendin, H., J.T. Maltsberger, A. Lipschitz, A.P. Haas, & J. Kyle. (2001). 'Recognizing and Responding to a Suicide Crisis'. *Annals of the New York Academy of Sciences*, 932 (1): 169–187.

Hepburn, A., & G. Bolden. (2013). 'The Conversation Analytic Approach to Transcription'. In T. Stivers & J. Sidnell (eds), *The Blackwell Handbook of Conversation Analysis*, pp. 57–76. Oxford: Blackwell.

Hepburn, A., & G. Bolden. (2017). *Transcribing for Social Research*. London: Sage.

Hill, D.J. (2011), 'What Is It to Commit Suicide?'. *Ratio*, 24: 192–205.

Hjelmeland, H. (2010). 'Cultural Research in Suicidology: Challenges and Opportunities'. *Suicidology Online*, 1: 34–52.

Hjelmeland, H. (2016). 'A Critical Look at Current Suicide Research'. In J. White, I. Marsh, M. Kral & J. Morris (eds), *Critical Suicidology. Transforming Suicide Research and Prevention for the 21st Century*, pp. 31–55. Vancouver: UBC Press.

Hjelmeland, H., & B.L. Knizek. (2010). 'Why We Need Qualitative Research in Suicidology'. *Suicide and Life-Threatening Behavior*, 40 (1): 74–80.

Hjelmeland, H., & B.L. Knizek. (2011). 'Methodology in Suicidological Research-Contribution to the Debate'. *Suicidology Online*, 2: 8–10.

Hjelmeland, H., & B.L. Knizek. (2019). 'The Emperor's New Clothes? A Critical Look at the Interpersonal Theory of Suicide'. *Death Studies*, 1: 1–11.

Hodge, R., & G. Kress. (1988). *Social Semiotics*. Oxford: Polity Press.

Hodge, R., & G. Kress. (1993). *Language as Ideology*. London: Routledge.

Holstein, J.A., & J.F. Gubrium. (2000). *Constructing the Life Course*. Lanham, MD: Rowman & Littlefield.

Hudzik, T.J., & K.E. Cannon. (2014). 'Introduction'. In K.E. Cannon & T.J. Hudzik (eds), *Suicide: Phenomenology and Neurobiology*, pp. 1–7. Heidelberg: Springer.

Hunter, E.C., & R.C. O'Connor. (2003). 'Hopelessness and Future Thinking in Parasuicide: The Role of Perfectionism'. *British Journal of Clinical Psychology*, 42 (4): 355–365.

Hutchby, I. (2001). 'Witnessing: The Use of First-Hand Knowledge in Legitimating Lay Opinions on Talk Radio'. *Discourse Studies*, 3: 481–497.

Hydén, L.C., & E.G. Mishler. (1999). 'Language and Medicine'. *Annual Review of Applied Linguistics*, 19: 174–192.

Ioannou, M., & A. Debowska. (2014). 'Genuine and Simulated Suicide Notes: An Analysis of Content'. *Forensic Science International*, 245: 151–160.

IOM (Institute of Medicine). (2001). *Health and Behavior: The Interplay of Biological, Behavioral, and Societal Influences*. Washington, DC: National Academy Press.

Isometsä, E.T. (2001). 'Psychological Autopsy Studies–A Review'. *European Psychiatry*, 16 (7): 379–385.

Ivanoff, A. (1989). 'Identifying Psychological Correlates of Suicidal Behavior in Jail and Detention Facilities'. *Psychiatric Quarterly*, 60: 73–84.

Jamison, K.R. (2004). *Noc szybko nadchodzi: zrozumieć samobójstwo, by mu zapobiec*. Poznań: Wydawnictwo Zysk i S-ka.

Jaworski, K. (2010). 'The Author, Agency and Suicide'. *Social Identities*, 16 (5): 675–687.

Jaworski, K. (2014). *The Gender of Suicide: Knowledge Production, Theory and Suicidology*. Burlington, VT: Ashgate.

Jefferson, G. (2004). 'Glossary of Transcript Symbols with an Introduction'. In G.H. Lerner (ed.), *Conversation Analysis: Studies from the First Generation*, pp. 13–31. Amsterdam: John Benjamins.

Jobes, D.A. (1995). 'The Challenge and the Promise of Clinical Suicidology'. *Suicide and Life-Threatening Behavior*, 25 (4): 437–449.

Jobes, D.A. (2016). *Managing Suicidal Risk: A Collaborative Approach*, 2nd edn. New York: Guilford.

Johannsen, W.J. (1969). 'Attitudes Towards Mental Patients'. *Mental Hygiene*, 25: 218–228.

Joiner, T.E., Jr. (2005). *Why People Die by Suicide*. Cambridge, MA: Harvard University Press.

Joiner, T.E., Jr. (2011). 'Editorial: Scientific Rigor as the Guiding Heuristic for SLTB's Editorial Stance'. *Suicide and Life-Threatening Behavior*, 41 (5): 471–473.

Kapur, N. & R.D. Goldney. (2019). *Suicide Prevention*, 3rd edn. Oxford: Oxford University Press.

Kelly, B.D. (2006). 'The Power Gap: Freedom, Power and Mental Illness'. *Social Science & Medicine*, 63: 2118–2128.

Kessler, R.C., G. Borges, & E.E. Walters. (1999). 'Prevalence of and Risk Factors for Lifetime Suicide Attempts in the National Comorbidity Survey'. *Archives of General Psychiatry*, 56 (7): 617–626.

Khan, A., S. Khan, R. Kolts, & W.A. Brown. (2003). 'Suicide Rates in Clinical Trials of SSRIs, Other Antidepressants, and Placebo: Analysis of FDA Reports'. *American Journal of Psychiatry*, 160 (4): 790–792.

Kinderman, P., J. Read, J. Moncrieff, & R.P. Bentall. (2013). 'Drop the Language of Disorder'. *Evidence-Based Mental Health*, 16: 2–3.

Kirmayer, L.J. (2012). 'Cultural Competence and Evidence-Based Practice in Mental Health: Epistemic Communities and the Politics of Pluralism'. *Social Science & Medicine*, 75 (2): 249–256.

Klonsky, E.D. (2019). 'The Role of Theory for Understanding and Preventing Suicide (But Not Predicting It): A Commentary on Hjelmeland and Knizek'. *Death Studies*, published online ahead of print 15 April 2019. doi: 10.1080/07481187.2019.1594005.

Kraus, A. (2003). 'How Can the Phenomenological-Anthropological Approach Contribute to Diagnosis and Classification in Psychiatry'. In B. Fulford, K. Morris, J.Z. Sadler & G. Stanghellini (eds), *Nature and Narrative: An Introduction to the New Philosophy of Psychiatry*, pp. 199–216. Oxford: Oxford University Press.

Kress, G. (2010). *Multimodality: A Social Semiotic Approach to Contemporary Communication*. Abingdon: Routledge.

Kress, G., & T. van Leeuwen. (1996). *Reading Images: The Grammar of Visual Design*. London: Routledge.

Kress, G., & T. van Leeuwen. (1998). 'Front Pages: (The Critical) Analysis of Newspaper Layout'. In A. Bell & P. Garrett (eds), *Approaches to Media Discourse*, pp. 186–219. Oxford: Blackwell.

Kress, G., R. Leite-García, & T. van Leeuwen. (1997). 'Discourse Semiotics'. In T. van Dijk (ed.), *Discourse as Structure and Process* (*Discourse Studies: A Multidisciplinary Introduction*, vol. 1, pp. 257–291. London: Sage.

Krzyzanowski, M., & B. Frochtner. (2016). 'Theories and Concepts in Critical Discourse Studies'. *Discourse and Society*, 27: 253–261.

Kutchins, H., & S.A. Kirk. (1999). *Making Us Crazy*. London: Constable.

Large, M., G. Smith, S. Sharma, O. Nielssen, & S.P. Singh. (2011). 'Systematic Review and Meta-Analysis of the Clinical Factors Associated with the Suicide of Psychiatric In-Patients'. *Acta Psychiatrica Scandinavica*, 124 (1): 18–19.

Leenaars, A.A. (1986). 'Brief Note on Latent Content in Suicide Notes'. *Psychological Reports*, 59: 640–642.

Leenaars, A.A. (1988). *Suicide Notes: Predictive Clues and Patterns*. New York: Human Sciences Press.

Leenaars, A.A. (1991). 'Suicide Notes and Their Implications for Intervention'. *Crisis: The Journal of Crisis Intervention and Suicide Prevention*, 12 (1): 1–20.

Leenaars, A.A. (1992). 'Suicide Notes of the Older Adult'. *Suicide and Life-Threatening Behavior*, 22 (1): 62–79.

Leenaars, A.A. (2002a). 'In Defense of the Idiographic Approach: Studies of Suicide Notes and Personal Documents'. *Archives of Suicide Research*, 6 (1): 19–30.

Leenaars, A.A. (2002b). 'The Quantitative and Qualitative in Suicidological Science: An Editorial'. *Archives of Suicide Research*, 6 (1): 1–3.

Leenaars, A.A. (2004). *Psychotherapy with Suicidal People: A Person-Centred Approach*. Chichester: John Wiley & Sons.

Leenaars, A.A. (2010). 'Edwin S. Shneidman on Suicide'. *Suicidology Online*, 1: 5–18.

Leenaars, A.A., & W.D. Balance. (1984). 'A Logical Empirical Approach to the Study of Suicide Notes'. *Canadian Journal of Behavioural Science/Revue Canadienne des Sciences du Comportement*, 16 (3): 249–256.

Leenaars, A.A., E.J. De Wilde, S. Wenckstern, & M. Kral. (2001). 'Suicide Notes of Adolescents: A Life-Span Comparison'. *Canadian Journal of Behavioural Science/Revue Canadienne des Sciences du Comportement*, 33 (1): 47–57.

Leenaars, A.A., D. De Leo, R.F. Diekstra, R.D. Goldney, M.J. Kelleher, D. Lester, & P. Nordstrom. (1997). 'Consultations for Research in Suicidology'. *Archives of Suicide Research*, 3 (2): 139–151.

Lemieux, A.M., D.M. Saman, & M.N. Lutfiyya. (2014). 'Men and Suicide in Primary Care'. *Disease-a-Month*, 60 (4): 155–161.

Lester, D. (1974). 'The Prevention of Suicide'. *Journal of the American Medical Association*, 228: 26–27.

Lester, D. (2000). *Why People Kill Themselves: A 2000 Summary of Research on Suicide*, 4th edn. Springfield, IL: Charles C. Thomas Publisher.

Lester, D. (2010). 'Qualitative Research in Suicidology: Thoughts on Hjelmeland and Knizek's "Why We Need Qualitative Research in Suicidology"'. *Suicidology Online*, 1: 76–78.

Lester, D. (2015). 'Dramatic Suicide Notes'. In D. Lester & E. Stack (eds), *Suicide as a Dramatic Performance*, pp. 21–39. New Brunswick, NJ: Transaction Publishers.

Lester, D., & S. Stack (eds). (2015). *Suicide as a Dramatic Performance*. New Brunswick, NJ: Transaction Publishers.

Linell, P. (2005). *The Written Language Bias in Linguistics: Its Nature, Origins and Transformations*. London: Routledge.

MacLeod, A.K., & A. Byrne. (1996). 'Anxiety, Depression, and the Anticipation of Future Positive and Negative Experiences'. *Journal of Abnormal Psychology*, 105 (2): 286–289.

MacLeod, A.K., & C. Conway. (2007). 'Well-Being and Positive Future Thinking for the Self Versus Others'. *Cognition and Emotion*, 21 (5): 1114–1124.

MacLeod, A.K., B. Pankhania, M. Lee, & D. Mitchell. (1997). 'Depression and the Anticipation of Positive and Negative Future Experiences'. *Psychological Medicine*, 27 (4): 973–977.

MacLeod, A.K., G.S. Rose, & J.M.G. Williams. (1993). 'Components of Hopelessness About the Future in Parasuicide'. *Cognitive Therapy and Research*, 17 (5): 441–455.

Mäki, N., & P. Martikainen. (2012). 'A Register-Based Study on Excess Suicide Mortality among Unemployed Men and Women during Different Levels of Unemployment in Finland'. *Journal of Epidemiol Community Health*, 66 (4): 302–307.

Mandrusiak, M., M.D. Rudd, T.E. Joiner, A.L. Berman, K.A. van Orden, & T. Witte. (2006). 'Warning Signs for Suicide on the Internet: A Descriptive Study'. *Suicide and Life-Threatening Behavior*, 36 (3): 263–271.

Maris, R.W. (2015). *Pillaged. Psychiatric Medications and Suicide Risk*. Columbia: University of South Carolina Press.

Maris, R.W., A.L. Berman, & M.M. Silverman. (2000a). *Comprehensive Textbook of Suicidology*. New York: Guilford.

Maris, R.W., A.L. Berman, & M.M. Silverman (2000b). 'The Theoretical Component in Suicidology'. In R. Maris, A. Berman & M. M. Silverman (eds), *Comprehensive Textbook of Suicidology*, pp. 26–61. New York: Guilford.

Marsh, I. (2010). *Suicide: Foucault, History and Truth*. Cambridge: Cambridge University Press.

Marsh, I. (2013). 'The Uses of History in the Unmaking of Modern Suicide'. *Journal of Social History*, 46 (3): 744–756.

Marsh, I. (2016). 'Critiquing Contemporary Suicidology'. In J. White, I. Marsh, M. Kral & J. Morris (eds), *Critical Suicidology. Transforming Suicide Research and Prevention for the 21st Century*, pp. 15–30. Vancouver: UBC Press.

May, A.M., & E.D. Klonsky. (2016). 'What Distinguishes Suicide Attempters from Suicide Ideators? A Meta-Analysis of Potential Factors'. *Clinical Psychology: Science and Practice*, 23 (1): 5–20.

May, A.M., E.D. Klonsky, & D.N. Klein. (2012). 'Predicting Future Suicide Attempts among Depressed Suicide Ideators: A 10-year Longitudinal Study'. *Journal of Psychiatric Research*, 46 (7): 946–952.

Mayo, D.J. (1986). 'The Concept of Rational Suicide'. *Journal of Medicine and Philosophy*, 11 (2): 143–155.

McCabe, R., R. Garside, A. Backhouse, & P. Xanthopoulou. (2018). 'Effectiveness of Brief Psychological Interventions for Suicidal Presentations: A Systematic Review'. *BMC Psychiatry*, 18 (1): 120.

McCabe, R., I. Sterno, S. Priebe, R. Barnes, & R. Byng. (2017). 'How Do Healthcare Professionals Interview Patients to Assess Suicide Risk?'. *BMC Psychiatry*, 17 (1): 122.

Meehan, P.J., J.A. Lamb, L.E. Saltzman, & P.W. O'Carroll. (1992). 'Attempted Suicide among Young Adults: Progress Toward a Meaningful Estimate of Prevalence'. *American Journal of Psychiatry*, 149 (1): 41–44.

Meinhof, U.H. (1997). '"The Most Important Event of My Life!". A Comparison of Male and Female Written Narratives'. In S. Johnson & U.H. Meinhof (eds), *Language and Masculinity*, pp. 208–228. Oxford: Blackwell.

Meinhof, U.H., & D. Galasiński. (2005). *The Language of Belonging*. Basingstoke: Palgrave Macmillan.

Meltzer, H., P. Bebbington, T. Brugha, R. Jenkins, S. McManus, & M.S. Dennis. (2011). 'Personal Debt and Suicidal Ideation'. *Psychological Medicine*, 41 (4): 771–778.

Menninger, K. (1938). *Man Against Himself*. New York: Harcourt, Brace & World.

Menz, F. (1989). 'Manipulation Strategies in Newspapers'. In R. Wodak (ed.), *Language, Power and Ideology*, pp. 227–249. Amsterdam: John Benjamins.

Mezzich, J.E., & C.E. Berganza. (2005). 'Purposes and Models of Diagnostic Systems'. *Psychopathology*, 38: 162–165.

Minois, G. (2001). *History of Suicide: Voluntary Death in Western Culture*. Baltimore, MD: Johns Hopkins University Press.

Mishara, B.L., & D.N. Weisstub. (2016), 'The Legal Status of Suicide: A Global Review'. *International Journal of Law and Psychiatry*, 44: 54–74.

Mishler, E. (1984). *The Discourse of Medicine: Dialectics of Medical Interviews*. Norwood: Ablex.

Morse, J., & J.J. Johnson. (1991). 'Towards a Theory of Illness'. In J.M. Morse & J.L. Johnson (eds), *The Illness Experience: Dimensions of Suffering*, pp. 315–342. Newbury Park, CA: Sage.

Mościcki, E.K. (1997). 'Identification of Suicide Risk Factors Using Epidemiologic Studies'. *Psychiatric Clinics of North America*, 20 (3): 499–517.

Münster, D., & L. Broz. (2015). 'The Anthropology of Suicide: Ethnography and the Tension of Agency'. In L. Broz & D. Münster (eds), *Suicide and Agency: Anthropological Perspectives on Self-Destruction, Personhood, and Power*, pp. 3–26. Abingdon: Routledge.

Neeleman, J., R. de Graaf, & W. Vollebergh. (2004). 'The Suicidal Process: Prospective Comparison between Early and Later Stages'. *Journal of Affective Disorders*, 82 (1): 43–52.

Nelson, I.A. (2010). 'From Quantitative to Qualitative: Adapting the Life History Calendar Method'. *Field Methods*, 22 (4): 413–428.

Nelson, I.A. (2017). *Why Afterschool Matters*. Camden, NJ: Rutgers University Press.

Nenonen, M., J. Mulli, A. Nikolaev, & E. Penttilä. (2017). 'How Light Can a Light Verb Be? Predication Patterns in V + NP Constructions in English, Finish, German and Russian'. In M. Luodonpää-Manni, E. Penttilä & J. Viimaranta (eds), *Empirical Approaches to Cognitive Linguistics: Analyzing Real-Life Data*, pp. 75–106. Cambridge: Cambridge Scholars Publishing.

Neuringer, C., M. Levenson, & J.M. Kaplan. (1972). 'Phenomenological Time Flow in Suicidal, Geriatric and Normal Individuals'. *Omega: Journal of Death and Dying*, 2 (4): 247–251.

NHS (National Health Service). (2019). 'A to Z of NHS Health Writing'. Available online: https://beta.nhs.uk/service-manual/content/a-to-z-of-NHS-health-writing#P (accessed 10 February 2020).

Nielsen, E. (n.d.). 'Mind Your 'C's and 'S's: The Language of Self-Harm and Suicide (and Why It Matters)'. *IMH Blog (Nottingham)*. Available online: https://imhblog.wordpress.com/2016/01/22/emma-nielsen-mind-your-cs-and-ss-the-language-of-self-harm-and-suicide-and-why-it-matters/ (accessed 10 February 2020).

Nock, M.K., I. Hwang, N.A. Sampson, & R.C. Kessler. (2010). 'Mental Disorders, Comorbidity and Suicidal Behavior: Results from the National Comorbidity Survey Replication'. *Molecular Psychiatry*, 15 (8): 868–876.

O'Carroll, P.W., A.L. Berman, R.W. Maris, E.K. Moscicki, B.L. Tanney, & M.M. Silverman. (1996). 'Beyond the Tower of Babel: A Nomenclature for Suicidology'. *Suicide and Life-Threatening Behavior*, 26 (3): 237–252.

O'Carroll, P.W., A.L. Berman, R.W. Maris, E.K. Moscicki, B.L. Tanney, & M.M. Silverman. (1998). 'Beyond the Tower of Babel: A Nomenclature for Suicidology'. In

R.J. Kosky, H.S. Eshkevari, R.D. Goldney & R. Hassan (eds), *Suicide Prevention: The Global Context*, pp. 23–39. Boston, MA: Springer.

O'Connor, R.C. (2011). 'The Integrated Motivational-Volitional Model of Suicidal Behavior'. *Crisis*, 32: 295–298.

O'Connor, R.C., H. Connery, & W.M. Cheyne. (2000). 'Hopelessness: The Role of Depression, Future Directed Thinking and Cognitive Vulnerability'. *Psychology, Health & Medicine*, 5 (2): 155–161.

O'Connor, R.C., & O.J. Kirtley. (2018). 'The Integrated Motivational–Volitional Model of Suicidal Behaviour'. *Philosophical Transactions of the Royal Society B: Biological Sciences*, 373 (1754): 20170268.

O'Connor, R.C., & J. Pirkis (eds). (2016). *The International Handbook of Suicide Prevention*. Chichester: John Wiley & Sons.

O'Connor, R., D. O'Connor, S. O'Connor, J. Smallwood, & J. Miles. (2004). 'Hopelessness, Stress, and Perfectionism: The Moderating Effects of Future Thinking'. *Cognition & Emotion*, 18 (8): 1099–1120.

O'Connor, R.C., S. Platt, & J. Gordon (eds). (2011). *The International Handbook of Suicide Prevention: Research, Policy and Practice*. Chichester: John Wiley and Sons.

O'Connor, R., & N. Sheehy. (2000). *Understanding Suicidal Behaviour*. Leicester: BPS Books.

O'Connor, R.C., R. Smyth, & J.M.G. Williams. (2015). 'Intrapersonal Positive Future Thinking Predicts Repeat Suicide Attempts in Hospital-Treated Suicide Attempters'. *Journal of Consulting and Clinical Psychology*, 83 (1): 169–176.

Oliffe, J.L., C.S. Han, J.S. Ogrodniczuk, J.C. Phillips, & P. Roy. (2011). 'Suicide from the Perspectives of Older Men Who Experience Depression: A Gender Analysis'. *American Journal of Men's Health*, 5 (5): 444–454.

Oliver, M. (1996). *Understanding Disability: From Theory to Practice*. New York: St Martin's Press.

Olson, R. (n.d.). *Suicide and Language*. Available online: https://www.suicideinfo.ca/resource/suicideandlanguage/ (accessed 10 February 2020).

ONS (Office for National Statistics). (2019b). Middle-Aged Generation Most Likely to Die by Suicide and Drug Poisoning'. ONS, 13 August 2019. Available online: https://www.ons.gov.uk/peoplepopulationandcommunity/healthandsocialcare/healthandwellbeing/articles/middleagedgenerationmostlikelytodiebysuicideanddrugpoisoning/2019-08-13 (accessed 10 February 2020).

ONS (Office for National Statistics). (2019a). *Suicide in the UK: 2018 Registrations*. Available online: https://www.ons.gov.uk/peoplepopulationandcommunity/birthsdeathsandmarriages/deaths/bulletins/suicidesintheunitedkingdom/2018registrations (accessed 10 February 2020).

Oquendo, M. A., & Baca-Garcia, E. (2014). 'Suicidal Behavior Disorder as a Diagnostic Entity in the DSM-5 Classification System: Advantages Outweigh Limitations'. *World Psychiatry*, 13(2), 128–130.

Ossowska, M. (1986). *Ethos rycerski jego odmiany*. Warsaw: Panstwowe Wydawnictwo Naukowe.

Padmanathan, P., L. Biddle, K. Hall, E. Scowcroft, E. Nielsen, & D. Knipe. (2019). 'Language Use and Suicide: An Online Cross-Sectional Survey'. *PLOS ONE*, 14 (6): e0217473.

Paris, J. (2007). *Half in Love with Death: Managing the Chronically Suicidal Patient*. London: Routledge.

Parker, I. (1989). *The Crisis in Modern Social Psychology – and How to End It*. London: Routledge.

Paykel, E.S., J.K. Myers, J.J. Lindenthal, & J. Tanner. (1974). 'Suicidal Feelings in the General Population: A Prevalence Study'. *British Journal of Psychiatry*, 124 (582): 460–469.

Phillips, J. (2005). 'Idiographic Formulations, Symbols, Narratives, Context and Meaning'. *Psychopathology*, 38: 180–184.

Phillips, J. (2019). 'The Dangerous Shifting Cultural Narratives Around Suicide'. *The Washington Post*, 21 March 2019. Available online: https://www.washingtonpost.com/outlook/the-dangerous-shifting-cultural-narratives-around-suicide/2019/03/21/7277946e-4bf5-11e9-93d0-64dbcf38ba41_story.html (accessed 10 February 2020).

Phillips, M.R., G. Yang, Y. Zhang, L. Wang, H. Ji, & M. Zhou. (2002). 'Risk Factors for Suicide in China: A National Case-Control Psychological Autopsy Study'. *The Lancet*, 360 (9347): 1728–1736.

Pokorny, A.D. (1974). 'A Scheme for Classifying Suicidal Behaviors'. In A.T. Beck, H.L.P. Resnik & D.J. Lettieri (eds), *The Prediction of Suicide*, pp. 29–44. Bowie: Charles Press.

Pokorny, A.D. (1983). 'Prediction of Suicide in Psychiatric Patients: Report of a Prospective Study'. *Archives of General Psychiatry*, 40 (3): 249–257.

Pokorny, A.D. (1993). 'Suicide Prediction Revisited'. *Suicide and Life-Threatening Behavior*, 23 (1): 1–10.

Pollack, L., & J.M. Williams. (2004). 'Problem Solving in Suicide Attempts'. *Psychological Medicine*, 34: 163–167.

Polski korpus listów pożegnalnych samobójców (Polish Corpus of Suicide Notes). (n.d.). Available online: http://www.pcsn.uni.wroc.pl/ (accessed 10 February 2020).

Poole, R., & R. Higgo. (2017). *Psychiatric Interviewing and Assessment*. Cambridge: Cambridge University Press.

Portzky, K. K. Audenaert, & C. van Heeringen. (2005). 'Adjustment Disorder and the Course of the Suicidal Process in Adolescents'. *Journal of Affective Disorders*, 87: 265–270.

Posner, J., B. Brodsky, K. Yershova, J. Buchanan, & J. Mann. (2014). 'The Classification of Suicidal Behavior'. In M.K. Nock (ed.), *The Oxford Handbook of Suicide and Self-Injury*, pp. 7–22. Oxford: Oxford University Press.

Posner, K., M.A. Oquendo, M. Gould, B. Stanley, & M. Davies. (2007). 'Columbia Classification Algorithm of Suicide Assessment (C-CASA): Classification of Suicidal Events in the FDA's Pediatric Suicidal Risk Analysis of Antidepressants'. *American Journal of Psychiatry*, 164 (7): 1035–1043.

Pridmore, S. (2000). *The Psychiatric Interview: A Guide to History taking and Mental Status Examination*. Amsterdam: Harwood Academic Publishers.

Pridmore, S. (2011). 'Medicalisation of Suicide'. *Malaysian Journal of Medical Sciences*, 18 (4): 78–83.

Quinlivan, L., J. Cooper, S. Steeg, L. Davies, K. Hawton, D. Gunnell, & N. Kapur. (2014). 'Scales for Predicting Risk Following Self-Harm: An Observational Study in 32 Hospitals in England'. *BMJ Open*, 4 (5): e004732.

Quinlivan, L. et al. (2017). 'Predictive Accuracy of Risk Scales Following Self-Harm: Multicentre, Prospective Cohort Study'. *British Journal of Psychiatry*, 210 (6): 429–436.

Rabkin, J.G. (1972). 'Opinions about Mental Illness'. *Psychological Bulletin*, 77: 153–177.

Reeves, A., M. McKee, D. Gunnell, S.S. Chang, S. Basu, B. Barr, & D. Stuckler. (2014). 'Economic Shocks, Resilience, and Male Suicides in the Great Recession: Cross-National Analysis of 20 EU Countries'. *European Journal of Public Health*, 25 (3): 404–409.

Richards, N. (2017). 'Old Age Rational Suicide'. *Sociology Compass*, 11 (3): e12456.

Rimkeviciene, J., J. O'Gorman, J. Hawgood, & D. De Leo (2016). 'Timelines for Difficult Times: Use of Visual Timelines in Interviewing Suicide Attempters'. *Qualitative Research in Psychology*, 13 (3): 231–245.

Ringel, E. (1987). *Gdy życie traci sens. Rozważania o samobójstwie*. Szczecin: Glob.

Roen, K., J. Scourfield, & E. McDermott. (2008). 'Making Sense of Suicide: A Discourse Analysis of Young People's Talk about Suicidal Subjecthood'. *Social Science & Medicine*, 67 (12): 2089–2097.

Rogers, J.R. (2001). 'Theoretical Grounding: The "Missing Link" in Suicide Research'. *Journal of Counseling & Development*, 79(1): 16–25.

Rogers, J.R. (2003). 'The Anatomy of Suicidology: A Psychological Science Perspective on the Status of Suicide Research'. *Suicide and Life-Threatening Behavior*, 31 (1): 9–20.

Rogers, J.R., & S. Apel (2010). 'Revitalizing Suicidology: A Call for Mixed Methods Designs'. *Suicidology online*, 1: 92–94.

Rogers, J.R., J.L. Bromley, C.J. McNally, & D. Lester. (2007). 'Content Analysis of Suicide Notes as a Test of the Motivational Component of the Existential-Constructivist Model of Suicide'. *Journal of Counselling and Development*, 85 (2): 182–188.

Rogers, J.R., & D. Lester. (2010). *Understanding Suicide: Why We Don't and How We Might*. Cambridge: Hogrefe.

Rosen, D.H. (1975). 'Suicide Survivors: A Follow-Up Study of Persons Who Survived Jumping from the Golden Gate and San Francisco-Oakland Bay Bridges'. *Western Journal of Medicine*, 122 (4): 289.

Rosenberg, M.L., L.E. Davidson, J.C. Smith, A.L. Berman, H. Buzbee, G. Gantner, G.A. Gay, B. Moore-Lewis, D.H. Millis, & D. Murray. (1988). 'Operational Criteria for the Determination of Suicide'. *Journal of Forensic Sciences*, 33 (6): 1445–1456.

Rudd, M.D. (2000). 'The Suicidal Mode: A Cognitive-Behavioral Model of Suicidality'. *Suicide and Life-Threatening Behavior*, 30 (1): 18–33.

Rudd, M.D. (2003). 'Warning Signs for Suicide?'. *Suicide and Life-Threatening Behavior*, 33 (1): 99–100.

Rudd, M.D. (2008). 'Suicide Warning Signs in Clinical Practice'. *Current Psychiatry, Reports*, 10 (1): 87–90.

Rudd, M.D., A.L. Berman, T.E. Joiner, M.K. Nock, M.M. Silverman, M. Mandrusiak, K. van Orden & T. Witte. (2006). 'Warning Signs for Suicide: Theory, Research, and Clinical Applications'. *Suicide and Life-Threatening Behavior*, 36 (3): 255–262.

Rudd, M.D., & T.E. Joiner. (1998). 'The Assessment Management and Treatment of Suicidality: Toward Clinically Informed and Balanced Standards of Care'. *Clinical Psychology: Science and Practice*, 5 (2): 135–150.

Rudd, M.D., T.E. Joiner, & M.H. Rajab. (2004). *Treating Suicidal Behavior: An Effective, Time-Limited Approach*. New York: Guilford.

Ruder, T.D., G.M. Hatch, G. Ampanozi, M.J. Thali, & N. Fischer. (2011). 'Suicide Announcement on Facebook'. *Crisis*, 32: 280–282.

Runeson, B.S., J. Beskow, & M. Waern. (1996). 'The Suicidal Process in Suicides among Young People'. *Acta Psychiatrica Scandinavica*, 93 (1): 35–42.

Rüsch, N., M.C. Angermeyer, & P.W. Corrigan. (2005). 'Mental Illness Stigma'. *European Psychiatry*, 20: 529–539.

Salem, T. (1999). 'Physician-Assisted Suicide: Promoting Autonomy – Or Medicalizing suicide?'. *Hastings Center Report*, 29 (3): 30–36.

Sanchez, F. (2010). *Understanding Suicide and Its Prevention: A Neuropsychological Approach*. Bloomington, IN: Xlibris Corporation.

Sand, E., K.H. Gordon, & K. Bresin. (2013). 'The Impact of Specifying Suicide as the Cause of Death in an Obituary'. *Crisis*, 43 (1): 63–66.

Sarangi, S., & L. Brookes-Howell. (2006). 'Recontextualising the Familial Lifeworld in Genetic Counselling Case Notes'. In M. Gotti & F. Salager-Meyer (eds), *Advances in Medical Discourse Analysis: Oral and Written Contexts*, vol. 45: Linguistic Insights. Studies in Language and Communication, pp. 197–225. Bern: Peter Lang.

Sarbin, T.R. (1986). *Narrative Psychology: The Storied Nature of Human Conduct*. Westport: Praeger.

Schrijvers, D.L., J. Bollen, & B.G. Sabbe. (2012). 'The Gender Paradox in Suicidal Behavior and Its Impact on the Suicidal Process'. *Journal of Affective Disorders*, 138 (1): 19–26.

Schwartz, D.A. (1979). 'The Suicidal Character'. *Psychiatric Quarterly*, 51: 64–70.

Scourfield, J., B. Fincham, S. Langer, & M. Shiner. (2012). 'Sociological Autopsy: An Integrated Approach to the Study of Suicide in Men'. *Social Science & Medicine*, 74 (4): 466–473.

Searle, J.R. (1969). *Speech Acts: An Essay in the Philosophy of Language*, vol. 626. Cambridge: Cambridge University Press.

Shea, S.C. (1998). *Psychiatric Interviewing: The Art of Understanding. A Practical Guide for Psychiatrists, Psychologists, Counselors, Social Workers, Nurses, and Other Mental Health Professionals*, 2nd edn. Philadelphia: W.B. Saunders Company.

Shiner, M., J. Scourfield, B. Fincham, & S. Langer (2009). 'When Things Fall Apart: Gender and Suicide Across the Life-Course'. *Social Science & Medicine*, 69 (5): 738–746.

Shneidman, E.S. (1985). *Definition of Suicide*. New York: John Wiley & Sons.

Shneidman, E.S. (1993). *Suicide As Psychache: A Clinical Approach to Self-Destructive Behavior*. Northvale, NJ: Jason Aronson, Inc.

Shneidman, E.S. (1996). *The Suicidal Mind*. New York: Oxford University Press.

Shneidman, E.S., & N.L. Farberow (eds). (1957). *Clues to Suicide*, vol. 56981. New York: McGraw-Hill.

Sikveland, R.O., H. Kevoe-Feldman, & E. Stokoe. (2019). 'Overcoming Suicidal Persons' Resistance Using Productive Communicative Challenges During Police Crisis Negotiations'. *Applied Linguistics*. doi: 10.1093/applin/amy065.

Silverman, M.M. (2006). 'The Language of Suicidology'. *Suicide and Life-Threatening Behavior*, 36 (5): 519–532.

Silverman, M.M. (2013). 'Defining Suicide and Suicidal Behavior'. In D. Lester & J.R. James (eds), *Suicide. A Global Issue. vol 1. Understanding*, pp. 1–30. Santa Barbara, CA: Praeger.

Silverman, M.M., A.L. Berman, N.D. Sanddal, P.W. O'Carroll, & T.E. Joiner. (2007a). 'Rebuilding the Tower of Babel: A Revised Nomenclature for the Study of Suicide and Suicidal Behaviors Part 1: Background, Rationale, and Methodology'. *Suicide and Life-Threatening Behavior*, 37 (3): 248–263.

Silverman, M.M., A.L. Berman, N.D. Sanddal, P.W. O'Carroll, & T.E. Joiner. (2007b). 'Rebuilding the Tower of Babel: A Revised Nomenclature for the Study of Suicide and Suicidal Behaviors Part 2: Suicide-Related Ideations, Communications, and Behaviors'. *Suicide and Life-Threatening Behavior* 37 (3): 264–277.

Silverman, M.M., & D. De Leo. (2016). 'Why There Is a Need for an International Nomenclature and Classification System for Suicide'. *Crisis*, 37 (2): 83–87.

Silverman, M.M., & R.W. Maris. (1995). 'The Prevention of Suicidal Behaviors: An Overview'. *Suicide and Life-Threatening Behavior*, 25: 10–21.

Silverman, M.M., & T. Simon. (2001). 'The Houston Case-Control Study of Nearly Lethal Suicide Attempts'. *Suicide and Life-Threatening Behavior*, 32: 1–84.

Sinclair, S. (2000). 'Disease Narratives: Constituting Doctor'. *Anthropology & Medicine*, 7 (1): 115–134.

Sinyor, M., A. Schaffer, I. Hull, C. Peisah, & K. Shulman. (2015). 'Last Wills and Testaments in a Large Sample of Suicide Notes: Implications for Testamentary Capacity'. *British Journal of Psychiatry*, 206 (1): 72–76.

Smith, P.N., K. Schuler, N. Fadoir, L. Marie, & N. Basu. (2019). 'Socio-Ecological Context and the Interpersonal Theory of Suicide: A Response to Hjelmeland & Knizek'. *Death Studies*. doi: 10.1080/07481187.2019.1586799

Smith, V. (2007). *Clean: A History of Personal Hygiene and Purity*. Oxford: Oxford University Press.
Sobell, L.C., & M.B. Sobell. (1992). 'Timeline Follow-Back'. In R.Z. Litten & J.P. Allen (eds), *Measuring Alcohol Consumption: Psychosocial and Biochemical Methods*, pp. 41–72. Totowa, NJ: Humana Press.
Sokero, T.P., T.K. Melartin, H.J. Rytsälä, U.S. Leskelä, P.S. Lestelä-Mielonen, & E.T. Isometsä. (2005). 'Prospective Study of Risk Factors for Attempted Suicide Among Patients with DSM–IV Major Depressive Disorder'. *British Journal of Psychiatry*, 186 (4): 314–318.
Sommer-Rotenberg, D. (1998). 'Suicide and Language'. *CMAJ: Canadian Medical Association Journal*, 159 (3): 239.
Soyland, A.J. (1994). 'Functions of the Psychiatric Case-Summary'. *Text*, 14 (1): 113–140.
Soyland, A.J. (1995). 'Analyzing Therapeutic Professional Siscourse'. In J. Siegfried (ed.), *Therapeutic and Everyday Discourse as Behavior Change: Towards a Micro-Analysis in Psychotherapy Process Research*, pp. 277–300. Norwood, NJ: Ablex.
Speed, E. (2006). 'Patients, Consumers and Survivors'. *Social Science & Medicine*, 62: 28–38.
Swales, J.M. (1990). *Genre Analysis: English in Academic and Research Settings*. Cambridge: Cambridge University Press.
Szanto, K., H.G. Prigerson, & C.F. Reynolds III. (2001). 'Suicide in the Elderly'. *Clinical Neuroscience Research*, 1 (5): 366–376.
Szasz, T. (1999). 'Suicide as a Moral Issue'. *The Freeman*, 49: 41–42.
Tagg, J. (1988). *The Burden of Representation: Essays on Photographs and Histories*, vol. 80. Minneapolis: University of Minnesota Press.
Titscher, S., M. Meyer, R. Wodak, & E. Vetter. (2000). *Methods of Text and Discourse Analysis*. London: Sage.
Twigg, J. (2000). *Bathing – The Body and Community Care*. London: Routledge.
Van der Vaart, W. (2004). 'The Time-Line as a Device to Enhance Recall in Standardized Research Interviews: A Split Ballot Study'. *Journal of Official Statistics*, 20 (2): 301–317.
Van der Vaart, W., & T. Glasner. (2007). 'Applying a Timeline as a Recall Aid in a Telephone Survey: A Record Check Study'. *Applied Cognitive Psychology: The Official Journal of the Society for Applied Research in Memory and Cognition*, 21 (2): 227–238.
Van Dijk, T.A. (1988). *News analysis. Case Studies of International and National News in the Press*. Hillsdale, NJ: Lawrence.
Van Dijk, T.A. (1993). 'Principles of Critical Discourse Analysis'. *Discourse & Society*, 4: 249–283.
Van Dijk, T.A. (1998). *Ideology*. London: Sage.
Van Heeringen, C. (2001). 'The Suicidal Process and Related Concepts'. In C. van Heeringen (ed.), *Understanding Suicidal Behaviour: The Process Approach to Research and Treatment*, pp. 1–15. Chichester: John Wiley & Sons.

Van Heeringen, K., K. Hawton, & J.M.G. Williams. (2000). 'Pathways to Suicide: An Integrative Approach'. In K. Hawton & K. van Heeringen (eds), *The International Handbook of Suicide and Attempted Suicide*, pp. 223–234. Chichester: John Wiley & Sons.

Van Leeuwen, T. (2008). *Discourse and Practice. New Tools for Critical Discourse Analysis*. Oxford: Oxford University Press.

Van Leeuwen, T., & R. Wodak. (1999). 'Legitimizing Immigration Control'. *Discourse Studies*, 1: 83–118.

Van Orden, K.A., T.K. Witte, K.C. Cukrowicz, S.R. Braithwaite, E.A. Selby, & T.E. Joiner Jr. (2010). 'The Interpersonal Theory of Suicide'. *Psychological Review*, 117 (2): 575–600.

Wasserman, D. (2015). 'The Suicidal Process'. In D. Wasserman (ed.), *Suicide: An Unnecessary Death*, pp. 27–38. Oxford: Oxford University Press.

Wasserman, D., & C. Wasserman (eds). (2009). *Oxford Textbook of Suicidology and Suicide Prevention*. Oxford: Oxford University Press.

Webb, D. (2011). *Thinking About Suicide. Contemplating and Comprehending the Urge to Die*. Ross-on-Wye: PCCS Books.

Wenzel, A., & M. Spokas. (2014). 'Cognitive and Information Processing Approaches to Understanding Suicidal Behaviors'. In M.K. Nock (ed.), *Oxford Handbook of Suicide and Self-Injury*, pp. 235–253. New York: Oxford University Press.

Werth, J.L. Jr. (ed.). (1999). *Contemporary Perspectives on Rational Suicide*. Philadelphia: Taylor & Francis.

White, J. (2017). 'What Can Critical Suicidology Do?'. *Death Studies*, 41 (8): 472–480.

White, J., & M. Kral. (2014). 'Re-Thinking Youth Suicide: Language, Culture and Power'. *Journal of Social Action for Counseling and Psychology*, 6 (1): 122–142.

White, J., I. Marsh, M.J. Kral, & J. Morris. (2016). 'Introduction: Rethinking Suicide'. In J. White, I. Marsh, M. Kral & J. Morris (eds), *Critical Suicidology. Transforming Suicide Research and Prevention for the 21st Century*, pp. 1–14. Vancouver: UBC Press.

WHO (World Health Organization). (1986). *Summary Report, Working Group in Preventative Practices in Suicide and Attempted Suicide*. Copenhagen: WHO Regional Office for Europe.

WHO (World Health Organization). (1998). *Primary Prevention of Mental, Neurological and Psychosocial Disorders. Suicide*. Geneva: WHO.

WHO (World Health Organization). (1992). The *ICD-10 Classification of Mental and Behavioural Disorders: Clinical Descriptions and Diagnostic Guidelines*. New York: WHO.

WHO (World Health Organization). (1993). The *ICD-10 Classification of Mental and Behavioural Disorders: Diagnostic Criteria for Research*. New York: WHO.

WHO (World Health Organization). (2018). 'Mental Health Atlas'. Available online: https://www.who.int/mental_health/evidence/atlas/mental_health_atlas_2017/en/ (accessed 10 February 2020).

WHO (World Health Organization). (2019). 'Suicide: One Person Dies Every 40 Seconds'. WHO, 9 September 2019. Available online: https://www.who.int/news-room/detail/09-09-2019-suicide-one-person-dies-every-40-seconds (accessed 10 February 2020).

Wierzbicka, A. (2003). *Cross-Cultural Pragmatics: The Semantics of Human Interaction*. Berlin: Walter de Gruyter.

Williams, J.M.G. (2014). *Cry of Pain. Understanding Suicide and the Suicidal Mind*, 3rd edn. London: Piatkus.

Williams, J.M.G., A.J.W. van der Does, T. Barnhofer, C. Crane, & Z.S. Segal. (2008). 'Cognitive Reactivity, Suicidal Ideation and Future Fluency: Preliminary Investigation of a Differential Activation Theory of Hopelessness/Suicidality'. *Cognitive Therapy and Research*, 32 (1): 83–104.

Wodak, R. (1999). 'Critical Discourse Analysis at the End of the 20th Century'. *Research on Language and Social Interaction*, 32: 185–193.

Yovell, Y., G. Bar, M. Mashiah, Y. Baruch, I. Briskman, J. Asherov, A. Lotan, A. Rigbi, & J. Panksepp. (2015). 'Ultra-Low-Dose Buprenorphine as a Time-Limited Treatment for Severe Suicidal Ideation: A Randomized Controlled Trial'. *American Journal of Psychiatry*, 173 (5), 491–498.

Zaśko-Zielińska, M. (2013). *Listy pożegnalne: w poszukiwaniu lingwistycznych wyznaczników autentyczności tekstu*. Wrocław: Wydawnictwo Quaestio.

Zethsen, K.K. & I. Askehave. (2006). 'Medical Communication: Professional-Lay'. In J.L. Mey (ed.), *Concise Encyclopedia of Pragmatics*, pp. 592–597. Oxford: Elsevier.

Zhang, J. (2016). *The Strain Theory of Suicide*. Riga: LAP Lambert.

Zhang, J., & D. Lester. (2008). 'Psychological Tensions Found in Suicide Notes: A Test for the Strain Theory of Suicide'. *Archives of Suicide Research*, 12 (1): 67–73.

Zhang, J., W.F. Wieczorek, Y. Conwell, & X.M. Tu. (2011). 'Psychological Strains and Youth Suicide in Rural China'. *Social Science & Medicine*, 72 (12): 2003–2010.

Ziółkowska, J. (2009). 'Positions in Doctors' Questions During Psychiatric Interviews'. *Qualitative Health Research*, 19 (11): 1621–1631.

Ziółkowska, J. (2014). 'Time and the Psychiatric Interview: The Negotiation of Temporal Criteria of the Depressive Disorder'. *Health*, 18 (2): 163–178.

Ziółkowska, J. (2016). *Samobójstwo. Analiza narracji osób po próbach samobójczych*. Warsaw: PWN.

Ziółkowska, J., & D. Galasiński. (2017). 'Discursive Construction of Fatherly Suicide'. *Critical Discourse Studies*, 14 (2): 150–166.

Index

absence of control 53–4, 61, 129–31, 134–7
acceptance 19, 73, 86, 112–13, 123, 124, 133, 178
active resistance 18
adjustment disorder 10
agency in suicide decision
    absence of control 53–4, 129–31, 134–7
    external force 50–2
    internal voice 52–3
    preparation and active role 56–64
    rendered in suicide letters 54–6
    time/intent 72–3
alcohol 56, 57, 77, 101, 104–6, 108, 128, 146, 147, 162
American Foundation for Suicide Prevention (AFSP) 4
American Psychiatric Association (APA) 6, 14, 49
anxiety disorder 39, 97, 98, 109
attempted suicide. *See* suicide attempt

bath (symbolism) 77
bereavement, and suicidality 5, 55, 98, 131, 180
biographic disruption 136
borderline personality disorder 10
breakup, as cause of suicide 98
British Office for National Statistics (ONS) reports 6, 137

Centers for Disease Control and Prevention (CDC) 21, 128
Christianity, attitudes/views on suicide 5
classification of suicide/suicidal behaviour 6–7, 26, 144
compassion 137, 148
completed suicide, classification 7, 21, 22
concentration, lack of 39
crying/moaning 32, 59, 81, 82, 87, 184 n.1

Declaration of Helsinki 18, 20
depression 9, 10, 39, 120, 147, 148, 151
disability, as cause of suicide 16, 53–4, 110, 131, 136
discourse, definitions 12–13, 14
distancing 50–1, 55, 56, 61–2, 152
'doing suicide' 23, 35–7, 84, 88, 89, 169, 174
drinking 56, 77, 101, 104, 105, 106, 107, 108, 128, 147
drowning 56, 57, 102, 106
drugs 39, 56, 146
DSM-V 6, 9, 14, 149

economic factors, and suicide risk 6, 137
epidemiology
    attempted suicide 4–5
    gender paradox 5
    suicide ideation 5
Eurostat 4

fate 32, 33, 131, 185 n.3
fear 52, 98, 130
felo de se (coroner verdict) 60
future orientation
    control over future lives 134–7
    peaceful and care-free future 125–9
    potential risk/recurrence of suicidal urges 129–32
    predictions and certainty level 120–5
    suicidological research 119–20, 132–7
Future Thinking Task (FTT) 120, 135

Grice's Cooperative Principle 72
guilt 39, 47, 48, 61, 98, 148, 170–1

hanging 35, 60, 107, 112
helplessness 31, 39, 98, 99, 119, 120
homosexuality 14

ideology 15
illness, and suicidality 5, 19, 49, 60, 62, 98, 110, 113, 127, 136, 148, 153
indeterminacy 7
integrated motivational-volitional model of suicidal behaviour 39
intent/intentionality 7–8, 25–6, 27, 29, 39, 45–6, 47, 48, 54, 60, 73–6, 87, 88, 89, 98, 133, 180
interpersonal theory of suicide 17, 98
'It's OK not to be OK' campaign 110
'It's OK to talk' campaign 110

labelling 19, 22
legal sanctions 60
life events 10, 146, 147
'long suicide' 73, 85–6, 88–9
loss, and suicidality 39, 98, 131
loss of consciousness 3, 57, 58, 112

marijuana 146
MeDLINE database 26
mental illness 5–6, 9, 14, 17, 19, 49, 153
modality/modalization 121–4, 145
multimodality. *See* visual representations of suicide

National Institute of Mental Health 26
non compos mentis (coroner verdict) 60

old age, and suicidality 53, 110
overdose 78

pain, and suicidality 39, 97–9, 104, 111, 112, 135, 136, 165, 180, 181, 182
passive acceptance 19
PMT 14
poison 27, 48, 51, 80, 102, 107, 128
preparations for suicide
    mental 100–1, 111, 112–13
    timescale 76–9, 89, 101
presuicidal syndrome 98
PubMed 26

reciprocity 3, 173
rejection, and suicidality 3, 39, 99, 165, 176
restless legs syndrome 14

'right to die' 110
risk factors 3, 5, 6, 10, 17, 39, 63, 172–3

schizophrenia 10
self-harm 7, 98, 104, 176
self-worth, absence of 39
shame 39, 98
sleeplessness 39
solitude 78, 82
'spiritual' concerns 112, 126
stigma/stigmatization 19, 55, 61, 62, 86, 113, 152, 171, 178, 179–80
substance abuse. *See* drugs
suicidal act
    cutting 105–6
    emotional and cognitive factors 97–9, 110
    and the future 125–9
    gouging 104–6
    hanging 107
    physicality of/last moments 104–9, 110–13
    rationality of 97–9, 109, 110
    ripping 105–6
    self-instructions/mental preparations for 99–104
    squeezing 105
    turning 105
Suicidal Behavior Disorder 6
suicidal fantasies 98
suicidal mode 39–40, 98, 112
suicide and suicidal behaviour
    acceptability of 112–13, 133
    attitudes towards 5
    classification/characteristics 7
    concept 9, 98–9
    definitions 7, 25–9, 45, 97–9
    emotional and cognitive factors 97–9
    goal of 135
    interpersonal theory 17
    language policy 177–81
    medicalization of 14
    as mental disorder 5–6, 14, 17, 18
    physicality of 104–9, 110
    rationality of 98–104, 110, 133–4
    risk factors 10, 17, 39–40
    Shneidman model 97–8
    statistics, global mortality rates 4–5, 46

terminology and classification 26–9
warning signs 39–40
suicide attempt
  agentive narratives 56–60, 104–9
  classification 7
  definition 8
  future orientation and 119–37
  and medical help 8
  'recovery' over 129–32
  recurrence of 129–32
  self-instructions/mental preparations for 99–104
  statistics 4
suicide crisis 39
suicide ideation
  classification 7
  epidemiology 5
  as mental disorder 6, 9
suicide letters/notes
  accounts of the future 119–37
  as act of communication with ulterior motives 87–8
  decision and agentic narratives 50–64
  future perspective 85–6
  intent 73–6, 88
  references to act of writing 82–4
  social practices 73
  of suicidal act and process 99–109
  suicide as time-extended process 29–37, 56–8, 181–2
  suicidological research into 2–3, 98–9, 132–7
  time/duration of suicide 71–90
  as 'ultrapersonal' 88
Suicide Notes (Leenaars) 98–9
suicide prevention
  biomedical model 6
  campaigns 110
  discourse analysis and 175–7
  strategies 2, 4, 38–9, 89, 90, 110, 111, 135, 137, 166, 175, 182
  suicidology and 4, 23, 39, 40, 61, 135
suicide process
  agency in 45–64
  concept 8–12
suicide process, discourse analysis
  approaches 1–2, 11, 12–16, 167, 172–5, 181–3
  data collection 18–21, 172
  and mainstream suicidology 16–18, 169–71
  vocabulary 21–3, 177–81
swallowing 59, 104, 105

teen suicide 80–1, 136
time of suicide
  and announcement of intent 73–6
  beginning of the process 71–3, 169
  end of the process/future perspective 84–7, 89–90, 170
  preparations 76–9
  time passing/waiting for death 79–84, 88–9, 105, 106, 111, 169

uncertainty 80, 98, 121, 123, 129–30, 132, 134
unemployment 6, 137
United Kingdom, suicide rates (ONS reports) 5, 6, 137
United States, suicide rates 5

visual representations of suicide
  discourse 143–5
  medical vocabulary, use of 147–56
  timelines, long- and short-term 145–67

warning signs, suicidal 39–40
water (symbolism) 77

www.ingramcontent.com/pod-product-compliance
Lightning Source LLC
Chambersburg PA
CBHW072108010526
44111CB00037B/2093